BEING A HUMAN BEING, I NEVER THOUGHT PEOPLE [WERE] GOING TO BE LIKE THAT, MAKING ME LIVE ALONE, GO NOWHERE, AND GET POOR PAY. BUT WHAT CAN YOU DO? YOU CAN'T DO NOTHING, EXCEPT YOU PLAY HARDER.

—Vic Power, All-Star first baseman, 1954–1965

BUT WHEN SOMEONE TRIES TO DISHEARTEN YOU—I KNOW I WAS LIKE THIS AND SO WAS [DON] NEWCOMBE—YOU'D TRY JUST THAT MUCH HARDER. AND WHEN YOU TRY HARDER, IT IMPROVES YOUR ABILITY.

—Roy Campanella, Hall of Fame catcher, class of 1969

I HAD MOST OF MY TROUBLE IN DANVILLE, VIRGINIA, IN THE CAROLINA LEAGUE IN '56. I THINK THAT'S WHY I HIT SO MANY HOME RUNS THAT YEAR, 51 OF 'EM AND 166 RBI'S. INSULTS PUSHED ME TO PLAY HARDER.

—Leon Wagner, All-Star left fielder, 1958–1969

GERALD EARLY
NATIONAL BASEBALL HALL OF FAME AND MUSEUM

PLAY HARDER

THE TRIUMPH OF
BLACK BASEBALL IN AMERICA

FOREWORD BY DAVE WINFIELD

TEN SPEED PRESS
California | New York

REMARKS ON THE OPENING
OF *THE SOULS OF THE GAME*

In the beginning, they played in the parks of the cold and crowded cities of the Northeast. They played in the sparse and scattered territories of the hot Southwest. They played on makeshift diamonds etched out on the windy prairies of the Great Plains and on snow-cleared outposts tucked deep in the valleys of the Rocky Mountain ranges. They played along the coastal lowlands of Maine. They played in Anaconda, Butte, and Helena, Montana. They played in New Orleans and in Nova Scotia. They played in Chicago, St. Louis, and Kansas City; Sioux City, Saint Paul, and Oswego. They played as ringers for the segregated hotels, where summer after summer they worked as butlers, bellhops, and bartenders. They played as businessmen on behalf of the barbershops that they owned. They played in Algiers, Louisiana, and Cadiz, Ohio. They played stationed at Fort Huachuca. They played between trips down the coal mines of Beaver Hill, Oregon. They played between their studies at Tuskegee, Howard, and Lincoln Universities. They called themselves the Fearless, the Wide Awakes, the Help Ups, the Resolutes, the Can't Get Aways, the Dolly Vardens, the Young Bachelors, the Homeboys, the Exiles. They called themselves the Stars, the Black Barons, the ABCs, the Monarchs, the Black Sox, the Crawfords, the Coconuts, the Cubans, the Plutos, the Grays. They called themselves the Giants, the Elite Giants, the American Giants, the Standard Giants, the Royal Giants.

They called themselves Dodgers, Braves, Cubs, Brewers, Expos, and—but of course—Giants.

Satchel Paige famously said, "Don't look back. Something might be gaining on you." This reflects not only his personal philosophy but also the resilience and forward-looking attitude that many Black baseball players had to adopt in the face of racial adversity. But now perhaps we can say, "Look back: something is gaining on you" and turn to not only face what's there but also embrace it as well. As you round the bases of the exhibit, take a moment to turn around and look back. Hopefully, something is gaining on you.

This exhibit opens a window to the past, offering a glimpse into the lives and legacies of the Black baseball players who did more than play a game, Black baseball executives who did more than administer the game, Black baseball fans who did more than watch the game, and Black baseball writers who did more than report on the game—they helped shape a nation.

For Black baseball is not only about excelling on the diamond; it is about the pioneers, community leaders, and advocates for justice whose contributions extend far beyond the boundaries of a ball field—for Black baseball touches the very soul of America.

Therefore, let us remember the enduring spirit of these people who gave themselves to the game with unwavering determination and dignity. Let their legacy inspire us to continue the work of making our world a more inclusive, just, and compassionate place. Long live baseball. And long live these beautiful souls of the game.

—Rowan Ricardo Phillips at the opening of the exhibit *The Souls of the Game: Voices of Black Baseball,* on which this book is based
NATIONAL BASEBALL HALL OF FAME AND MUSEUM, MAY 24, 2024

CONTENTS

FOREWORD

by Dave Winfield

Baseball was not just my favorite sport when I was a young boy growing up in Minnesota in the 1950s and 1960s, but it was the number one sport in America, in terms of both participation and respect. Even more than football, basketball, soccer, and golf, baseball caught my attention at a very early age and became the sport that my brother Steve and I played more than any other.

The lessons we learned from baseball were many: teamwork, being on time, and not making excuses. We learned how to prepare, how to put in the hard work, and how to win. I always knew that if I brought my best to the field and tried to make myself better every day, it would carry me through life.

Those lessons opened the door to higher education at the University of Minnesota, led to a successful career in baseball and business, and took me all over the world, where I have met the most interesting people, from local residents to multiple U.S. presidents.

But as a child playing the game, I saw baseball as simply about having fun. I knew that I had found something I loved, but I could never have imagined that it would love me back in the ways it has.

This game has taken me to six big league teams in both leagues, on both coasts, and in many different countries. I was blessed to play Major League Baseball (MLB) for twenty-two years, make twelve All-Star teams, win seven Gold Glove Awards and six Silver Slugger Awards, and earn election to the National Baseball Hall of Fame on the first ballot.

But I'm equally as proud to have gained the personal respect of my teammates and to have become the first athlete to have their own charitable foundation, in service of others. You can imagine, over the last half century, who I've met and what I've experienced.

OPPOSITE Dave Winfield parlayed his athleticism and determination into a twenty-two-year career in the big leagues. But it was the lessons he took from the game that led him to Cooperstown.

I've stood on the shoulders of some of the greatest to ever play the game, and many of those who embraced me looked like me. They had similar life experiences, which helped me imagine that I could be successful, too.

As a professional player, I was humbled and delighted to meet many of my heroes and follow in their footsteps. Legendary Negro Leaguers (who were even better human beings) Satchel Paige, Monte Irvin, Joe Black, John "Buck" O'Neil, Cool Papa Bell, Mamie "Peanut" Johnson, Hank Aaron, and Willie Mays, as well as Rachel Robinson (the wife of Jackie Robinson), have guided me on this journey. My life and career have intersected with the best who played and influenced the game I love.

That is why, as a former San Diego Padres player and executive, I helped create Negro Leagues tributes at the ballpark for ten years. In 2008, I suggested the idea of hosting a Negro Leagues draft within Major League Baseball so that these heroes could be honored while they were still alive.

In 2006, I got chills as I sat on the stage in Cooperstown when seventeen players from the Negro Leagues, chosen through a special election, were rightfully honored with a plaque in the gallery. Then, in 2022, I was truly humbled to give a speech on behalf of John W. Jackson, aka Bud Fowler—the very first African American to play professional baseball—when he was inducted into the Hall of Fame. Just forty-eight hours earlier, we had visited his grave to pay our respects; he was laid to rest in 1913 an hour outside of Cooperstown, where he grew up and now lives on forever.

I am very proud to say that there are now thirty-nine Negro Leagues men and women—players, executives, and owners—who have been inducted into the Hall of Fame in recognition of their accomplishments, beginning with Satchel Paige in 1971. In 2020, Major League Baseball formally recognized seven different Negro Leagues as "major leagues," adding the statistics of more than 3,400 players from 1920 to 1948 to the official records.

As a student of history, I knew that a career in baseball mirrored the issues facing everyday Black Americans in the workplace. Fowler and players like Moses Fleetwood Walker and his brother Weldy played together with white teammates before the color line was created. Racism and Jim Crow laws reared their ugly heads for a couple of generations before Jackie Robinson ultimately integrated baseball—or reintegrated it for good—in 1947.

When things did not go their way, Black players from Bud to Jackie simply *played harder*. Back then, they had no choice but to do so.

Yet, four decades later, a prominent major league general manager said out loud what many people in the sport thought, "that [Black people] may not have some of the necessities" to be the manager or GM of a club. This statement reflected the misguided and miseducated thinking of the day and didn't reckon with the fact that limiting the access of "others" to privilege and opportunities kept change from happening earlier and at an increased pace.

I was my team's player representative for the Major League Baseball Players Association (MLBPA) in sixteen of my twenty-two years in the big leagues. As a Black player in a leadership and advocacy position, I faced many hurdles, but today I can look back and see that my input made a difference in the game and the workplace.

But our work is not yet done.

With the declining number of Black players on the field, Black fans in the stands, and Black people playing the game for recreation or a potential career, MLB has responded in a number of ways, including various diversity and inclusion initiatives, that are seeing some positive results.

Over the last decade, the MLBPA has taken the next step toward leadership as well, not only for all baseball players but for players in other professional men's and women's sports. In fact, through the leadership of Tony Clark, the MLBPA has extended its work into other industries, both domestically and internationally, setting an example for other unions of how to stand up for their members. After a fourteen-year big league career, Tony became the MLBPA's fourth executive director and the first Black person to hold the position. He has advanced the playing conditions, pay, business opportunities, and protections of the 1,200-plus MLBPA members while bringing 5,600 minor league players into the union—a phenomenal feat.

There is a direct line from Tony Clark, Bill Lucas, and Bob Watson to Dusty Baker, Cito Gaston, Dave Roberts, and other minorities being allowed to make their own profound mark in this country and in the world of Major League Baseball. Needless to say, Black opportunities have led the way for other players of color and international players to participate and thrive, including one of today's biggest superstars, Shohei Ohtani.

But there are those who would choose to erase American history, including Black history. I am not one of them. Thankfully, there are now countless books, videos, documentaries, and museums that showcase this history, none of which existed when I was a youth. It is critical to understand history so that we know where we've come from, where we stand today, and where we can go in the future. This helps us avoid past mistakes and enables us to move forward.

That is why I'm so proud to contribute to *Play Harder: The Triumph of Black Baseball in America* by Dr. Gerald Early, the renowned scholar, award-winning author, essayist, culture critic, and professor of African and African American studies. Together, we were on the advisory committee of the National Baseball Hall of Fame and Museum's Black Baseball Initiative, of which this new book is a part. Another centerpiece of the initiative is an exhibit focused on the lived experiences of being Black and being involved in this wonderful game. *The Souls of the Game: Voices of Black Baseball* reveals the deep connections between baseball and Black America and is truly worth a visit to Cooperstown.

Both the exhibit and this book provide countless examples of Black people being given an opportunity and proving that they can make things better, improving our game and our country, for thousands who have followed them onto the ball field and millions more who follow them as citizens of our great country. It is a long and decorated lineage, and it is one of my greatest accomplishments to have been a part of this historical journey.

OPPOSITE Dave Winfield during Induction Weekend in 2001, when he entered the Hall of Fame.

TO ME BASEBALL IS CAMELOT,

THAT MYSTICAL DREAM TO WHICH WE ALL ASPIRE. THERE ARE KINGS, QUEENS, PRINCES AND PRINCESSES, DUKES, AND KNIGHTS. REINTERPRET IN BASEBALLESE, OWNERS, MANAGERS, COACHES, AND THE KNIGHTS OF THE DIAMOND—THE BALLPLAYERS.

—Art Rust Jr., Black American baseball fan and sportswriter, *Recollections of a Baseball Junkie*

INTRODUCTION

THE BASEBALL THAT BLACK PEOPLE CREATED

Play Harder is the story of Black Americans and baseball. For more than 150 years, Black people have played "the long game": developing their skills as youngsters; mastering the trade as professionals; creating teams; constructing, against long odds, the business model of leagues or what is called organized baseball; promoting the game to their fans; and, finally, breaking the long-standing color barrier in the sport. The title of this book itself—*Play Harder*—was a phrase Black players used to motivate themselves when facing adversity. "Play harder" was an expression of aspiration, determination, willpower, and courage. It acknowledged the fierce demands of high-level athletic competition, as well as Black people's difficult history in a racist America with an uneven playing field in all walks of life. The old saying among Black folks was that one had to be twice as good to get half as far as a white person. In this regard, "play harder" could be considered a sort of motto, a two-word pep talk for Black people.

Sportswriter Art Rust Jr.—who's right to suggest that baseball is a sort of Camelot—became an ardent fan of the game as a youngster when his Jamaican father, who immigrated to the United States at nineteen, switched his sports allegiance from cricket to baseball. There was something mythical about Black baseball in the heyday of the Negro Leagues. Owners like Effa Manley, Cumberland Posey, Gus Greenlee, and J. B. Martin were like queens and kings. Their meetings and disagreements were fodder for Black newspapers. Managers and masterminds like Rube Foster, Buck O'Neil, C. I. Taylor, and Dave Malarcher were the princes and dukes, the shapers of players and plays. And, of course, the great players like Oscar Charleston, Josh Gibson, Satchel Paige, Willie Wells, Biz Mackey, Cool Papa Bell, and Buck Leonard were the knights, the Lancelots, Gawains, and Percivals of the realm. All of these people were larger than life, the subject of gossip, rumor, and Black newspaper columns, as if they were movie stars. For a certain period, Black baseball was a world, a cosmos unto itself. For its adherents, it had the power of a religion.

Roy Campanella was fifteen years old when he debuted for
the Washington Elite Giants of the Negro National League in
1937. Eleven years later, Campanella played his first game for
the Brooklyn Dodgers. He is shown here circa 1950.

Not all Black people felt so positive about the game, however. The great Rube Foster told his half brother Bill not to play baseball. "That's no life for you," he said. At fifteen, and already a professional, Roy Campanella came home at two in the morning from a doubleheader with the Baltimore Elite Giants. His mother was incensed, distraught with worry. She hit him with a leather strap while berating him, "You're getting to be a bum, just like the rest of those baseball bums!" She called him a "bum" over and over as she struck him several times before she began to cry. Campanella's mother was not unusual as a Black parent perplexed by the attraction of a seemingly worthless game that produced no practical skills for employment—an itinerant job for which, as Campanella wrote, "[the] bus was our home, dressing room, dining room, and hotel"; a job that did not seem to advance the race, and, for the devout, violated the Sabbath. Why would Black people waste their time watching baseball? Why would a Black person want to make a living from something so frivolous? She wanted her son to finish high school. He never did. For her, baseball had bewitched him. For young Campanella, with the great Negro Leagues catcher Biz Mackey as his coach, baseball was the best school he could have. And it was labor. As he said, he wasn't "just *playing* at catching, but *working* the position." Labor that fulfilled him and not just labor for labor's sake. Despite her misgivings and dislike of the game, Campanella's mother let him play baseball. She realized, after a point, how much it meant to him.

Rust loved white baseball, too, although he knew that the white stars "were for the most part bigots," and that they were "probably the sorriest idols I had." But idols they were until his father finally took him to a Negro Leagues game in 1938 when he was ten. When he saw the Black players, he had new heroes. Rust, about to enter college, "nearly cried" when Jackie Robinson signed with the Brooklyn Dodgers in 1945. On September 23, 1949, Fawcett Comics put out the first of six comic books devoted to "Jackie Robinson, Baseball Hero." A Black man as a comic book hero! Robinson had become the biggest crossover Black hero in American popular culture at the time.

Play Harder is about what it means to be a Black baseball hero—and what it costs. Many think that Robinson's early death in 1972 at the age of fifty-three was the price he paid for his heroism. Moses Fleetwood Walker, who played on an integrated team at Oberlin College in the 1880s, was the last Black man to play white major league baseball until Robinson. Walker struggled after his baseball career ended—he moved from occupation to occupation and went to prison for a year for mail theft, a charge he fought bitterly. Houston Astros phenom flamethrower J. R. Richard had a stroke on the field in 1980. At the time, his record was 10 wins, 4 losses, 4 shutouts, and a 1.90 ERA. He was one of the greatest pitchers of his generation. He would never pitch for the Astros again. He lost his money, his family through divorces, his bearings through depression, and wound up homeless, living under a bridge for several months. Often, to understand what the game means to Black people is to learn not what it feels like to win but what it feels like to lose.

Play Harder tells the narrative of Black baseball from the end of the Civil War to today's effort by Major League Baseball (MLB) to attract more African Americans to the game. The Negro Leagues sit at the center of this history, the fulcrum that torques the machine. But what happened in the roughly fifty-five years of Black baseball before the formation of the Negro National League in 1920 and what has happened in the nearly eighty years of integrated baseball since 1947 are just as important as the approximately forty-year period, starting in 1920, when the administrative, economic, and cultural spasms of the Negro Leagues produced two powerful eras of Black organized baseball.

The Negro Leagues are central to the story of Black baseball, but as *Play Harder* reveals, they are not, by any means, the whole story. Black baseball of the late nineteenth and early twentieth centuries saw isolated instances of integration on the field, at least right after the Civil War, and attempts to organize professional teams and leagues after the end of Reconstruction. But when the Negro Leagues organized Black baseball at last, they aspired to be the force by which white major league baseball's color line would be broken and reached that goal by preparing a cadre of trained Black men who could play with the best white players. The story does not end there: when the white major leagues integrated, effectively ending the Negro Leagues, African Americans eventually wanted a greater role in the everyday operation: as managers, administrators, and even owners, the very jobs they held in the Negro Leagues. This struggle for parity continues today.

Chapter 1 tells the story of Black baseball in the nineteenth century, from the Reconstruction era until the eve of World War I, starting with early amateur Black baseball organizers like Octavius Catto in Philadelphia and Frederick Douglass's sons in Washington, D.C. It also covers the organization of the first Black professional teams. This chapter, like every other, profiles a few key players of the era. Here it is Bud Fowler and Moses Fleetwood Walker, who spent most of their careers playing on white teams until the relentless push of Jim Crow drove them from otherwise white baseball.

Chapter 2 centers on the creation of the Negro National League (NNL) in 1920, the era of the New Negro Renaissance, which produced Black figures as diverse as Marcus Garvey and Langston Hughes. The story focuses on Rube Foster, the father of Black organized baseball, and his rival, Ed Bolden, who formed the Eastern Colored League as a competitor to the NNL. There are up-close and personal profiles of Satchel Paige and Cool Papa Bell.

Chapter 3 focuses on the aftermath of World War II, the rising importance of civil rights on the national stage, as well as Jackie Robinson and the integration of the Brooklyn Dodgers, a move that changed baseball forever. Robinson's legacy in the history of the game is touched on in the remaining chapters as well. The chapter also examines the state of the Negro Leagues immediately before and after integration occurs.

Chapter 4 looks at the interaction of Latino and Black American players, providing a brief account of Latino players who participated in the Negro Leagues. It also explores the story of Black American Negro Leagues players who played in Latin America in the winter and who jumped their teams to play there during the regular season. The chapter concentrates on the experiences of Dominican outfielder Felipe Alou, who became a key player for the San Francisco Giants in the early 1960s, one of the most racially diverse teams in major league history. Alou's and Puerto Rican slugger Orlando Cepeda's relationship with the Giants' African American superstar Willie Mays—and their ambivalence about Mays as a clubhouse leader—is explored as well.

Chapter 5 is about the impact of the racial rebellions across urban America in the 1960s, and the growing militancy of some Black athletes as Black Power increasingly became the political rallying cry of African Americans. Profiles include an examination of Jackie Robinson's post-baseball career, the career of Dick Allen in Philadelphia, Hank Aaron's mid-career with the Braves, and Curt Flood's legal challenge to baseball's reserve clause. It also covers the changes in baseball, including expansion and the advent of television, and how they affected ongoing integration in the game.

Chapter 6 examines Black players in the major leagues from the 1970s to the 1990s, the advent of free agency, and the continued expansion of Major League Baseball. Reggie Jackson and Dave Winfield are highlighted as well as Darryl Strawberry and Dwight Gooden. Hank Aaron's pursuit of Babe Ruth's home run record later in his career and the death of Jackie Robinson are covered, too. The chapter ends with the advent of Black managers in corner offices, including Bill White's reign as the president of the National League.

Chapter 7 deals with Black baseball up to current times, focusing on Black people's loss of interest in the game and seeming estrangement from it. Barry Bonds and Ken Griffey Jr. are profiled. And the ongoing pursuit of equity in management ranks is explored. A section is devoted to MLB's efforts to increase the number of Black players.

There are also spotlight essays interspersed throughout the book, vignettes dealing mostly with certain individuals such as Duke Ellington and his adventures with baseball in Washington, D.C., as a child, Black baseball figures like Sol White and female Negro Leaguer Toni Stone, major Black MLB stars like Vada Pinson and Vida Blue, and such topics as barnstorming in the early decades of the twentieth century as well as the connection between hip-hop and baseball today.

"You have to be a man to be a big-leaguer," Roy Campanella famously said, "but you have to have a lot of little boy in you too." That is the paradox of this game: to grow up without ever growing up. Ralph Ellison, in his great novel, *Invisible Man*, framed it with his character Trueblood as "to move without moving." The grand illusion of baseball is that, for a while, this seems possible, even actual, that something can change without changing, that the game is what it has always been, that the players are what they always were.

It is my hope that the readers of *Play Harder* will be forever grateful to the Black men and women who gave so much to our nation through this game. Walt Whitman was right: "the game of ball is glorious."

Early Black teams, like the Spartans from Virginia, pictured here circa 1890, offered opportunities for African Americans to play baseball on a professional level.

CHAPTER 1

CHILDREN, GO WHERE I SEND THEE

THE BEGINNINGS OF BLACK BASEBALL

1865–1910

BASEBALL
WAS MY GAME . . .

—Novelist, diplomat, poet, and NAACP field secretary
James Weldon Johnson, who cowrote "Lift Every
Voice and Sing," the Black national anthem

From the end of the Civil War to World War I, African Americans experienced extraordinary change. In one respect, they went from being enslaved people to citizens, from slavery to freedom, in a complete redefinition of a people. The ratifications of the Thirteenth Amendment (December 1865), which ended slavery; the Fourteenth Amendment (July 1868), which granted citizenship; and the Fifteenth Amendment (February 1870), which granted Black men (but not yet women) the right to vote, radically changed the civic and political status of Black people in an amazingly short period of time. In addition, the Civil Rights Act of 1866 ensured equal protection under the law, and the Civil Rights Act of 1875 banned racial discrimination. Black leaders obtained political office in some Southern states, including sixteen who were elected to Congress, two who served in the U.S. Senate, and two who served briefly as governors during Reconstruction (1865–1877), the period when the United States experimented with being a multiracial democracy.

But if the elevation of Black Americans during Reconstruction was a revolution, it was met by a fierce counterrevolution on the part of white Southerners who vehemently and violently opposed any change in the status of Black people. White Southerners utterly opposed the Freedmen's Bureau, a federal agency established to help newly freed African Americans obtain fairer wages and better employment conditions from their former enslavers; the bureau also established, in conjunction with the American Missionary Association, some HBCUs (historically Black colleges and universities). But its main work ended in 1869, and the bureau closed for good in 1872, at which time it had not had nearly enough time to achieve the goal of helping a mostly impoverished people become self-supporting citizens.

White Southerners formed terrorist organizations, like the Ku Klux Klan, that brutally intimidated Black citizens and created Black Codes to nullify African Americans' new rights. Barely a year after the end of the Civil War, in May 1866, Memphis erupted in one of the worst racial pogroms of the Reconstruction period. White people, provoked because Black soldiers had stood up to racist white (mostly Irish) policemen, rampaged through the Black community of Memphis, killing 46 Black people, injuring over 75, and burning to the ground every Black school and church in the city. The Colfax Massacre in Louisiana in 1873 resulted in the murder of somewhere between 62 and 153 Black citizens who had surrendered after resisting a white attempt to take over the local courthouse. Despite Frederick Douglass's efforts as the last president of the Freedman's Savings Bank, including lending it $10,000 to keep it afloat, the bank's failure in 1874 destroyed the faith of millions of Black people in the country's financial institutions. The lack of will on the part of the federal government and "the friends of the Negro" to enforce the social and economic changes that Reconstruction had promised left Black Americans feeling betrayed, powerless, and further impoverished by the 1880s. With the failure of Reconstruction, Black people were no longer fully empowered citizens but political and social ciphers. As Malcolm X once told a Harlem audience, "You're nothing but an ex-slave." The Confederates may have lost the Civil War, but the southern counterrevolutionists won the race war that followed.

Out of this cauldron of hope, then chaos and repression, Black people gave the world spirituals and ragtime and, in 1900, their own national anthem, "Lift Every Voice and Sing." Segregated and virtually exiled, the all-Black Twenty-Fourth and Twenty-Fifth Infantry regiments, two of the regiments known as the Buffalo Soldiers, and the Ninth and Tenth Cavalries fought in the grim wars in the West against Native Americans. Black units also fought in Cuba and the Philippines during the Spanish-American War. It can hardly be said that Black people did not serve their country, even as their country scarcely acknowledged them. They built schools and churches and started newspapers. The literacy rate among Black people in 1870 was 18.6 percent. It had jumped to 55.5 percent by 1890. Between 1890 and 1900, the number of Black physicians and dentists nearly doubled, thanks to

OPPOSITE A Black team from Morris Brown College, one of the earliest historically Black colleges and universities, located in Georgia, circa 1899.

BASE BALL.

MR. EDITOR:—A match was played between the Henson Base Ball Club of Jamaica, and the Unknown, of Weeksville, at Jamaica, L. I., on Tuesday, Nov. 15th, which resulted in another victory for the Henson. The following is the score:

HENSON.	O.	R.	UNKNOWN.	O.	R.
Johnson, c.	2	10	Poole, p.	4	4
Henson, p.	4	6	H. Smith, c.	1	8
Vanwyck, s. b.	3	4	Ricks, f. b.	4	5
Hanke, f. b.	4	5	Anderson, s. b.	2	6
G. Anthony, t. b.	0	9	J. Thompson, t. b.	4	3
Ferris, s. s.	3	4	J. Smith, s. s.	2	4
Wilmore, c. f.	2	8	A. Thomson, r. f.	2	6
J. Anthony, r. f.	4	4	Wright, c. f.	5	3
Hewlett, l. f.	2	4	Johnson, l. f.	2	8

RUNS MADE IN EACH INNING.

Innings	1	2	3	4	5	6	7	8	9	
Henson	6	1	6	17	3	9	3	9		—54
Unknown	7	5	4	4	7	0	2	3	11	—43

SCORERS.—Henson Club, Wm. Austin; Unknown, Wm. Johnson.

UMPIRE—Charles English.

Even before the start of the Civil War, Black teams were playing baseball; shown here is the earliest known box score between two all-Black teams. It was printed in the December 10, 1859, edition of the *Anglo-African*, about a game played between the baseball club called the Unknowns and the Henson Baseball Club on Long Island, New York.

HBCUs. Surely, Black citizens were climbing a steep hill, but they were willing to do so, in part because so many of them believed in this country, even if the country did not believe in them. Alas, between 1890 and 1900, 1,217 African Americans were lynched—a form of white social engineering at its most brutal. For Black citizens, believing in this country was not easy.

And most notably, perhaps quixotically, groups of Black athletes, against considerable odds but with firm dedication, played baseball. During Reconstruction, during the launch of the Jim Crow era, when local and state laws legalized segregation in the South, and at the nadir of race relations at the turn of the twentieth century, they organized teams and sought competition with great energy. Nay, even more—there were Black people in America who loved baseball more than just about anything else.

FREDERICK DOUGLASS AND SONS

In his 1845 *Narrative of the Life of Frederick Douglass, an American Slave*, Douglass wrote in some detail about the holiday periods on the plantation, the week between Christmas and New Year's Day. During the holiday season, some enslaved people were permitted to earn money in order to improve their condition or to save up for their ever-elusive freedom. "But by far the larger part," Douglass observed, "engaged in such sports and merriments as playing ball, wrestling, running foot-races, fiddling, dancing, and drinking whisky; and this latter mode of spending the time was by far the most agreeable to the feelings of our masters." Douglass asserted that the masters wanted the enslaved to waste the holidays, to not be productive or seek any form of self-improvement. Douglass's theory was that the master wanted this small taste of freedom to be a dissolute, gluttonous experience to warp the enslaved peoples' sense of what freedom was and to make them more amenable to returning to work when the holiday ended.

Two things in this passage are notable. First, among their activities, the enslaved people played a ball game of some sort that historian Michael E. Lomax claims was a form of rounders or town ball. If this is true, it would mean that an early version of baseball was played on some Southern plantations in border states in the 1830s, which was when Douglass was enslaved in Maryland. (He escaped in 1838.) Second, Douglass disapproved of the various sports the enslaved people played, as well as "fiddling" and "dancing." He classed all these activities with "drinking whisky," which Douglass, a firm temperance supporter, abhorred. Douglass thought that any activity that pleased the owners was not in the enslaved peoples' interest. Besides, these activities seemed frivolous, not in any way moving the enslaved mentally and emotionally toward freedom, nor in any way opposing the system of slavery. In fact, to Douglass's way of thinking, they reinforced it.

But whatever Douglass thought of sports on the plantation during slavery, he saw matters differently with the advent of freedom. His youngest son, Charles, who was twenty-three years old in 1867 when he started working for the Freedmen's Bureau, was a fervent player. More than that, he was an organizer on a Black

team in Washington, D.C., called the Alerts, immediately after the Civil War, when Black baseball teams began appearing in the East. Indeed, when Charles's father attended an Alerts game, it made headlines in New York: "Fred Douglass Sees a Colored Game." Many government workers like Charles Douglass played baseball (or "base ball," as it was written at the time). In fact, the White House lawn was a popular site for play. Despite Black interest in a game that had a considerable white following and much white participation, there was no mixing of the teams and not much interracial play. Racial lines had already been drawn.

Douglass helped his son Charles raise money for the team, and for Black baseball generally, by writing a letter urging Black Washingtonians to support the Alerts team. He donated his own money as well. When his son switched teams to become the president of the rival Black Washington team, the Mutuals, joining his brother, Frederick Jr., Douglass Sr. switched his allegiance as well, becoming an honorary Mutual in September 1870. It is not overstating to say that Douglass was a baseball man. He attended games, supported his sons' involvement, and even played catch with his grandchildren.

Douglass's support gave Black baseball an imprimatur of race approval as an activity that uplifted the race. It was not frivolous for Black men to pursue this sport as an avocation, or even as a vocation. Baseball conveyed a kind of Black social capital. Black men as ballplayers were seen as entrepreneurs, as "manly" (which they were not when enslaved), as supporting a meritocracy and having standards of excellence, and as being role models to Black children. They were also playing the American game and thus underscoring their identification as American and their right to make such a claim. After the debacle of the 1857 *Dred Scott* Supreme Court decision, which held that Blacks were not citizens and were never intended to be, such a claim was not to be taken lightly. If the Black public could not make a claim as Americans, what could they make a claim to being? For Black people after the Civil War, playing baseball was not *a* way to *a* future, but *the* way of *the* future.

OPPOSITE Orator, author, and Black leader
Frederick Douglass, whose son Charles Douglass
organized the Alerts, a Black team in Washington, D.C.,
after the end of the Civil War.

BASEBALL AND THE BLACK ELITE

In his pathbreaking sociological study *The Philadelphia Negro* (1899), W. E. B. Du Bois mentions "the cold-blooded assassination" of "an estimable young teacher, Octavius V. Catto." Du Bois footnotes the entire article in *The Philadelphia Tribune* (a Black newspaper) chronicling Catto's murder and his funeral, which covers nearly three full pages of his book. Catto, a race activist, was killed on October 10, 1871, election day in Philadelphia, where a fierce battle between Democrats and Republicans took place in the races for mayor, district attorney, and city controller. Black men in Philadelphia, nearly all Republican, had been given the right to vote two years earlier, and this was the first election to put their new right to the test. Aided by the police, white toughs and vigilantes, mostly members of the Irish working class and the Democratic Party, roamed the streets, physically intimidating Black voters. Catto, who had closed his school, the Institute for Colored Youth, early in the afternoon because of the unrest, was shot to death by a white "peacekeeper" near Eighth and South Streets as he was preparing to join his Black National Guard unit. Catto was armed, but never had a chance to use his weapon, as he was shot at nearly point-blank range.

Catto, arguably, had one of the biggest funerals ever afforded a Black man to that point in American history. The Philadelphia City Council closed the government's various departments to permit employees to attend the funeral. Most of the important Republican leaders of the city were there. He was given an honor guard, and his body lay in state at the City Armory. Thousands crowded the streets to pay their respects, many having come from New York City, Washington, D.C., and Baltimore. The *Philadelphia Tribune* article that Du Bois ran in full said much about Catto, except one thing: in addition to his roles in the military, as an educator, and as a Black civic leader, he was a baseball player. Du Bois never mentioned it, either.

Catto's team was the Pythians, which premiered in 1866, as much a social club as a baseball outfit. Club members rented rooms at the Institute for Colored Youth, where the strict rules included no gambling, no liquor, no profanity, and no conduct that would redound unfavorably to the race. These men were largely mixed-race and would have been considered the Black Philadelphia elite. Du Bois would have called them "the Talented Tenth," just the sort of college-educated Black elite he felt was necessary to lead the race. The Pythians were gentlemen of breeding, and playing baseball was meant to enhance their respectability. Other Black clubs called themselves the Blue Stockings or the Giants, but the Pythians showed their cultural aspiration in their name, a reference to ancient Greece and the Olympic Games. As with the white clubs of the period, the Pythians, like the Mutuals and the Alerts in Washington, were amateurs, not professionals. These men, for the most part, were not common laborers but, like Charles Douglass, had white-collar jobs. They had the leisure time and the money to play baseball.

Like Washington, Philadelphia had an active and long-standing Black elite with two aims: to serve as a bridge or liaison to white elites, and to be exemplars to lower-class Black citizens. In essence, the Black leadership class tried to balance two pursuits: gaining access to white institutions and organizations in an effort to remove racial stigmas and gain equal civic and economic opportunity; and creating Black institutions and enterprises that showed self-reliance, intelligence, the solidarity of the race, and a commitment to self-improvement.

That Catto was an activist is hardly surprising. According to Daniel R. Biddle and Murray Dubin in *Tasting Freedom*, the entire leadership of the Pythians came from "abolition and Underground Railroad families," the antebellum Black activist elite that included fugitive slave lecturers, writers, and organizers like James W. C. Pennington, William Wells Brown, and Frederick Douglass.

The Pythians acquitted themselves well against rival Black teams in Philadelphia, a city that would remain a hotbed of Black baseball through the days of the Negro Leagues. They played both the Mutuals and the Alerts, in Philadelphia and Washington, in games that were not only competitive but highly social, as the home team would always host a huge meal after the game. To be a successful Black team required that the Pythians be highly organized, with a committee to secure a field and umpires (a challenge for Black teams that would continue into the Negro Leagues era, as white teams controlled baseball spaces), a committee responsible for transporting the team if they were the visitors, a committee to work on the after-game feast or picnic if the Pythians were the host, and a committee to select a trophy or prize for the opposing team. The team practiced twice a week and held monthly meetings; for Catto, an additional obligation was running the Institute for Colored Youth. Dues were five dollars a year. The drawn-out schedule of meetings and practices indicates that early Black baseball was played at a leisurely pace as an amateur game. When it became professional, many more games would be played to try to keep both the league and individual teams afloat.

In October 1867, Raymond J. Burr, the Pythians' vice president, attended the convention of the Pennsylvania Association of Amateur Base Ball Players (PAABBP), held in Harrisburg. Baseball at this time held a number of conventions and meetings, local, statewide, and national, as it stabilized and codified its rules and established league affiliations. The Pythians had applied for full membership in the PAABBP. They had had a successful 1867 season, becoming one of the best Black clubs in the country. Their play received regular press in the *Sunday Mercury* and *The Philadelphia Inquirer.* Burr was the only Black person at the convention, but was treated courteously, even collegially at times. However, the Pythians' application was denied—in fact, Burr withdrew it when it was clear that it had no chance of success. Had the Pythians been a white club, their acceptance would have been pro forma.

The reason for the rejection was purely racial, as granting a Black team membership would have been tantamount to recognizing Black men as equals; most white Northerners were not keen to do this, in part because such a gesture would have stymied sectional reconciliation. The Civil War was over, and there was now no reason for Southern and Northern white people to foster hard feelings against one another. If the source of any hard feelings was the status of the freed and newly created Negro citizen, the easiest solution was to keep the Black population as a subordinate, inferior group, socially and politically. This accommodation of the South by the North made Reconstruction half-hearted and was the reason it ultimately failed. For baseball's future, as white Northerners saw it, getting white Southerners committed to the game as the National Pastime was crucial. This feeling only intensified in the latter part of the nineteenth century as white Southerners propagated the myth of the Lost Cause, which made them seem

OPPOSITE Octavius Catto captained his team, the Pythians, in Philadelphia in the years immediately following the Civil War; an active proponent for racial equality, he was tragically killed during a race riot on election day, October 10, 1871.

OCTAVIUS V. CATTO,

like tragic heroes rather than traitors. And so, the Pythians' failed try at PAABBP membership was the first official step in the codified segregation of baseball.

At the 1867 National Association of Base Ball Players (NABBP) convention, the nominating committee issued a statement barring the membership of any Black club or any club with a Black member. This move appeased NABBP president Arthur Gorman, a founding member and a pro-Union Democratic Southerner from Maryland. He was also a star player with the Washington Nationals, which was formed in 1859 and recognized as America's first "official," high-caliber, nationally known baseball team. Gorman served only one year as the NABBP president, solely as a postbellum gesture of reconciliation. He was, as author Ryan Swanson perceptively, if wryly, points out, "'an affirmative action' hire," as he was selected solely because he was a white Southerner. The NABBP's ban of Black teams and players was the second major precedent that eventually led to a segregated baseball system in the United States. This segregation in the sport was to grow, reaching its peak by the mid-1880s, even before Jim Crow was fully nationalized and made constitutional with *Plessy v. Ferguson*'s "separate but equal" decision in 1896.

The death of Catto was the end of the Pythians. The club seemed to lose heart and direction, not only because of the death of its most important leader but especially because of the way he died. But Black baseball soldiered on, its story just beginning. A new class of Black ballplayers was coming, the men who played for money—the professionals.

FOWLER, FLEET, AND THE END OF INTEGRATED BASEBALL

The NABBP faced a great deal of dissension in its efforts to harness baseball after the Civil War. Apathy and disputes were common. But the biggest threat to the NABBP was the rise of professional baseball. The Cincinnati Red Stockings announced in 1869 that they were a fully professional baseball team, and they recruited players from around the country to play for a salary. Of course, many teams had been paying players, but Cincinnati's announcement changed baseball forever. Professionals appealed to the fans—indeed, to the general public—and they would come to define and dominate the game. In 1883, with the creation of the National Agreement that formally recognized two major leagues, the National League and the American Association, and one high minor league, the Northwestern League, "Organized Baseball" was officially established. A minimum salary was set, a season with a set number of games was scheduled, and the same supplier of baseballs and equipment, A. G. Spalding, was used across the leagues. And as the reserve clause now began to be used, players became contractually tied to their clubs and could not jump from club to club, as many were wont to do.

Black players were not entirely shut out of the major leagues or the movement toward professionalization. They continued to form their own clubs and played against each other and even against white teams. There were even Black players on white teams. According to historian Leslie Heaphy, "before 1890 seventy African American names appeared on white, professional rosters." But this fact doesn't tell the whole story, as Black players were being relentlessly squeezed out of the white game by the mid-1880s.

On August 10, 1883, the Chicago White Stockings of the National League stopped in Toledo, Ohio, to play the Toledo Blue Stockings of the Northwestern League. Player-manager Adrian "Cap" Anson and owner A. G. Spalding objected to the presence of Toledo's Black catcher, Moses Fleetwood Walker. Anson, then the greatest player in professional baseball, made it clear that he would not take the field "with no damned nigger." But Toledo insisted that Walker play,

Bud Fowler traveled the country in search of
opportunities to play the game he loved; he is pictured
here (*top row, center*) in 1885 with a Keokuk, Iowa,
team, one of the many he played with.

unless the White Stockings wanted to lose their share of the gate by forfeiture. "We'll play this here game," Anson said, "but we won't play never no more with the nigger in." Anson's declaration signaled another step toward the end of Black players in white organized baseball.

☽☾

The members of the Black "sporting" crowd, as they were called, were a strong fraternity—athletes, musicians, singers, songwriters, dancers, gamblers, women of the night, and sharpies of various kinds. They had in common that they were either entertainers or the hustler types who adhered to them. They were not entirely respectable to the middle-class or churchgoing Black community, but some were among the most famous and admired Black people of their day. They earned more money than the average Black worker, and their work was generally far more interesting. Most were creatives of one sort or another, living by their training, their hard-earned skills, or their wits. Even among the Victorian types in the Black community who were consumed by the idea of respectability, the "sporting crowd" was at least grudgingly given their due. They were also highly peripatetic. Their work frequently required travel around a circuit of venues. But probably no one of this Black Bohemia during the post–Civil War era was quite as peripatetic as Bud Fowler. If a common phrase was "George Washington slept here," it could be paraphrased as "Bud Fowler played here."

He was born John Jackson, in Fort Plain, New York, in 1858, but would become known in the world of professional baseball as Bud Fowler. He learned to play growing up in, appropriately, Cooperstown. If it was thought that pitcher Satchel Paige was the ultimate traveling man during his days in the Negro Leagues, he had nothing on Fowler. According to one historian, Fowler "played in 13 different professional minor leagues in an 18-year period." He also played for a number of semipro teams and in such places as Stillwater, Minnesota; Keokuk, Iowa; Pueblo, Colorado; Crawfordsville, Indiana; and Topeka, Kansas. "He played on crossroads farm teams, in mining camps, in pioneer settlements of the West, and in cities in the East," writes one scholar. Fowler's motto could have been "Have Bat, Will Travel."

Fowler's wanderlust shows how widespread the baseball craze was during and after Reconstruction, empowered by the railroad, which contributed greatly to making baseball a national game after the Civil War. His travels also show the fluidity of the race situation, as Fowler played, for a significant part of his career, on white teams. When Fowler was not playing baseball, he was a barber. Barbering was considered one of the most important professions for a Black man in the nineteenth century, as the clientele was largely white. Indeed, barbers were numbered among the Black elite. Being a barber helped Fowler's baseball career by putting him in contact with white people of influence.

Fowler left some teams for better pay and others because they went bankrupt and disbanded, a common occurrence in nineteenth-century baseball for both Black and white teams. Still others he left because of racism. To be sure, Fowler was a good player; otherwise, he would not have found such steady employment over the course of his career. But in 1887 Fowler was released by the Binghamton Bingos of the International League, despite hitting .350, because of his race. He was the last Black player to be driven from white organized baseball. He signed the next year with the New York Gorhams, with whom he played until 1891.

The Gorhams were a Black professional team whose rivals for a time were the Cuban Giants, the first Black professional team. Formed in 1885, the Giants were the powerhouse Black team of their time. The Cuban Giants—who were not Cubans but Black Americans—were meant to take Black baseball to the next level, achieving a new standard of excellence, by being like the Cincinnati Red Stockings, with players paid a regular salary, not a portion of the game's gate receipts. During his time with the Gorhams, Fowler, a promoter to the hilt, ballyhooed a competition called the "Colored League" championship, although there was no "colored league" at the time. The Cuban Giants took the bait and played the Gorhams for this "title," which was much like the invented "colored" titles in late nineteenth-century Black boxing circles, in 1887 and 1888.

In 1894, Fowler became the manager of the Black professional team in Adrian, Michigan, the Page Fence Giants, who were meant to be the new powerhouse of Black baseball. The new manager bragged that twelve of his players were college-educated, respectable men. Fowler was key among Black baseball players in the nineteenth century in cultivating an image of clean living and fair play, which was their attempt to distinguish themselves from the rest of the Black sporting world of which they were a part. Not only was Fowler present at the point of creation of Black professional baseball but he was a major force in its conception. He died in 1913, so he was not part of its future as an "organized" sport, but he helped set the stage.

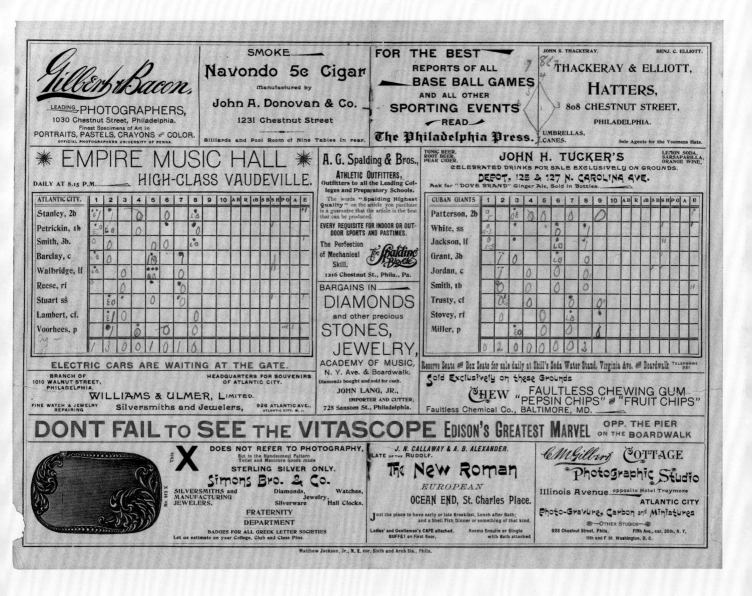

A scorecard from a July 23, 1896, game between the first
professional all-Black club Cuban Giants and an Atlantic
City collegiate team, which fielded white players.

Moses Fleetwood Walker, who played baseball at Oberlin College while a student there in the late 1870s—and whose brother Weldy (also sometimes known as Welday) played there as a member of the class of 1885—was the last Black player for a major league club in the nineteenth century. Walker's father was a physician, another indication of how many Black players in these early days of Black baseball came from relatively privileged backgrounds. That Walker was a student at Oberlin is hardly surprising. The college was coeducational at a time when that was unusual, it was radically abolitionist before the Civil War, and it had always admitted Black students. Walker continued his baseball career at the University of Michigan, which recruited him from Oberlin. Black men playing baseball who had gone to college was not as uncommon as one might expect for a people just freed from slavery.

When he signed to play professionally with the Toledo Blue Stockings in 1883, Walker doubtless was more educated than nearly all of his white teammates. Often referred to as Fleet, he was described as the perfect gentleman, a demeanor he needed to play among white players. Toledo left the Northwestern League for the American Association in 1884, transforming it from a high minor league to a major league team. Walker played in fifty-four games in 1884 and hit .251. His brother joined the team briefly—playing in ten games and hitting .222—though they were not believed to be on the field at the same time. Fleetwood Walker's offense wasn't as important as his defense: he was a catcher, the most demanding position on the field, at a time when hand injuries were common because players usually wore thin, unpadded gloves or no gloves at all.

Playing on white teams was difficult. Umpires often called borderline plays against Black players. Racial slurs from opposing players and the fans were common, and opposing pitchers frequently threw pitches at Black batters. Sharpened spikes and high, vicious slides were so common that, according to many sources, Fowler invented wooden shin guards to use when playing the field. A pitcher on Walker's own team refused to acknowledge his signs and threw anything he wanted, making Walker's life miserable trying to catch for him. The pitcher confessed years later that Walker was the best catcher he ever threw to.

When the Chicago White Stockings returned to Toledo to play the Blue Stockings in July 1884, Cap Anson got what he wanted. Walker did not play. What a

Oberlin College, located in northeast Ohio, was integrated from its early
years, and its sports program reflected that. Both Moses Fleetwood
Walker (*seated on the left*), and his brother Weldy (*standing, third from
the left*) can be seen in this team photo from that era.

difference a year made! Toledo could not make it as a major league team, endured
a terrible season, and returned to the minors in 1885—without Moses Fleetwood
Walker. In 1908, Walker published a book called *Our Home Colony*, advocating that
Black people immigrate to Africa because, he argued, they had no future in the
United States. At the time, he owned a movie theater in Cadiz, Ohio, that featured,
among other entertainments, the popular racist minstrel shows of the era, which
he hated, but he had to give the customers what they wanted.

SOL WHITE: BLACK BASEBALL'S FIRST HISTORIAN

King Solomon White, born in Bellaire, Ohio, in 1868, was a key figure in the early history of Black baseball. Sol White, as he was commonly known, played with and managed several Black teams, from the Pittsburgh Keystones, part of the short-lived National Colored Base Ball League, where he started in 1887, to the Cuban Giants and then Philadelphia Giants in 1903, where he began his managing career. Most influential, however, was his contribution to the study of Black baseball. He wrote what is considered to be the first history of Black players in the game, *History of Colored Base Ball.* Also known as *Sol White's Official Base Ball Guide*, it was published in 1907.

White's academic career prepared him for this pivotal contribution. The August 7, 1909, editions of *The Broad Ax*, published in Chicago, and *The Freeman*, published in

OPPOSITE Sol White's *History of Colored Base Ball*
documented some of the earliest heroes of Black baseball and
remains one of the seminal works on the history of the sport.

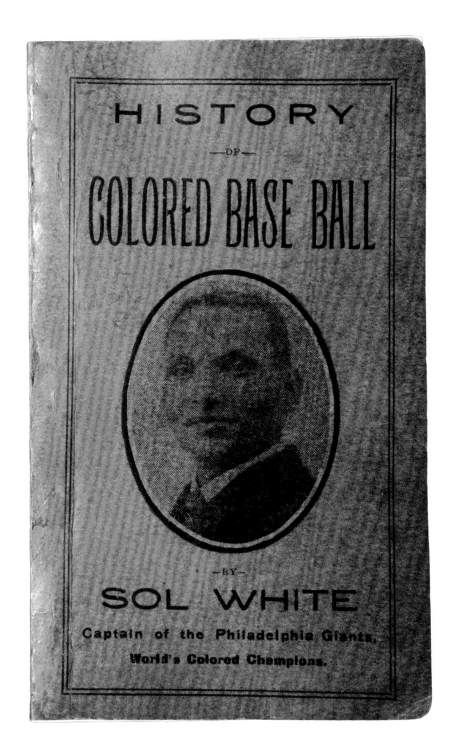

HISTORY

—OF—

COLORED BASE BALL

—BY—

SOL WHITE

Captain of the Philadelphia Giants,
World's Colored Champions.

Indianapolis, reported, "Captain White enjoys the reputation of being the only professional Negro player who is a college graduate, having been educated at Wilberforce University, which is the oldest institution in America for the education of Afro-Americans." Available academic records from Wilberforce for 1895–1896 and 1896–1897 show that the twenty-seven-year-old theology major got his sheepskin by taking classes in reading, grammar, arithmetic, physiology, spelling, U.S. history, geography, and elocution (formal speaking). On a scale of 1 to 10, White earned grades ranging from 8.7 to 9.5.

White put his intellectual leanings to work in writing *History of Colored Base Ball*. One passage reveals "I have endeavored to follow the mutations of colored baseball as accurately as possible, from the organization of the first colored professional team in 1885, to the present." The result was a 128-page history with 57 timeless images of legendary personalities.

Four years after elder statesman W. E. B. Du Bois had declared in *The Souls of Black Folk* that "the problem of the twentieth century is the problem of the color line," White's history served as the genesis for serious study of Black baseball before organized league play began in 1920. This slender work, published as a pamphlet measuring 5¾ by 3½ inches, can be described as an almanac, a memoir, and a tutorial, with chapters written by Andrew "Rube" Foster on "How to Pitch" and Grant "Home Run" Johnson on "The Art and Science of Hitting." The *Baltimore Afro-American* of May 11, 1907, called it "unique, in that no history of the popular pastime, as played by colored men, has ever before been written. No one knows more of the progress of the game better than he, and he writes most entertainingly. In addition to the full tale of the progress of the game there are nearly a hundred [*sic*: fifty-seven] half-tone pictures of old time and present-time colored players. The book is on sale wherever the Philadelphia Giants are playing."

White published his writings in the *New York Amsterdam News* in 1929 and later in *The New York Age* (1930–1939). An article in the *Age* on January 17, 1931, sang the praise of future Hall of Fame second baseman Frank Grant. And on January 24, 1931, and August 5, 1939, White gave the highest accolades to another second baseman, Bill Monroe. His account of a perfect game pitched in 1903 by Danny McClellan graced the pages of the June 3, 1939, edition of the *Age*. Without Sol White's editorial scrolls, many players of color might have gone unrecognized, unnoticed, and underappreciated.

Upon retiring from active play, White became secretary of the infant Columbus Buckeyes of the newly created Negro National League in 1920. He later managed the short-lived Cleveland Browns in 1924. White spent his last days in a baseball uniform with the Newark Stars in 1926, co-managing and coaching with Andy Harris.

In 1927, *Pittsburgh Courier* writer Floyd J. Calvin described White as "high strung, still he is a calm, quiet man now who likes to read good books." Calvin added, "His object in telling his story is to let some of the younger fellows know something of what is behind them—something of the struggles that have made possible the improved conditions of the present."

Calvin characterized White as "one man who has given his life, unselfishly, to the game purely for the love of it. He gave up all of his money in order to keep his players together. Some others went into the game to make money, but Sol takes greater pride in having watched the game develop to where it is today, although he has no money to show for it."

Added commentary came from *Pittsburgh Courier* writer W. Rollo Wilson in his "Sports Shots" article on October 3, 1931: "An old fan recently told me that in his opinion the three men who could teach the most to others were John Henry Lloyd, Chappie Johnson, and Rube Foster. Well, they all played under Sol White."

White lived out his remaining years at 207 West 140th Street in New York City, where he enjoyed reading and working as an elevator operator. He died a pauper and was buried in an unmarked grave at Frederick Douglass Memorial Park on Staten Island. Dr. Jeremy Krock led fundraising efforts that culminated in a 2014 ceremony, roughly sixty years later, with a tribute read by John Thorn, the official historian for Major League Baseball, and a headstone placed on grave 18 in section G, row 7. ⚐

BY LARRY LESTER

Members of the Philadelphia Giants gather around white
sportswriter and team owner Walter Schlichter for a studio
shot in 1909, later mislabeled as the 1906 club. One of the
greatest players to ever grace the diamond, John Henry
"Pop" Lloyd is pictured standing, second from the right.

A NEW NEGRO
FOR A NEW CENTURY

In December 1886, the National League of Colored Base Ball Players convened in Pittsburgh, a sign of Pittsburgh's growing importance in the world of Black baseball, which would reach its apogee in the 1930s. Bud Fowler helped to write the constitution. Philadelphia, Cincinnati, Baltimore, Washington, Louisville, and Pittsburgh were represented. At a second meeting in March, the structure of the league was finalized: New York, Boston, and Philadelphia would be in the eastern division, and Pittsburgh, Baltimore, and Louisville would be in the western division. "The League, on the whole," Sol White wrote, "was without substantial backing and consequently did not last a week. But the short time of its existence served to bring out the fact that colored ball players of ability were numerous."

It was the first attempt to form a Black league. It would not be the last. Another league—the National Association of Colored Baseball Clubs of the United States and Cuba, which consisted of the Brooklyn Royal Giants, the Cuban Giants, Abel Linares's Cuban Stars of Havana (who were actually from Cuba), and the Philadelphia Giants—lasted from 1907 to 1910. Its fusion of Latino and Black American players would become a major feature of Black baseball in the United States and the Caribbean in the decades to come.

Even though Black players were eliminated from white organized baseball, independent Black teams continued to develop into the twentieth century. The Cuban X-Giants (mostly made up of players from the Cuban Giants), Chicago Unions, Wilmington Giants, Columbia Giants, Philadelphia Giants, and Leland Giants were among the noted Black teams before the emergence of Rube Foster's Chicago American Giants in 1911. These teams often played before white audiences, as the Black populations of most northern American cities at this time were usually not big enough to support a Black team. They also played against white teams, which necessitated periods of clowning—making comical, exaggerated plays on the field, joking around with the opposition, making harmless fun of the umpire—to lessen any white hostility, especially if the Black team was winning. The teams developed not only a Black fan base and star players, from

John Henry "Pop" Lloyd to Grant Johnson, but also a stream of young Black men who devoted themselves to mastering the game. By 1906, there was no question that Black baseball was here to stay.

Establishing a league that would endure was the next step in the development of Black baseball. Without a league, Black baseball would lack the organizational power to direct the nature of its game and the movement of its players. Also, without a league, Black baseball had little hope of becoming anything more than regional. The ambition to create a national Black game matched the aspiration of the early twentieth-century Black leadership to see Black people become part of the larger population, a national *people*, not simply a regional or isolated Southern *folk*. Black teams needed a league not only to show white teams that they could organize one but to show themselves. Part of this transformation of Black base-ball was made possible by the departure of Black citizens from the South. Leaving rural life for the cities in the Great Migration, they became a truly modern people for whom baseball would become central both culturally and economically. A set of circumstances, a historical moment, and an ineluctable fate would intersect with the abilities and destiny of one particular Black man, Rube Foster, who would achieve what, in the nineteenth century, had seemed impossible: a sustained league of organized Black baseball.

In 1924, Moses Fleetwood Walker was living in Cleveland. He briefly owned a movie house there, as he had in Cadiz. But running a movie theater was expensive those days and the profits less than earlier in the twentieth century. Four years prior, in 1920, his wife of twenty-two years died. On a questionnaire from Oberlin, an effort by the school to track down former students, he wrote that his education there was "excellent" and he listed first among his occupations "Professional Base Ball."

He lived on the same street as Hooper Field, where the newest entry of the Negro National League, the 1924 Cleveland Browns, played sometimes. On May 11 at 1:25 p.m., Fleetwood Walker died of lobar pneumonia. He suffered only a matter of hours. Many are curious if Walker ever wandered down to the stadium to watch the Browns play and wonder about Negro Leagues baseball. Would he have been remembered as the surviving Black knight of the old era of baseball, the last Black major league player, one of the last players in the white world of baseball? The Cleveland Browns died by the end of the 1924 season. So ended our knight.

Fleetwood Walker, one of the most celebrated of all early
Black players, who played with and against white players,
retired from baseball in the late 1880s, around the time that
the first Negro League, the short-lived National League of
Colored Base Ball Players, first convened.

CHAPTER 2

THE
NEW NEGRO
AND THE
LEAGUES
1920-1945

AS I HAVE ELSEWHERE SAID . . . THERE IS LITTLE RACE PREJUDICE IN THE AMERICAN DOLLAR.

—Booker T. Washington, *The Negro in Business*, 1907

A Universal Negro Improvement Association parade in Harlem, New York, August 1920.

On April 27, 1919, the dark-skinned Jamaican former printer Marcus Garvey, the head of the Universal Negro Improvement Association and African Communities League (UNIA-ACL), asked Black Harlemites to support his Black Star Line, a shipping company. As Garvey said in his newspaper, *Negro World*, "There is a White Star Line owned by white men, there will be a Black Star Line owned by black men." Garvey was a Black Pan-Africanist who was going to redeem the Black diaspora and unshackle the Black American. He was, at the height of his fame, arguably the most famous Black man in the world, more famous than W. E. B. Du Bois, who was the editor of *The Crisis*, the house organ of the National Association for the Advancement of Colored People (NAACP). Du Bois was also a fellow Pan-Africanist, the most renowned Black scholar in the world, and Garvey's most implacable and intense rival. Garvey believed in the power of business, of enterprise, to restore the race. His steamship line was meant to engage Black people in international trade. Garvey knew nothing about ships or shipping lines, but he did not let that stop him. Du Bois, who ridiculed the scheme, thought it should have.

The response to this quixotic venture was overwhelming. So much money poured in that Garvey's operation could not keep proper track of it. Buying shares in the Black Star Line was a point of racial pride, and investing in it was touted as investing in the future of the race, a demonstration of one's belief in the destiny of the race. Supporting it was a sign that Black people could organize a business on a large scale, as white people could.

In 1920, a year after the Black Star Line was launched, Andrew "Rube" Foster, a Black American with a grand strategy, was certain that he could organize a baseball league and that Black people would support it. After all, many of the teams, and the men who could run them, already existed. Black baseball was not a pipe dream but a reality, much more so than Garvey's Black Star Line. Black men knew how to play baseball, and Rube Foster knew everything there was to know about baseball, about how to play it and how to manage a team. He knew what a league should be and how to bring it about. It was simply a matter of organizing, the key to Black people's future in the post–World War I world. It was the age of the "New Negro," the age of redefinition, when Black people, the Black world, could throw off the shackles of white oppression, re-form their identities, and succeed at anything they set their minds to, if they organized. And a major step was *organized* baseball, which white observers said Black people could not do. White people believed that Black people were too disorganized to ever become truly professional. The 1920s would be a new age of Black organizing, and a new age of Black rivalry.

THE BLACK BASEBALL TITAN ORGANIZES IN CHICAGO

Rube Foster set his sights on Chicago, which, in some respects, might not have seemed the best place to play Black baseball. The summer of 1919 had featured some of the worst racial violence of the twentieth century, particularly in Chicago, where hostilities lasted from July 27 to August 3. Thirty-eight people died and scores were injured in what was, in effect, a race war. On the other hand, other American cities weren't any less racist, and Chicago, despite the violence, was a magnet for migrating Black Southerners.

The Chicago Defender, the nation's most widely circulated Black newspaper, did not advocate Black migration from the South in 1915. It changed its tune, however, in 1916, when thousands of Black Southerners began to leave as the boll weevil wrecked cotton crops—and the market for cotton—leaving many Black families without work. The Great War also had reduced European immigration to the United States to a trickle, resulting in a severe labor shortage in the North. Perhaps most important, though, was continued lynching and racial oppression in the South, which made life unbearable for Black families. By the winter of 1916–1917, the *Defender* calculated, 250,000 Black people had left the region. In the spring of 1917, the *Defender* declared May 15 the day of the Great Northern Drive, aiming to encourage one million Black Southerners to depart for the North. The Great Migration would reshape the United States and redefine Black Americans, truly creating the "New Negroes."

With so many Black people moving north, a Black baseball entrepreneur like Foster saw a great opportunity. It was simple: more Black migrants going to major northern cities could support Black baseball teams as fans. There would be substantial Black- and white-owned small-business infrastructure—barbershops, churches, beauty salons, restaurants, newspapers, taverns, clubs, grocery stores, cleaners, haberdashers, boardinghouses—to support a pastime like baseball.

An air of optimism underlay Foster's vision. His new league was meant to show that Black leaders could organize and maintain a national business supported by Black patrons. And the league was meant to train and prepare a class of athletes to be ready for entry when the major leagues integrated, as Foster felt sure would happen sooner or later.

Andrew "Rube" Foster was born in Calvert, Texas, on September 17, 1879, a preacher's kid. His Christian upbringing surely affected his values and beliefs: that there is a right order of things, that hard work is rewarded but is worthwhile in and of itself, that adversity must be overcome by effort, and that fairness is essential in a just world. These beliefs dovetailed nicely with how he viewed the world as a Black man and with his sense of sportsmanship. Foster was a baseball man through and through. He knew nothing else. After quitting school in the eighth grade, he defied his father by playing baseball, particularly on Sunday. For him, baseball was the ship and the rest of what the world had to offer was the sea.

He was a star pitcher, but he was also a leader of men. In 1902, Foster joined the Chicago Union Giants, and it was in Chicago that he would make his career. He later joined the Chicago Leland Giants, where he became the manager. After the 1910 season, in partnership with white tavern owner John Schorling, the son-in-law of Chicago White Sox owner Charles A. Comiskey, Foster formed the Chicago American Giants. Schorling, who had long been involved with Black baseball, arranged for the team to take over South Side Park, former home of the White Sox, and remodeled it to accommodate about nine thousand fans. With this foundation, Foster's team became a significant sports attraction, sometimes outdrawing the Cubs and the White Sox. Knowing how to attract talent and how to train and deploy it, Foster made the Chicago American Giants the powerhouse Black ball club of its era. And it would become the cornerstone of Foster's league.

Foster was convinced that Black baseball had no future unless a league was formed. A league would provide a regular schedule, an established set of rivals, governance and administration to maintain rules and order, and control over players, preventing them from moving willy-nilly from team to team. Escalating park rental costs were working against independent Black teams, Foster argued; formed into a league, they would be able to negotiate lower fees. The league would attract more fans because a league would offer a structured season, giving the fans a narrative by which to interpret the fortunes of the teams. Many Black players feared that the formation of a league would suppress salaries, but Foster asserted that players would make more money because more fans would be attracted to the games. Fans would come to league games after seeing that Black baseball was run by *professionals* and played by *professionals*.

Andrew "Rube" Foster—a star pitcher as a player—formed the Chicago
American Giants in 1910 and founded the Negro National League in 1920.

With the signing of its constitution, the Negro National League (NNL) was established on February 13, 1920, in Kansas City, with Foster as president and secretary. He was also the owner of the American Giants and the booking agent for the league. The owners who signed included two Black baseball legends in their own right—C. I. Taylor of the Indianapolis ABCs and J. L. Wilkinson of the Kansas City Monarchs—along with Joe Green of the Chicago Giants, Lorenzo S. Cobb of the St. Louis Giants, and Tenny Blount of the Detroit Stars. In addition to these teams, the Dayton Marcos and the itinerant Cuban Stars rounded out the eight-team league in its first year. Wilkinson was the only white owner. The franchise fee was $500 (about $7,800 today).

Foster received no salary as the president of the league but instead a 5 percent return on all booking fees. Serving as league president, booking agent, and team owner was a conflict of interest for Foster, but as the league had been his idea, he wanted to exercise complete control over it. This, naturally, caused problems over the six years that Foster ran the league; other owners accused Foster of being a dictator, although there was never a concerted effort to oust him. Foster almost certainly felt that a "strong man" leader had to dominate if the league was to be successful. In this sense, the league seemed an expression of Foster's drive, a triumph of his will.

Despite having a league, teams still had to barnstorm and play against non-league clubs as they traveled during the season to be financially stable. Not owning their own playing venues, they had to lease stadiums, and this made scheduling games a challenge. As a result, some teams played more league games than others. Among other grievances against him, Foster was accused of setting the most profitable schedule for his own team. This view was reinforced by the fact that for the years the league was under Foster's leadership, the American Giants were usually the best team. At first, teams, not the league, had to provide the umpires for their games. This, too, caused problems, with umpires being accused of favoritism, depending on which team hired them. Also, Black fans complained about the use of white umpires, feeling that white officials should not be making decisions about the play on the field in a Black baseball league. In response, Foster added seven Black umpires from other cities, but many were poorly trained, and some did not even know the rules of the game. While white umpires found it hard to control the games, Black umpires fared no better. It was equally difficult to get some of the Negro League players to stop acting like ruffians, intimidating umpires and even assaulting them. Black baseball was a hard game played by tough men, just as white baseball was at the time.

The Negro National League was a midwestern circuit. The sheer distance between each city, compared to the relative proximity of major East Coast cities, made operating the league a logistical challenge. And Black East Coast teams did not find traveling the Midwest circuit of the NNL to be profitable. Like most new leagues, teams dropped out, unable to balance their finances to keep things going. Foster continually had to replace teams to keep the league balanced competitively, for after all, a sports league is selling competition: on any given day in a given league, any team should have a decent chance of beating any other team. For instance, after the death of owner C. I. Taylor in 1922, the Indianapolis ABCs went wobbly. In 1922, the St. Louis Giants were replaced by the St. Louis Stars. Ball clubs from Cleveland and Pittsburgh lasted only one season. The Memphis Red Sox joined the league in 1924, left in 1926, but returned in 1927.

Replacing troubled franchises added to Foster's stress, and in 1926 he had a nervous breakdown and was confined to Kankakee State Hospital, an asylum in Illinois. His behavior had been growing increasingly erratic over the previous year. On May 26, 1925, Foster was nearly asphyxiated in his Indianapolis rooming house by a gas leak. He was discovered and rescued barely in time by some of his players. Did he suffer brain damage from his prolonged exposure to carbon monoxide poisoning? He was never himself again, and the Negro National League floundered without him. On December 9, 1930, he died while in confinement. Just months before, *The Chicago Defender* wrote that it was "his long hours and hard work plus the worry of running … the league" that cost Foster his health. Perhaps he did work himself to death. The Negro National League closed down after the 1931 season.

But Foster's death was not the end of the Negro Leagues. It was only the end of the beginning.

The Chicago American Giants, under the
leadership of Rube Foster (*center*), were one
of the top Negro Leagues teams of their era.
They are pictured here in 1916.

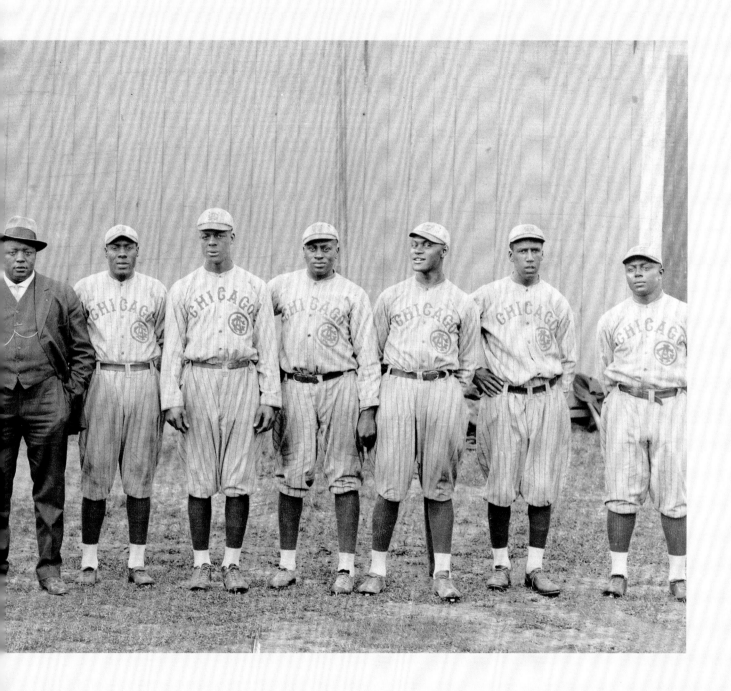

BARNSTORMING BLACK BASEBALL

On a hot July day in 1913, the Chicago Union Giants arrived in Oelwein, Iowa, to play the local nine in a barnstorming game before a large hometown crowd. Fans were in for a treat, as their club was playing a team hailed by the local press as the "fastest colored team in the world." Such was the life of a Black baseball team, barnstorming across the United States, playing whoever would be willing to meet them on the ball field.

Barnstorming was the lifeblood of Black baseball. From the late nineteenth century through the mid-1950s, it was often the only way many communities could watch the great stars they read about in the Black newspapers. Before the creation of the Negro Leagues in 1920, Black teams barnstormed all over the country. Later, in a typical Negro Leagues season, about a third of a team's games were played under the auspices of the league, while the rest were barnstorming or exhibition games. These types of games were the reason so many Black teams existed.

Barnstorming served the economic purpose of helping Black teams meet their daily expenses and stay afloat from year to year. Gate receipts often helped to

The Page Fence Giants, sponsored by the Page Woven
Wire Fence Company, were based in Adrian, Michigan,
and often traveled by train during their barnstorming trips.
They are shown here in 1895.

Members of the St. Paul Gophers proudly position
themselves in front of a scoreboard in Hibbing,
Minnesota, May 22, 1909. The Gophers were one
of the country's top Black barnstorming teams.

enhance players' salaries as they traversed the country in buses and cars to their scheduled contests. They played games in every small town that had a team or a field. The Cuban Giants from New York City played throughout the Northeast and Midwest just to make expenses. The Homestead Grays played local ball clubs as they traveled across Ohio on their way to play the Chicago American Giants in their home park. They also played other Negro Leagues teams in cities like Canton and Zanesville, Ohio, in contests that did not count in their league record. The Kansas City Monarchs often traveled with a team sponsored by the House of David, a Michigan-based religious order, so that they had a regular opponent—much like today's basketball-playing Harlem Globetrotters, who for years have traveled with the Washington Generals. These types of games made up the bulk of the schedule for Black ballplayers, starting in the 1880s. Without such contests, many teams would never have survived, and the men couldn't have made a living as ballplayers.

Most barnstorming games in the nineteenth and early twentieth centuries took place in local parks, on school ball fields, and in minor league parks—all modest spaces. Black teams were forced to rent stadiums from white ball clubs and would not have their own ballparks until later. Clubs like the Cuban Giants and Chicago Unions barnstormed around their regions starting in the 1880s. In the 1910s, barnstorming began to take teams across the country—led by the All-Nations team (a club owned by J. L. Wilkinson, who later owned the Kansas City Monarchs)—and south of the border, as the Indianapolis ABCs did in 1915 on their trip to Cuba. By the 1930s, barnstorming all-star teams played against big major league barnstorming teams in the offseason, led by stars such as Bob Feller and Dizzy Dean. Jackie Robinson and Roy Campanella had their own barnstorming teams after they established themselves with the Brooklyn Dodgers.

Traveling teams experienced all that America had to offer, both the good and the bad. Most teams had to travel by bus or car to reach many of the small towns where they played. Often, they had to drive through the night to get to the next game on time, taking turns sleeping and driving. This, at times, led to accidents, as players fell asleep driving. Players hung their uniforms out the windows to dry because there were no places to wash and dry them. Many towns, owing to racist Jim Crow restrictions forcibly separating the races, had nowhere for Black ballplayers to sleep, eat, or even wash up. Teams would have to go to the back doors of restaurants to get food or have the lightest-skinned player pump their gas. Everywhere they traveled, teams ran the risk of being harassed and forced to move on because they were not welcome. Given the difficulties associated with such travel, the quality of play witnessed by the fans was even more amazing.

Another challenge for barnstorming teams was scheduling. Schedules for teams constantly changed, as booking agents and traveling secretaries were on the lookout for the next game. Most Black clubs tried to play at least one game every day and even a doubleheader or two on the weekend, when they might have the best crowds. With no formal leagues to play in until 1920, Black teams like the Cuban Giants, the Chicago Unions, and the Page Fence Giants took every game they could book. In 1896, the Unions played games across Indiana, Illinois, Wisconsin, Michigan, and Iowa within a two-month span. In just the month of May 1895, the Page Fence Giants played in St. Paul, Minnesota; Benton, Wisconsin; Rock Island, Illinois; Fort Wayne, Indiana; Davenport and Sioux City, Iowa; and Delphos and Lima, Ohio. This relentless schedule for barnstorming teams continued even after the formation of the Negro National League in 1920.

In October 1927, the Homestead Grays took part in a four-game barnstorming series for the second year in a row with the American League Barnstormers. All the games were played at Forbes Field in Pittsburgh, but since the white Pirates were in town playing the New York Yankees, the games for the Grays weren't prioritized and therefore weren't consecutive. News reports estimated crowds nearing twenty thousand for one of the games. Between games, the Grays barnstormed locally and then set out with the American League players on a trip through Ohio, playing in Youngstown, Zanesville, Columbus, and Springfield. Thousands of fans got the thrilling opportunity to see players such as Biz Mackey and Martín Dihigo play in their local stadium. An entire trainload of fans made the trip from Pittsburgh to see the game in Youngstown, Ohio.

Barnstorming trips not only introduced local fans to players and teams they might never have been able to see; they also gave local players a chance to test their skills, at times resulting in recruitment to Negro Leagues clubs. A trip through the Deep South to play the Montgomery Grey Sox or the Tennessee Brown Rats opened up the possibility for local players to be seen by managers from the North.

Barnstorming was done not only by celebrated teams such as the Monarchs and the Grays but also by lesser-known teams like the Dayton Marcos and semipro Black teams that loved the game. In 1928 the Havana Red Sox played in front of 4,500 fans in Jersey City, New Jersey, winning a doubleheader from the locals before heading out on a barnstorming tour through the South. They won, 4–2, in Newport News, Virginia, and then headed directly to Beaufort, North Carolina, where they defeated the locals, 10–2. They got to spend three days in Wilmington, North Carolina, playing the local Colored Giants, winning one game and tying another. Next on their tour came South Carolina, Georgia, and Alabama, ending in Louisiana, all in one week.

Kansas City Monarchs pitcher Ernest Johnson described Midwest barnstorming for author Brent Kelley in *"I Will Never Forget": Interviews with 39 Former Negro League Players*. "We played everybody. Back in those days just about every town of any size had their own baseball team. During that time, especially in Minnesota and Iowa, you had a lot of teams that were stocked with college ballplayers and guys that had been to the major leagues or been in minor-league ball and they were playing in these smaller towns. That's who we played."

As Johnson implied, Black barnstorming spread baseball fever to remote locations. On the road, the teams helped promote the Negro Leagues and gave white fans exposure to players who didn't look like them. In a telling paradox, Black barnstorming, while a result of discrimination, ultimately helped to integrate the game. ⚑

BY LESLIE HEAPHY

BAREFOOT BOY WITH CHEEK (OF TAN) BECOMES A PITCHING ACE

As Leroy Paige explained in his autobiography, his mother "didn't put real big store by book learning." She didn't mind very much if he didn't attend school. He took full advantage of this indulgence by, in fact, barely going to school at all. His mother was much more interested in young Paige working and probably gave him the dickens when he failed to bring home any money. The pressure of contributing to the family income—a household in which he was the seventh of twelve children—resulted in, among other things, his famous nickname. He began carrying bags for travelers at the train depot. He didn't make much carrying one bag at a time, so, using a pole and some rope, he figured out a way to carry three or four bags at once. Other kids said he looked like "a walking satchel tree." And Satchel Paige was born.

His mother was a washerwoman and his father a gardener, though he preferred to be called a landscaper. Even at a young age, once his older brother had introduced him to sandlot baseball, Leroy made it clear to his father that his ambition was to be a baseball player. He knew he would be a pitcher. He was the only boy in his environs who could kill birds with unerring accuracy by throwing rocks at them. He could also chuck rocks at people with deadly precision.

It was throwing rocks in intense battles with gangs of white boys—as well as shoplifting and truancy—that, on July 26, 1918, landed Paige in the Alabama Reform School for Juvenile Negro Law-Breakers, a reformatory for troubled Black boys in Mount Meigs. "Maybe I got into all those fights because I wasn't real smart and didn't take too good to books. But maybe it was because I found out what it was like to be a Negro in Mobile. Even if you're only seven, eight, or nine, it eats at you when you know you got nothing and can't get a dollar. The blood gets angry. . . . Those fights helped me forget what I didn't have. They made me a big man in the

OPPOSITE Pitcher Satchel Paige, shown here circa 1946, was a legend not only of the Negro Leagues but of all baseball. The path from Alabama would take him to many pro and semipro teams, including the Kansas City Monarchs, and across countries, where he thrilled fans of the game.

The 1936 Negro National League champions, the Pittsburgh
Crawfords, kneel in front of their bus at Greenlee Field. Satchel
Paige is pictured second from the right. The photo is mistakenly
labeled as "1935," an error uncovered by Hall of Fame researchers
investigating the details of the image.

neighborhood instead of just some more trash." If he had not become a ballplayer, he might have wound up in prison or dying a violent death at a young age; "a big bum, a crook," as Paige put it. He was actually a rather cheeky boy who became a shrewd showman as an adult.

The Mount Meigs reformatory was run by Booker T. Washington disciple Cornelia Bowen. Washington, unlike his ideological rival W. E. B. Du Bois, seemed more interested in sports and knew about the leading Black athletes of the era, like boxer Jack Johnson, jockey Isaac Murphy, and cyclist Major Taylor. Washington, who died in 1915, had been supportive of the idea of a Black baseball league and was much impressed with J. L. Wilkinson's multiracial All-Nations Baseball Club, "composed of a Japanese, an Indian, a woman first baseman, and a Negro pitcher." Even more important for Satchel Paige, Washington believed that baseball could be useful in rehabilitating wayward Black boys. It was at Mount Meigs that Paige, there for five years, learned not just about personal hygiene—or the "gospel of the toothbrush," as Washington disciples put it—and choir singing, as well as a bit about reading. Most important, he learned about the fundamentals of baseball. There he developed his skills as a ballplayer. He was six feet, three inches tall, about 150 pounds, with an electric arm and a blazing fastball. When he left Mount Meigs, he was seventeen and a half years old.

Paige's brother Wilson, a solid pitcher and catcher himself, got his younger sibling his first baseball job right out of Mount Meigs in 1924, pitching for the semipro Mobile Black Tigers. Satchel was an immediate sensation. He threw nothing but fastballs, trusting on location and slight alterations in speed. Although he would develop a curveball several years later, he was the epitome of a power pitcher—but one with breathtaking control.

By 1926, he had acquired his most famous showboating stunt: bringing in his outfielders, especially if he was playing for a poor-fielding team, and striking out the opposing side. Though it drove the crowd into a frenzy every time he did that, his teammates did not always like it, as baseball is a team sport, not a soloist's art. Also, by 1926, at the age of nineteen, Paige was already doing what would become his habit: jumping from team to team to get the highest salary. He signed with the Chattanooga White Sox of the Negro Southern League, a lower-level rival of Foster's Negro National League, in the spring of 1926, fulfilling his dream of becoming a professional baseball player. He was playing for the New

Orleans Black Pelicans before the 1926 season ended, then returned to the Black Lookouts for a salary of $275 a month. In 1927, he jumped to the Birmingham Black Barons of the Negro National League, a far better team than the Lookouts, for $450 a month. In 1929, he was invited to play winter ball in Cuba, and he would continue to play winter ball for nearly the rest of his multi-decade career.

With the onset of the Depression, the Negro National League had collapsed at the end of the 1931 season, but Paige surely did not. He hustled, pitching for the Cleveland Cubs, the Homestead Grays in Pittsburgh, the Nashville Elite Giants, the Baltimore Black Sox, and many semipro teams. Paige was a gate attraction. The teams he played for as they barnstormed across the country from 1929 through 1931 had him pitch nearly every day for a few innings. But Paige needed another organized Black baseball league as the platform for his skills and fame. Pittsburgh would become the place that provided it.

Businessman and illegal lottery operator William Augustus "Gus" Greenlee, owner of the Pittsburgh Crawfords, built his own stadium in 1932. One of the very few Black baseball team owners with his own venue, he wanted to challenge Cumberland Posey's powerhouse Homestead Grays. With the coming of Greenlee, the Negro National League was revived in 1934. Greenlee had seen Paige pitch for the independent Homestead Grays in 1931, and to beat his rival, he signed the pitcher himself in 1932. Paige would become the new NNL's biggest star in the 1930s, with some assistance from Greenlee's promotion of both him and super-star catcher Josh Gibson. Satchel Paige would enjoy some of his biggest triumphs during that decade, and he would also suffer a mysterious injury that came close to ending his career. But Paige, despite his unparalleled ability, did not resurrect Black organized baseball—the return of rivalry did.

THE RIVAL

Unlike his league rival Rube Foster, Ed Bolden never played baseball. He spent his entire adult life, beginning in 1904, working at the United States Post Office (USPS). By most accounts, he was an exemplary worker.

How Bolden was able to be an owner, general manager, and publicist of a Black baseball team and, for a time, president of a league, all while maintaining full-time employment, is astonishing. Like Foster, Bolden suffered mentally; he would have two mental breakdowns, not one, as Foster did. Bolden suffered organizational defeats and would be out of baseball for periods of time, but he always returned, determined to make his mark on the game.

Bolden's adventures in Black baseball began in 1910 with the Hilldale Daisies. The Hilldale Athletic Club, a Black amateur baseball team located in Darby, Pennsylvania, advertised itself in May 1910 as available for games "with all 14- and 15-year-old traveling teams." The manager was nineteen-year-old Austin Devere Thompson, whose fourteen-year-old brother played for the team. It was a team of teenagers—the players ranged in age from fourteen to seventeen—who worked in the local community and played a sport in their free time to earn a little money and keep themselves occupied. It was a way to stave off boredom, to gather as a group doing something productive. Unlike the boys' semiskilled or unskilled jobs, playing baseball was a craft that required specialized skills and involved the use of equipment, or "tools." To play amateur baseball was something like being a member of a guild. Moreover, the players wore uniforms, which gave them an identity.

How Edward Bolden became involved with Hilldale is murky. He had been asked to keep score at one of Hilldale's games, though why he was asked is unclear. Had he some connection to the team or some of its players? He was twenty-nine years old and married, with a daughter. He was an adult among boys. He was five seven and weighed less than 150 pounds, a small man who dressed stylishly. But he had the ability to gain the boys' respect. When Bolden replaced Thompson as the manager of the team, Hilldale began its rise. It became clear that he had

Ed Bolden was one of the driving forces behind
Black baseball in the 1920s and 1930s.

Belt buckle awarded to the Hilldale club,
the 1923 Eastern Colored League Champions.

ambitions for the club, that he wanted to transform it into a professional team. He became known as "the Chief."

While Foster had *The Chicago Defender* as his megaphone for the promotion of Black baseball in Chicago and the Negro National League, Bolden had *The Philadelphia Tribune*, the city's most prominent Black newspaper, and his association with the Black elite. The Black leadership class of Philadelphia supported his baseball efforts and vouched for his character. This support was essential in overcoming any bourgeois thinking that sports in general, and baseball in particular, were disreputable, unworthy of the race's push for uplift.

At the time of Bolden's emergence as a Black cultural leader in Philadelphia and Foster's rise in Chicago, jazz, ragtime, and blues were becoming important forms of Black American popular music. Feelings among the Black population about these art forms were not monolithic. Many felt that this secular music was the devil's music, and many were also opposed to baseball being played on Sunday. Black popular music of the time was considered low-class by many in the Black bourgeoisie, who worried that it stigmatized the race. Some of these same people felt similarly about sports. Of course, a considerable part of the Black populace

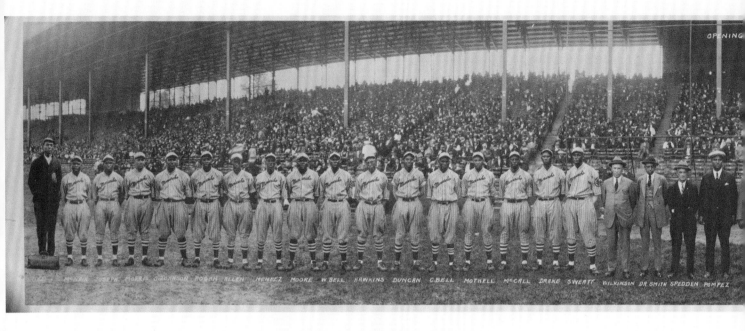

Matchups between Black baseball teams were common in the
1920s, including legendary contests like the 1924 Colored World
Series between the Hilldale Daisies and the Kansas City Monarchs.

thought the opposite and saw a rising Black presence in sports as a way forward
in the war against racism and segregation. The rise in Black urbanization, which
was making organized Black baseball and the spread of Black popular music possible, was shifting lifestyles and values. The Black population's internal culture
war created a challenge for baseball mavens like Foster and Bolden, pushing them
to win the hearts and minds of the Black public during a time of great social and
cultural change.

   Year by year, Bolden raised the standard of performance for Hilldale. He incorporated the team, making himself president, in 1917. It was the same year he began
to sign professional players. Hilldale also began to play barnstorming games against
white big league players as well as Black professional teams like the Cuban Stars
and Foster's Chicago American Giants, the latter contests drawing huge crowds.
Bolden continued to sign top players, including Judy Johnson, and his team began
to make a profit. Hilldale also played benefit games to help Black communities in
various ways. Bolden said that Hilldale "has financed more colored boys thru [sic]
college, given more money to charity and war benefits and lifted to a higher plane
Negro ball players and other athletes than any institution of its kind in the United
States." By the mid-1920s, the Hilldale Daisies were the best Black team in the East.

It would become the best Black professional team in the country, a powerhouse that enabled Bolden to form his own circuit—the Eastern Colored League—to rival Rube Foster's Negro National League.

When Foster established the Negro National League in 1920, he incorporated it in Pennsylvania, New York, and Maryland. He wanted to form two circuits, midwestern and eastern. While Foster sought partnerships, he also wanted to vanquish rivals. He saw Bolden as a potential threat, and it was inevitable that the two would clash. Bolden had signed three players from Foster's Chicago American Giants, and Foster wanted to trim Bolden's sails for doing that. This was already a sign of the discord that would afflict Black professional leagues as they raided each other's rosters and players jumped teams in order to maximize their salaries. Meanwhile, the white big leagues were a successful cartel with the power of a monopoly. Black baseball was never able to rein in competitiveness in a way that would allow them to monopolize a market.

Bolden, to prevent his roster being raided by the NNL, became an associate member in 1921. He didn't like the restrictions that the NNL placed on playing non-NNL eastern teams under the control of Jewish booking agent Nat Strong—it being common for Jewish businessmen to be involved in Black enterprises—and

Bolden thought that travel to play Black midwestern NNL teams was onerous and expensive. He also resented Foster for seeming to run the schedule in a way that financially favored his American Giants. What's more, the NNL was struggling. Attendance and revenue were down, and three clubs—the Bacharach Giants, Cleveland Tate Stars, and Pittsburgh Keystones—bit the dust. Bolden withdrew from the NNL in December 1922. In partnership with Strong, he then formed the Mutual Association of Eastern Colored Baseball Clubs, also known as the Eastern Colored League (ECL), that same month with six clubs: Hilldale, the Baltimore Black Sox, Cuban Stars, Brooklyn Royal Giants, Lincoln Giants, and Atlantic City Bacharachs. Bolden was appointed chairman of the commission that ran the league. Unsurprisingly, Foster and Bolden began to attack each other in the press.

The ECL had a profitable 1923 season. Hilldale was the most formidable club in the league, winning 137 games and the pennant. The team won the ECL pennant again in 1924 and, working out an agreement with the NNL, played a "colored" World Series against the NNL champion Kansas City Monarchs, losing in a ten-game matchup. Hilldale turned the tables in 1925, winning the ECL pennant again and dominating the Monarchs in the World Series, winning five of six.

This was Bolden's and Hilldale's zenith. Despite winning the championship, Hilldale was losing money. Also, Black fans and the Black press skewered Bolden for his use of white umpires. More and more, he was criticized as a race traitor. His partnership with Strong intensified this charge. However, Black baseball affairs on the field did not improve with Black umpires, as with Foster's NNL. Fights in the stands and on the field were common. If anything, some Black umpires felt that they were even less respected than white umpires. Bolden, like Foster, was accused of manipulating the management of the ECL to favor his team. There were calls for him to step down as league chairman. In September 1927, crumbling under a variety of pressures, he collapsed completely. After recovering in a month, he withdrew Hilldale from the ECL, in 1928. Shortly after, the league itself collapsed.

Bolden formed the American Negro League (ANL) in 1929, but it folded in 1930, with Bolden's use of white umpires still causing controversy. The issue became especially touchy with the start of the Great Depression in 1929. Many wondered: How could Bolden be a "race man" when he wouldn't employ Black umpires? Bolden also tried to dissolve the Hilldale corporation, but the board of directors bought him out. Despite the Depression, however, Black baseball soldiered on. In 1933, with the formation of the new Negro National League, Bolden would return.

THE TRICKSTER

James Nichols, the legendary speedster outfielder who became known as Cool Papa Bell, began his professional baseball life as a left-handed pitcher. Being a southpaw secured him a job forever, as long as he was able to get left-handed hitters out. In 1922, when he first faced the murderously aggressive and muscular left-handed star Oscar Charleston, considered by baseball analyst Bill James the best overall player in Negro Leagues history, Bell struck him out on three pitches, a knuckleball and two curves. That made his teammates on the St. Louis Stars take notice. Bell had struck out not merely a superstar player but a myth: Charleston, who beat up a whole regiment of Cuban soldiers while playing winter ball in Havana (it was actually just one soldier); Charleston, who ripped the hood off a Ku Klux Klan member when accosted by a group of the white terrorists (totally apocryphal); Charleston, who bashed NNL umpires in the face when he disagreed with their calls (true); Charleston, who slid into bases spikes high, looking to intimidate (true).

Bell was nineteen when he struck out Charleston, but he pitched with the experience of a man who was forty. He was, however, only a passably decent pitcher. How long was he going to fool a beast like Charleston throwing that kind of stuff? If Satchel Paige for the first several years of his professional career threw nothing but fastballs, Bell threw nothing but junk, curves and knuckleballs. In 1938, when Paige hurt his arm and thought his career was over, Bell taught him to throw knucklers and curves. "Look, Satchel," Bell told him, "why don't you learn how to pitch? You don't throw a curve, you don't have control of it. And you have to have a change-up. As hard as you throw you'd really fool the batter." That's trickster pitching, not macho pitching: fooling a batter rather than simply overpowering him.

Bell pitched against Rube Foster's American Giants, and with his speed he thwarted Foster's attempt to pressure the Stars' defense by constantly bunting. Indeed, Bell turned the tables completely by bunting successfully when he was down in the count by two strikes and a foul bunt would have been an automatic strikeout. It caught the opposition flat-footed. Tricky baseball, indeed! His manager and teammates dubbed him "Cool" because of his unflappable nature, "Papa" being popularized in blues songs of the day, like singer Bessie Smith's "Hard Driving Papa" and "Worn Out Papa Blues." Rube Foster was so impressed with Bell that he bought him an expensive pair of spikes. For Foster, Bell was not simply a talented player. He was innovative. He was a thinking player. Foster even tried to trade for Bell. The Stars knew they had a good thing in Bell and nixed the deal.

Candy Jim Taylor, one of the winningest managers in Negro Leagues history, took over the reins in St. Louis in 1923. He became Bell's favorite manager. He also changed Bell as a player. Bell's speed was extraordinary, and so were his instincts as a base runner. Taylor wanted that element in the game on an everyday basis because, as the saying goes, speed never goes into a slump. After Bell hurt his arm, the switch became complete in 1924: he stopped pitching and played center field. Taylor also decided to make Bell, who was a natural right-handed hitter, a switch-hitter. The reason was simple: with Bell's speed, it was important to get him a few steps closer to first base by having him bat on the left side of the plate. Also, facing far more right-handed than left-handed pitchers, Bell could use batting from the left side as an offensive advantage. Taylor also instructed Bell not to swing hard, but to punch the ball over the infield, or chop the ball off the plate and run like the dickens. With Bell's speed, putting the ball in play like that put enormous pressure on the defense. He became one of the best contact hitters in professional baseball.

When the hard-nosed shortstop Willie "Devil" Wells joined the St. Louis Stars in 1924, along with Mitchell Murray, Willie Bobo, and Dewey Creacy, the Stars became a formidable team. In 1925, they played the Kansas City Monarchs for the Negro National League championship, but lost the series by one game. In 1928, the Stars won the championship, beating the Chicago American Giants, partly aided by the fact that the incapacitated Rube Foster no longer ran the team. Bell hit .407 with eleven hits in that series.

Bell, the Mississippi kid who joined his ball-playing brothers to work at the St. Louis Independent Packing Company, became a bigger star than any of his siblings. From 1928 through 1931, the Stars won the Negro Leagues championship three years out of four, and many consider the 1930 Stars to be the greatest Negro Leagues team ever. But the Negro National League was falling apart after the death of Foster and from the ravaging of Black incomes with the onset of the Depression. Not even J. L. Wilkinson's innovative introduction of portable lights in 1930, allowing working people to attend night games, could save the league once the novelty wore off. At the time of their collapse, the Negro Leagues, including

Legendary Negro Leagues base runner Cool
Papa Bell began his career as a pitcher, throwing
knuckleballs and curveballs that allowed him to
fool even the most experienced batters.

Cool Papa Bell's baserunning attracted fans to Negro Leagues games; he is shown here sliding into third base for the Homestead Grays against the Baltimore Elite Giants in 1943.

the Negro National League, the Eastern Colored League, and the Negro Southern League, had produced stars—players who were written and talked about, players whose barnstorming teams played against white "all-star" teams and beat them consistently.

The Negro Leagues made Black baseball an ongoing concern and a true attraction, and the players became household names throughout much of the Black community. Many of the players had become so well known as individuals that when the sharp young Black businessman Gus Greenlee introduced the East-West All-Star Game in 1933, that game, not the Negro Leagues World Series, became the showcase of Black baseball. In some respects, the stars became more important than the teams they played for or the leagues they played in.

Entertainment was key, much as in today's game with its loud music, kiss cams, and fireworks. Bands played and players clowned. There was a taint of minstrelsy about the games sometimes as players did comic acts. Black patrons generally loved the entertainment that surrounded the games; the game was not enough. Satchel Paige, who always pitched seriously even when he was clowning around, developed his slow shuffle and southern Black drawl in front of Black audiences who loved his act, as they did actor Stepin Fetchit and trumpeter-singer Louis Armstrong. It was only when these men became crossover stars, performing the same act for white audiences, that Black patrons began to ridicule them as Uncle Toms.

Despite its flaws, the Negro Leagues had showcased athletic excellence and organizational aspiration in the age of the New Negro Renaissance. By 1934, the center of gravity had shifted to Pittsburgh, where Greenlee would build a powerhouse called the Crawfords and become the rival of fellow Black Pittsburgh baseball owner Cumberland Posey, whose Homestead Grays were also a powerhouse.

Greenlee, a numbers king and former bootlegger, could think big, including Satchel Paige. In Smoketown, with its grand parade of talent—from bandleader Earl Hines to Robert Vann, editor of the *Pittsburgh Courier*, one of the most important Black newspapers, and cartoonist Jackie Ormes, the first Black woman to have a syndicated comic strip—Black folks had to believe that anything was possible, even during the Depression.

By this time in Pittsburgh, there was a young, powerful catcher named Josh Gibson, who had signed with the Crawfords in 1928. Everybody would hear of him when the second Negro National League hit its stride.

Cool Papa Bell was one of baseball's best players
of the 1920s and 1930s with the St. Louis Stars. The
future Hall of Famer (*seated fourth from right*) is shown
with the 1930 Stars team that included additional
Cooperstown-bound players Mule Suttles (*standing,
far left*) and Willie Wells (*standing, second from left*).

PITTSBURGH, THE END OF PHILADELPHIA, AND THE DEATH AND RESURRECTION OF SATCHEL PAIGE

In 1934, Ed Bolden was back in the game with the Philadelphia Stars. He sold a half-interest in the team to Jewish entrepreneur Ed Gottlieb. This assured Bolden of bookings, but some Black fans complained that Black baseball should be completely controlled by Black owners—a dream that was rarely realized. Sportswriter W. Rollo Wilson was named the salaried commissioner of the revamped Negro National League, an operational step forward. The teams in the new NNL that year besides the Stars were the Chicago American Giants, the Nashville Elite Giants, the Pittsburgh Crawfords, the Cleveland Red Sox, and the Newark Dodgers. Among the associate members were the Homestead Grays and the Bacharach Giants.

The Philadelphia Stars rolled to a championship showdown with the Chicago American Giants. But controversy arose in Game 6 when umpires were physically attacked by Stars players. Chicago protested to the commissioner that the guilty players should be banned from the rest of the series, but Bolden threatened to pull his team from the series if this occurred. He had the juice—nothing happened to the Stars players. The Stars went on to win the series, although both sides were unhappy with the outcome. It looked for a moment like the shift of power to the east in Negro Leagues baseball was going to occur in Philadelphia, but it did not. The Stars never played for another championship during the remainder of Bolden's life. He died in 1950. The shift was to Philadelphia's sister city and western rival, Pittsburgh.

Through the 1930s and 1940s, Pittsburgh, Pennsylvania, would be the nucleus of the Black baseball world, which stretched south into the Caribbean. At Greenlee Field on the Hill and at nearby Forbes Field, visiting squads played against two of Black baseball's flagship franchises. "Coming to Pittsburgh was a big thrill," Hall of Famer Monte Irvin recalled. "You see, the Pittsburgh Crawfords and the Homestead Grays dominated baseball at that time." With stellar baseball, stunning jazz, and the *Pittsburgh Courier* trumpeting these exploits, the Hill—a

Josh Gibson, who joined the Pittsburgh Crawfords in 1928 at
age sixteen, would become a star in the Negro Leagues.

neighborhood rising above downtown Pittsburgh, where newcomers to the city
had long settled—was dubbed the "Crossroads of the World."

While J. L. Wilkinson's Kansas City Monarchs dominated the Negro American
League, winning five championships in eight years between 1939 and 1946,
the Grays and the Crawfords set the standard for Negro National League play.
Combined, they won more than a dozen NNL titles; the Homestead Grays won
nine of those titles and showcased some of baseball's most iconic figures. Seven
of the first eleven Negro Leaguers elected to the Hall of Fame played for one or both
clubs, and their owners have become among the most storied Black businessmen
in American history. Cumberland Posey was inducted into the Hall of Fame in 2006.

But as much as the Grays and Crawfords captured the flair of the Black game,
they played deeper roles for African Americans. The Great Migration had expanded

Pittsburgh and its environs were a growing industrial center and
a magnet for Black migrants during the early twentieth century.
The city was the focus of the Negro Leagues universe between
the two world wars, featuring top teams like the Pittsburgh
Crawfords and the Homestead Grays that called it home.

Black Americans' realm of possibility, but also exacerbated internal tensions and posed new problems. Now concentrated throughout the country's major cities, baseball, remarkably, encouraged solidarity and pride in urban Black communities.

As Pittsburgh's Black population tripled in the early twentieth century, they confronted an array of difficulties. The city was ill prepared to accommodate the influx of newcomers. Most migrants from the South made their way to the Hill, while others moved into nearby mill towns to work in the steel industry. Divided by the city's hills and rivers, Black Pittsburghers could not marshal their potential economic and political clout.

Another dilemma was bad timing. Pittsburgh's industries plateaued after World War I, and many migrants came too late to get jobs that would allow them to help brothers or sons get work as easily as European immigrants had done. Frequent layoffs made buying homes and bequeathing them to children difficult. Unable to put down roots, many moved on.

Moreover, differences based on place of birth, class, skin color, occupation, and education troubled Black Americans. The differences between the "OPs"—Old Pittsburghers, who had grown up in the city—and recent migrants who journeyed northward to escape rural poverty and violence were vexing. Some OPs feared that less-educated, less-skilled rural migrants would cast them in a bad light, diminishing their status.

These frictions were evident in baseball. An 1890s wave of migrants from Virginia's Shenandoah Valley had created the Homestead Grays. Many players held skilled or semiskilled jobs at the Carnegie Steel Works. Homestead-born Cumberland Posey Jr. joined them in 1911. His father, Cumberland Willis Posey Sr., was a river pilot whose entrepreneurial drive made him the region's most prominent Black businessman. Known by his shortened name "Cum," Posey Jr. was a gifted all-around athlete who led off and patrolled the outfield as the Grays became the premier Black club in Pittsburgh.

Posey captained, managed, and ultimately owned the team. Adding top players from the region, and some from beyond it, including aging hurler Smokey Joe Williams, the Grays took on all comers. Crowds swelled, and in 1926 their record after 114 games was a startling 102 wins, 6 losses, and 6 ties. Posey proved himself off the field, too, as a promoter and leader. He wrote for the *Pittsburgh Courier*, served on Homestead's school board, and would make the Grays one of the longest-running franchises in Negro Leagues history.

"Homestead Grays of 1931"
4-3-31
Coloreld Champions

The Homestead Grays were based in Pittsburgh and became one of the most dominant teams in the game in the late 1930s and early 1940s, finishing first in the Negro National League nine straight times from 1937 to 1945.

The Pittsburgh Crawfords were a Negro Leagues dynasty; two of the most famous stars to play with the team included Josh Gibson (*far right*) and Satchel Paige (*second from right*).

The Crawfords were not OPs, but sons of the Great Migration. In 1926, Teenie Harris, later renowned for his photography, merged the Black players on two integrated teams on the Hill to compete in a city tournament. Though these young men played with and against white players when on their own, league play dictated segregated teams. They took their name from the Crawford Bath House, a city-run center that helped newcomers adjust to urban life. Their parents, from the Deep South, held unskilled jobs and lacked the education that those who formed the Grays enjoyed. But that did not dampen their athletic potential. After winning the tournament, the Crawfords stayed together, energized by the chance to play and the celebrity it brought.

Both the Grays and Crawfords emerged on local sandlots, where thousands came to see them, often tossing change into a passing hat. Gus Greenlee, who provided the Crawfords' first uniforms and served as the Hill's de facto banker, became their benefactor. Supporting the Crawfords was a way he gave back to the community.

As their captain, Harold Tinker, whose family migrated from Alabama, pushed the Crawfords to become good enough to defeat the Grays. Among the ballplayers Tinker recruited with that end in sight was Josh Gibson, a sixteen-year-old he saw playing on the city's Northside. Impressed by Gibson's fielding, Tinker thought: "This boy is a marvel." Then Josh came to bat. "He hit the ball out of existence. They didn't even go after it. It went over a mountain. I said to myself, 'This is part of my plan. He needs to be with us.'" Afterward, Tinker asked Gibson to join the Crawfords at Ammon Field on the Hill. "Those people up there went wild over him, and so did we, from the very first day." With Gibson in the lineup, the Crawfords were ready to challenge the Grays. But Posey, always scouting for talent, persuaded Gibson to join his club before booking the Crawfords. Gibson would return to the Crawfords, however, from 1932 through 1936.

Though the Crawfords lost to the Grays the first two times they played, Satchel Paige came on in relief in their third encounter with the Grays ahead by three runs. "And I'll tell you," Tinker recounted, "they hardly hit a foul ball off Satchel the rest of the game. He was throwing nothing but aspirin tablets—fastballs. He hadn't developed all that fancy stuff then." Decades later, Tinker smiled as he sat in Central Baptist Church on the Hill, where he preached, recalling that the Crawfords rallied and, "by the grace of God, that's when we beat the Grays."

A bat used by Josh Gibson, circa 1930s. As Harold Tinker, the
Pittsburgh Crawfords captain who recruited Gibson, commented
on his batting ability, "He hit the ball out of existence."

But Greenlee couldn't withstand a raid from Ciudad Trujillo, a Dominican ball club linked to Rafael Trujillo. The state-of-the-art dictator's minions persuaded Paige, Gibson, Bell, and half a dozen other Crawfords to jump to the island in the spring of 1937 by offering them substantial salaries. This star-studded team won the island championship, but back in the States the Crawfords never recovered. Greenlee was deeply angered and blamed "the race" for not properly supporting his team. He was also angry with Satchel Paige, who led the departure in 1937 and then went to Venezuela and Mexico in 1938. As a result of the demise of the Crawfords, Greenlee lost Greenlee Field and turned to managing boxers.

In the spring of 1938, Paige's arm hurt so much that he could not pitch anymore, and he feared his career was over. Given how often he pitched, it was surprising that he was not waylaid sooner by an arm ailment. Now, despite his desperation, no Negro Leagues team would do anything for Paige, who had behaved as though he transcended any team and burned them too often. Only Wilkinson of the Kansas City Monarchs came to his aid, and that was because Paige still drew fans. He did tricks and stunts with a traveling subsidiary of the Monarchs. He also played first base, not well. He returned to pitching, but he was ineffective and in constant pain. By himself, Paige did not put the Crawfords out of business, but he contributed to the team's demise. Some in the Negro Leagues felt that Paige's bad arm was karma.

Gus Greenlee returned to the game in 1945, launching the United States League. At this time, there were three other Negro Leagues in existence: the Negro American League, the second Negro National League that he had started in 1933,

and the Negro Southern League, originally organized in 1920. His revived Pittsburgh Crawfords won the title in 1946, the United States League's second and final season. Meanwhile, Cum Posey died in 1946 and Josh Gibson succumbed in January 1947 at the age of thirty-five. The Grays won the last Negro Leagues World Series ever played, beating the Birmingham Black Barons and their teenage center fielder Willie Mays in 1948. They barnstormed for a few more seasons, but Pittsburgh was no longer the crossroads of Black baseball.

As for Satchel Paige, something miraculous happened some months later. The team trainer, Frank "Jewbaby" Floyd, had just given Paige an arm massage. The arm, to this point, had not responded to any treatments, ointments, incantations, or physicians. Paige thought his situation was hopeless. But just as unexpectedly as Paige was stricken, he was cured. In 1939, his arm recovered. He would go on to have several good years with the Monarchs from 1940 to 1947. He had done his penance. Besides, as Paige accurately, if self-servingly, said, "Even with those guys jumping off [to the Dominican Republic], the Negro Leagues didn't come close to busting up. That bust-up came when the major leagues started raiding Negro clubs and just giving them a few pennies or nothing and killing off attendance."

War in Europe broke out in the same year that Paige got his groove back. In 1941, the United States would join the war. Before the end of the 1940s, the National and American Leagues would be integrated, and amazingly, considering his age, Paige would be one of the first Black players to get the call.

Rob Ruck has contributed substantially to this section.

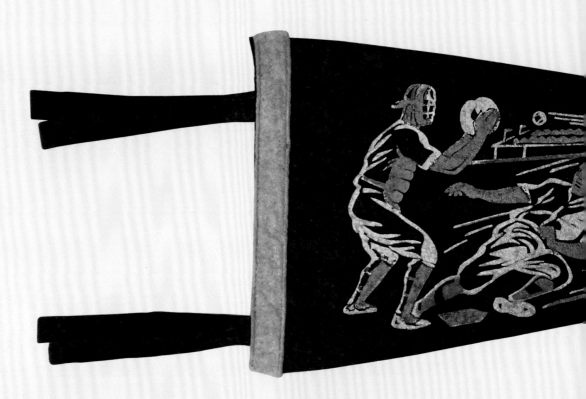

The Negro Leagues teams, such as the Philadelphia
Stars and the Homestead Grays, were some of the most
successful Black businesses of their era, attracting
millions of fans to games across the country.

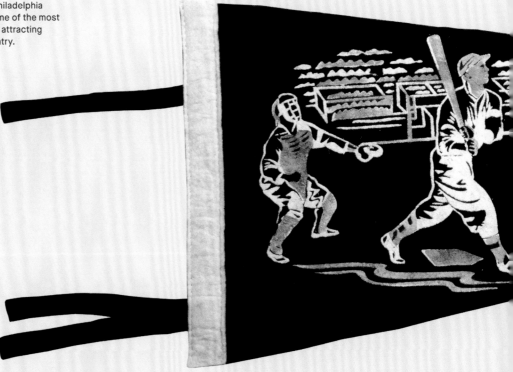

PHILADELPHIA
STARS

HOMESTEAD
GRAYS

THE ALL-AMERICAN BOY AND BLACK BASEBALL FANS IN WASHINGTON

The great jazz bandleader and composer Duke Ellington told two stories in his memoir, *Music Is My Mistress*, about his love of baseball growing up in Washington, D.C., in the early twentieth century. The first is about playing in vacant lots around town as a youngster:

> There were many open lots around Washington then, and we used to play baseball at an old tennis court on Sixteenth Street. President Roosevelt would come by on his horse sometimes, and stop and watch us play. When he got ready to go, he would wave and we would wave at him. That was Teddy Roosevelt—just him and his horse, nobody guarding him.

Ellington, born in 1899, grew up a Black middle-class kid in a family who taught him manners, proper speech, and the importance of respectability and racial pride. His family was very status-conscious, and the fact that his parents did not find baseball degrading suggests something important about the status of the game among many "striving" Black families at the time.

Bandleader Duke Ellington (batting), whose passion for baseball dated to his young years in Washington, D.C., is seen here in 1955 playing with band members at a stop on a tour in Florida in front of their segregated motel.

Ellington follows this story almost immediately with another:

Washington was in the American League and every day I had to see the game. The only way for me to do that was to get a job at the baseball park. I succeeded in getting one and had my first experience of stage fright. I had to walk around, in and out and in front of all those people, yelling, "Peanuts, popcorn, chewing gum, candy, cigars, cigarettes, and score cards!" I soon got over my nervousness, although the first day I missed a lot of the game hiding behind the stands. By the end of the season, I had been promoted to yelling, "Cold drinks, gents! Get 'em ice cold!" I was so crazy about baseball. It's a wonder I ever sold anything. The opportunity to walk around there, looking at those baseball heroes, whose pictures were a premium in the cigarette packages, meant a lot to me.

There was much to celebrate at Griffith Park during the period Ellington probably worked there. The Washington Senators had joined the American League in 1901, two years after Ellington was born, when Ban Johnson declared it part of the majors, challenging the hegemony of the National League. Pitcher Walter Johnson, the Senators' first superstar, was in his heyday during Ellington's youth: Johnson never won fewer than twenty games in the 1910s, and only twice during that span did he have an ERA over 2.00. Also, the stadium was new—the steel-and-concrete park had opened in 1911, the same year that the old wooden stadium burned down. The original, called National Park after the Senators' previous name, was located in a Black neighborhood in northwest D.C. near Howard University and was constructed mostly by Black workers. The new park was built only a short distance away, on Seventh and U Streets, and in 1923 the name was changed to Griffith Stadium, after the Senators' owner, Clark Griffith.

Black Washingtonians were big fans of the Senators, and during the team's glory years in the 1920s they filled the right-field seats. This wasn't the only place they could sit—the park was officially integrated—but it was the only place they felt comfortable. Probably because of the park's location, Black fans felt no less identification with the team than white supporters did. Griffith Stadium "became a meeting ground for middle-class, intellectual, and working-class African Americans." Cumberland "Cum" Posey, owner of Pittsburgh's Homestead Grays of the Negro National League, found D.C.'s sizable Black fan base irresistible and in 1940 arranged for the Grays to play half their home games in Griffith Stadium. At first, Negro Leagues' ownership was reluctant to have a team play there because Black fans seemed too loyal to the Senators, but Posey's move paid off. Within two years, the Grays were earning more revenue than any other team in the Negro Leagues.

Noted Black sportswriter and D.C. native Sam Lacy pushed hard for Griffith to integrate the Senators, with the U Street Black community behind the call. There had even been some noise about boycotting and picketing the stadium in 1938 to push the issue of integrating the Senators, but nothing came of it. Griffith did allow interracial exhibition games to be played at the park in 1942, but did not do much else to integrate the team. Griffith passed control of the team to his son, Calvin, who moved it to Minnesota in 1960 because, as he told a local Lions Club in 1978, "you've got good, hardworking white people here."

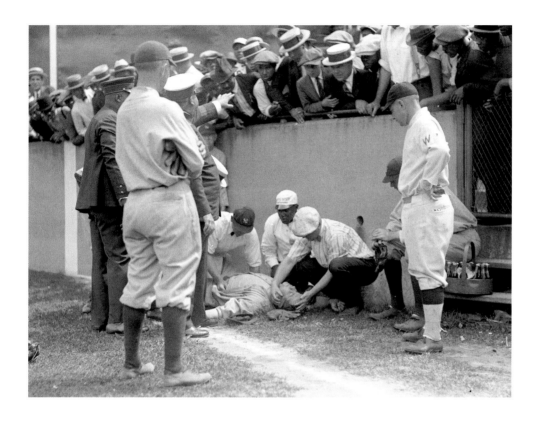

Griffith Stadium was a baseball mecca in Ellington's Washington, D.C. Shown
here are fans, Black and white, as Babe Ruth is being evaluated after being
knocked out running into a concrete wall on July 6, 1924.

In his memoir, Ellington never mentions that the Senators were an all-white team,
that Griffith Park was in a Black neighborhood, or whether he worked only among
the Black fans. Instead, he conveys his love of baseball, uncomplicated by social
considerations or realities. He tells his story from the perspective of a boy for whom
baseball transcended race. Johnson and his white teammates were Ellington's heroes,
too. He was a typical American boy entranced by the all-American game. ⚑

BY GERALD EARLY

CHAPTER 3

MR. ROBINSON'S NEIGHBORHOOD

THE RISE OF INTEGRATION

1945–1960

AND HERE'S SOMETHING ELSE. [ROBINSON'S] ONLY THE FIRST, BOYS, ONLY THE FIRST! THERE'S MANY MORE COLORED BALLPLAYERS COMING RIGHT BEHIND HIM AND THEY'RE HUNGRY, BOYS. **THEY'RE SCRATCHING AND DIVING.** UNLESS YOU WAKE UP, THESE COLORED BALLPLAYERS ARE GONNA RUN YOU RIGHT OUT OF THE PARK.

—Dodgers manager Leo Durocher,
on his opposition to the white players'
petition against playing with
Jackie Robinson

The double-V campaign expressed the hopes of African Americans that, having worked to defeat Nazism during World War II, civil rights might be won at home upon their return. Shown here are Black soldiers in an artillery unit in November 1944 in Belgium.

In 1946, the United States was trying to return to normal after nearly four years of war. For Black Americans, however, there would be no returning to "normal," or to how things were racially, as whites understood it, before the war. African Americans had fought the war with the hope of victory on two fronts—a double-V campaign not just over Asia and Europe but over racism at home. For them there was no turning back, no matter how persistently many white Americans tried to keep the prewar racist status quo.

Isaac Woodard Jr. (*center*) was beaten and blinded by the South Carolina police just hours after his discharge from the army after serving in World War II. Here he is in August 1946 at New York's Hotel Theresa guided by heavyweight champion Joe Louis (*left*) and author Neil Scott, to discuss a fundraising event for blind African Americans.

BUS STOP

On February 12, 1946, twenty-six-year-old U.S. Army Sergeant Isaac Woodard Jr. boarded a bus in Augusta, Georgia, on his way to Winnsboro, South Carolina, his home. He had finished three years in the service, stationed in the Pacific Theater. Woodard was in uniform when he got into a brief altercation with the bus driver about being permitted to use the facilities when the bus came to an unofficial rest stop. It was not an unusual request, but the white bus driver claimed that Woodard's attitude was a bit too assertive. In Batesburg, South Carolina, the driver stopped the bus to have the police remove Woodard, whom he deemed an unruly passenger. Lynwood Shull, Batesburg's police chief, struck Woodard over the head with his blackjack as Woodard tried to explain what happened. According to Woodard, when he wrested the blackjack from Shull, another officer, Elliot Long, pulled his gun and threatened to shoot him. Woodard dropped the blackjack, at which point, Shull savagely beat Woodard into unconsciousness. When he was taken to court the next day to pay his fine for "drunk and disorderly conduct," a fine of $44, all the cash he had on his person, he could not see. The beating had permanently blinded him.

President Harry Truman was disturbed by the acts of violence against Black veterans, such as Woodard experienced, on their return from the war. After fighting against a racist Germany, race relations at home, instead of being better, had actually worsened. In response, Truman's attorney general, Tom Clark, did something unprecedented. He filed federal charges against Shull. The government lost the case, but it marked the beginning of the federal government seeing its role differently in regard to race. On December 5, 1946, Truman issued Executive Order 9808, which established the multiracial President's Committee on Civil Rights. And more change was coming: in the summer of 1947, a tiny number of Black baseball players were going to show the world that they could play in the same big leagues as white players.

JACKIE ROBINSON, NEGRO LEAGUER

Jackie Robinson left the army in 1944 on a medical discharge following his court-martial for insubordination when he was told to sit in the back of a military bus. He found himself, at the age of twenty-five, in precisely the same position he was in before he received his draft notice in March 1942. He left UCLA without a degree in 1941 and became a star collegiate athlete with no place to play. His grades were poor. His girlfriend, Rachel Isum, who would become his wife in 1946, rebuked him for failing to finish. Between 1941 and when he received his draft notice, Robinson tried to find a career. He was never strongly interested in academics, as he felt that a Black man had little possibility of using those kinds of skills. He simply did not think that a college degree meant that much. "I tried to talk him out of it," Rachel Robinson later said. "He was so close to finishing."

Before entering the army, Robinson tried to make it in some realm as a professional athlete, but the options were few for Black athletes. The highest level of professional football was off-limits for Robinson. The National Football League had drawn the color line in the 1920s, and it would not be crossed until Kenny Washington signed with the Los Angeles Rams on March 21, 1946. By that time, Robinson was preparing to play with the Brooklyn Dodgers' minor league team, the Montreal Royals. Robinson tried other professional football leagues: he was a bust with the Hollywood Bears because of his bad ankle, and he lasted only a season, until December 1941, with the Honolulu Bears. Unhappy with his performance and homesick, he had been hoping to become an athletic director before the army called.

He fulfilled that hope in 1945, after his army stint, when he became athletic director at Samuel Huston College, a small Black United Methodist Church school that was teetering on the brink of bankruptcy. But the pay was too low for him to stay. His only alternative at that point was to consider playing in the Negro Leagues.

OPPOSITE Jackie Robinson was exonerated after being court-martialed in 1944 while serving in the army for refusing to move to the back of a bus.

Although football was his number one sport in college—the sport with which he became most associated as a college student—and basketball was number two, Robinson had also played baseball, and he continued to play the sport while in the army. He was more successful playing baseball at Pasadena Junior College than at UCLA, where his one season as a shortstop was dismal. But baseball, because of the Negro Leagues, offered the only viable option to make a living playing a sport.

Robinson chose to play for the Kansas City Monarchs, the only Negro Leagues team owned by a white man, for the 1945 season at $400 a month. J. L. Wilkinson, the owner, was well respected among other league owners and among the Black movers and shakers in Kansas City. Wilkinson first introduced night baseball in 1930 through a system of gas-powered portable lights mounted on trucks. He also formed the All-Nations team in 1912; arguably the most diverse professional team ever, it included Black, white, Asian, Native American, and Latino players, and one woman, something that deeply impressed Booker T. Washington. Wilkinson was something of a visionary. Robinson, as a famous college athlete, would be a good gate attraction, but there was also a sense that someone like Robinson might be a candidate to integrate major league baseball. After the war, many in the Black press and Black baseball felt that the integration of the majors was imminent. The Monarchs themselves were one of the storied franchises of the Negro Leagues, having employed at various times such Hall of Fame players as pitcher Satchel Paige and base-stealing center fielder James Cool Papa Bell. Those men carried themselves as aristocratic, well-groomed professionals.

With the team's regular shortstop injured, Robinson stepped into his old college position, even though his arm was not strong enough. He made many errors but was able to use the tips he got from his teammates to improve at the position. Robinson survived, in fact succeeded, as a professional player because of his athleticism and his intelligence, not because of his (limited) baseball experience. He honed his skills even more while barnstorming with a Black team in Venezuela that winter. Unfortunately, Robinson's Kansas City Monarchs statistics are unclear. No one knows precisely what they are because, as Robinson noted, no one was sure what counted as league games. He was chosen to be the starting shortstop at the 1945 East-West All-Star Classic, where he went 0-for-5. It is estimated that Robinson hit .375 and played in about thirty-four league games.

But Robinson was not a good fit for the Negro Leagues. Having attended not only college but white schools, and having played with white athletes, he had different feelings about how an elite athlete should be treated. He disliked the practical joking (he took himself very seriously), the long rides on rickety buses, the terrible Jim Crow hotels, the haphazard scorekeeping, and the unprofessional umpiring. To his teammates, at times, he seemed almost priggish and self-righteous, although he made it a point always to respect them. As a high-performance athlete, he thought he was playing under humiliating, degrading conditions. These were the conditions that Black people had to put up with in a racist, segregated America. There was nothing empowering about it, as far as Robinson was concerned, and the falsely constructed solidarity was nothing to be proud of.

In April 1945, Robinson participated in a workout for a white major league team—the Boston Red Sox—along with two other Negro Leaguers, Marvin Williams and Sam Jethroe. It was arranged by Black sportswriter Wendell Smith. The tryout was a bust, a dog and pony show. The Red Sox had no intention of signing any Black players, and Robinson was angry that his time had been wasted. Meanwhile, Smith, on his way back from Boston, stopped in New York to talk to Brooklyn Dodgers general manager Branch Rickey about Robinson. Rickey had been mulling the idea of signing some Black players since 1943. As he learned more about Robinson, he became interested. By late August, just as Robinson was about to quit the Monarchs in disgust, he was invited to meet with Rickey. On August 28, 1945, after meeting with Rickey for two hours, Robinson signed a contract binding him to the Brooklyn Dodgers. Whatever Robinson may have thought of the Negro Leagues, without having had such a platform, he would never have been discovered. Negro Leagues baseball was good enough to draw the attention of white baseball men. Robinson owed it that much and he knew it.

On that day Robinson changed not only the course of his own life but also white major league baseball, Negro Leagues baseball, and America itself forever.

Jackie Robinson and Rachel Isum married in 1946 and soon after
left for spring training in Florida. They encountered discrimination
each step of the way from California to Daytona Beach.

LONG DAY'S JOURNEY INTO NIGHT

On February 28, 1946, Jackie and Rachel Robinson left Los Angeles for the Dodgers' spring training camp in Daytona Beach, Florida. They arrived at their stopover in New Orleans without incident. But upon entering Jim Crow land, the journey went sideways. First, they were bumped from their flight, and one hour later they found that their next flight had left without them. Unable to get service at the restaurants in the airport, they went without eating. Finally, a cab took them to a dilapidated and impoverished Black hotel. Nearly twelve hours after their arrival in New Orleans, they were able to board a connecting flight to Pensacola, Florida, but were bumped again. When they finally boarded a flight in Pensacola, they were told that they had to disembark because the plane had weight issues, despite the fact that white passengers were able to take their seats. White people in Jim Crow land were always served before Black folk.

In the end, the Robinsons took a sixteen-hour bus ride to Daytona. They were told by the driver to sit in the very last row of the bus. As the bus went on, working-class and farming Black folk filled the back to overflowing, while seats in the front of the bus, designated for white passengers, were empty. "I had never been so tired, hungry, miserable, upset in my life as when we finally reached Daytona Beach," Rachel Robinson said.

Robinson was livid the entire way. He thought seriously about going back to California. He didn't, but clearly the desegregation of professional baseball was not going to be easy.

BLACK BASEBALL
ON THE PRECIPICE

The Negro National League (NNL) and Negro American League (NAL) endured their share of problems in the 1940s. One of the biggest challenges was preventing their players from jumping to different teams or to the Mexican League, which, for a time, was a serious threat. They also suffered some of the same problems that afflicted white professional baseball during the war years, but because the Black leagues faced more precarious finances, the problems were far more intense. Gas and tire rationing added to the problems of travel that Blacks already faced because of pervasive racism, even in the North. The military draft reduced the number of available Black players, who were part of a smaller aggregate than players in the white leagues. Black baseball was still subject to the availability of white-owned facilities, which made a balanced schedule across the entire season impossible. Black teams still needed to barnstorm extensively in order to make money because league games didn't produce enough revenue. And on top of it all, owners still found it difficult to work together well for the good of their leagues.

Nevertheless, Negro Leagues baseball was profitable through 1946. In fact, it was more profitable than it had ever been in the 1930s, or during its first iteration in the 1920s, in large part because Black income rose as a result of wartime employment, particularly in the defense industry. The crowds were also larger than they had ever been, because the Black community needed the diversion of baseball more than ever. Despite all the obstacles it had to overcome simply to field teams on a consistent basis, Black baseball endured, even thrived.

In 1946, Robinson's first year with the Brooklyn Dodgers organization, the NNL had six teams: the Homestead Grays (playing home games at both Pittsburgh's Forbes Field and Washington, D.C.'s Griffith Stadium), the Newark Eagles, the Baltimore Elite Giants, the Philadelphia Stars, the New York Cubans, and the New York Black Yankees. The NAL, which was the geographic equivalent of a western division and a southern division, included the Cleveland Buckeyes, the Birmingham Black Barons, the Kansas City Monarchs, the Chicago American Giants, the Cincinnati-Indianapolis Clowns, and the Memphis Red Sox. Adding to the economic

The East-West All-Star Game, or East-West Baseball Classic, was played in Chicago's Comiskey Park, and occasionally in other cities, showcasing the talent of both the NNL and the NAL. Shown here is the program from the 1946 game.

This stadium seat is from Comiskey Park, where the East-West All-Star Game was played almost every summer during the contest's twenty-nine-year existence.

OFFICIAL SOUVENIR PROGRAM

EAST WEST BASEBALL CLASSIC

COMISKEY PARK • AUGUST 18

25¢

EAST WEST PROGRAM PUBLISHERS

challenges facing the leagues was the distance between teams in the NAL, which was greater than in the eastern-focused NNL, giving the latter an advantage. The greater distances made play between the two leagues difficult and costly, as it had always been since the earliest attempts at Black organized baseball.

A high point was the East-West All-Star Game, the big event of Black baseball since the game's inception in 1933, the same year as the white major leagues' first All-Star Game. In 1946, however, two All-Star Games took place: one on August 15 at Griffith Stadium, the home of the Washington Senators, the second time in the game's history that the All-Star Game was played in the East; and the second on August 18 at Chicago's Comiskey Park, where the showcase had almost always been played. Even though traditionally the game had largely been under the control of the NAL, there was now a push to play an All-Star Game in the East because the NNL was trying to control it, or at least share it with the NAL. The huge Black baseball fan base in Washington made playing the game there in 1946 sensible. But more than 45,000 fans showed up for the game in Chicago, while 15,000 were on hand in the District. In the crowd at Griffith Stadium was Jackie Robinson, there between games for the Brooklyn minor league team for which he then played. The following year, 1947, East-West All-Star Games in both the Midwest and the East drew well: the Chicago game attracted more than 48,000, while the one at the Polo Grounds in New York, with 38,400 in the stands, was the best-attended Black All-Star Game ever held outside of Chicago.

This was about the only good news for the Negro Leagues in 1947. Attendance had declined significantly across the leagues, and the owners had no way to stop it. The East-West All-Star Game would continue until 1962, but it never again achieved the numbers of 1947. Indeed, by 1950 attendance would be half that of 1947, and by 1954 it would be down to 10,000. The revenue of the Kansas City Monarchs, one of the most storied of all Negro Leagues teams, would drop from roughly $156,000 in 1946 to $83,000 in 1948. The leagues limited players' salaries in 1948 to $6,000 per month per team, a 25 percent reduction that alienated players. The Black Yankees moved from the Bronx to Rochester, New York, largely because of the expense of renting Yankee Stadium but also because the New York market could no longer support two Black teams. As a result, Alex Pompez's Black Cubans had New York all to themselves. This cost-cutting and team shifting, however, did not help.

Negro Leagues team owners were stunned by how quickly things got worse. They could not believe that their fan base would abandon them so completely and

During the Jim Crow era, the annual *Negro Motorist Green Book* guided Black
travelers to welcoming establishments as they navigated a segregated country.
As seen here from the 1949 *Green Book*, fans packed Chicago's Comiskey Park to
see the brightest Negro Leagues stars play in the East-West All-Star Game.

so fast. Attendance at regular Negro Leagues games during 1948 dropped to a range
of 700 to 1,700 customers, making it financially impossible for many of the teams
to continue operation. The Negro National League died at the end of that year. The
revamped Negro American League soldiered on until 1960, but it was, in effect,
zombie baseball, a league that refused to acknowledge its own death. The reason
for this demise was simple: the white major leagues had abolished the color line,
albeit tentatively but steadily, in the late 1940s, and as far as Black fans were concerned, Black baseball leagues weren't needed anymore. If the old saying is true
that people vote with their feet, then Black people overwhelmingly rejected segregated baseball after being given the alternative of an integrated version of the sport.

Effa Manley, the outspoken owner, along with her husband Abe, of the Newark
Eagles, despondently said, "The Negro fan would rather watch Doby, Robinson,
Campanella, and Paige than a Negro league game any time." She complained that
the Black press promoted the Black players in the majors far more than they did the
Negro Leagues. But as historian Neil Lanctot points out, the Negro Leagues them-
selves were never very good at promoting their game. Manley knew the nature of
Black businesses during the age of segregation—that is, both their strengths and
their disadvantages—and what angered her most was the lack of support, by the
Black press and the Black public, that she felt was owed to Black businesses.

EFFA MANLEY: THE WOMAN WHO TOLD JACKIE ROBINSON HE WAS WRONG

When Jackie Robinson criticized Negro Leagues baseball in the June 1948 issue of *Ebony*, he ruffled the feathers of one of its foremost proponents, Newark Eagles co-owner Effa Manley.

Robinson's 1947 debut with the Brooklyn Dodgers was a watershed moment in baseball history, and Black fans, both the passionate and the casual, looked to him to share his insights on not only the game but the world itself. Prior to integrating major league baseball, Robinson played for five months with the Kansas City Monarchs, the Negro Leagues team that produced more major league players than any other Black team.

In his 1948 *Ebony* essay, which he titled "What's Wrong with Negro Baseball?," Robinson wrote, "The bad points range all the way from the low salaries paid players and sloppy umpiring to the questionable business connections of many of the team owners." Addressing criticism that he had been "stolen" by Branch Rickey, Robinson said that whether or not he could have played elsewhere, he would have left Kansas City owing to the state of Negro Leagues baseball. Robinson also complained about the uncomfortable buses, dingy and dirty sleeping accommodations, and lack of discipline surrounding the team.

By most accounts, what Robinson wrote was accurate, but Manley felt that he had betrayed the Negro Leagues. Ever since 1933, when she married businessman Abe Manley, Effa had worked extensively in the Newark Eagles' club operations. Along with organizing civil rights events, such as an anti-lynching campaign, and supporting "Don't Buy Where You Can't Work" protests coordinated by the Citizens League for Fair Play, she was known for tirelessly advocating for better salaries, accommodations, and scheduling for her players. "It's too bad the other [Negro Leagues] owners didn't go along with her on many of her proposals," said Monte Irvin, one of Manley's star players. Manley's activism and passion could be felt in her staunch defense of the leagues. She emphasized how the players were just as talented as their contemporaries in white baseball and how important the leagues were in and of themselves. Manley appreciated the style of play and the role that Black baseball played in the community in building wealth and social capital.

When Robinson took to the Black press to voice his frustrations about the leagues' disorganization and ethical lapses—"Negro baseball needs a housecleaning from top to bottom," he wrote—Manley shot back.

In a rebuttal published in the August 1948 issue of *Our World* titled "Negro Baseball Isn't Dead!," Manley exclaimed, "I charge Jackie Robinson with being ungrateful. He is where he is today because of Negro baseball. I believe that he never would have been noticed if it were not for the people and the teams he derides." She even went so far as calling the pioneering baseball legend "ungrateful and more likely stupid."

Manley felt that Robinson had betrayed the Negro Leagues and thus responded with a vociferous defense. Her reaction was not just that of an owner and a businessperson, but that of an ardent believer in Black baseball's importance. As such, she viewed Robinson's comments as a personal affront to the men he had briefly played alongside. "I do not think it's fair for a half-baked statement to come from irresponsible members

Effa Manley, who helped turn the Newark
Eagles into a Negro Leagues powerhouse,
was a fierce supporter of the leagues.

of our race and have it stand unchallenged. I think an apology is due the race that nurtured him—yes, the team and league which developed him," she continued.

At a time when women were not commonly seen in roles such as hers, and were certainly not known for speaking up, Manley often found herself confronting powerful men in and around baseball. She once told Dodgers owner Branch Rickey that she could "make trouble" for him after he lured pitcher Don Newcombe away from her team in 1946. And she did make trouble when Rickey signed Monte Irvin—so much trouble that Rickey finally dropped Irvin's contract and Irvin wound up with the New York Giants. Manley made it clear that she expected compensation for any of her players if they left for the white major leagues, a promise she pursued when center fielder Larry Doby joined Bill Veeck's Cleveland Indians in 1947.

Challenging Jackie Robinson over his put-down of the Negro Leagues was one of many examples of how fiercely Manley advocated for Negro Leagues baseball. Though she was known as a shrewd businesswoman, she never backed down from a fight. Manley's combative personality might be partly explained by her background growing up in Philadelphia with five siblings in what may have been a racially mixed Black family. In fact, some believe that Manley may have had white parentage. Born in 1900 and making her way as a white-looking "Black" person in a racist society made her assertive within both white and Black circles. She would battle with anyone—regardless of their standing within the baseball community—to defend what she loved. It was her passion that forged her legacy.

After the major league color barrier was broken, Manley feared that the demise of the Negro Leagues was imminent. She suggested that they become a minor league, not only to continue the pipeline for the development of Black players but also to allow the leagues and their teams to continue to be viable.

With the Manleys at the helm, the Newark Eagles won the 1946 Negro World Series. It would be their first and only league title. The Manleys sold the team in 1948, and it would disband after the 1951 season.

In the spring of 1947, writer and activist Wendell Smith of the *Pittsburgh Courier* reported from Havana, Cuba—where Robinson, Newcombe, and Roy Campanella were participating in spring training—that Robinson would be elevated from the Montreal

Royals to the Brooklyn Dodgers before the major league season started. After the news broke, William G. Nunn, managing editor of the *Courier*, wrote, "The 'Iron Curtain' which has prevented Negroes from participation in major league baseball has been lifted!"

But by the end of 1950, just two years after Manley's blunt rebuttal of Robinson, Smith was reporting on the declining status of the Negro Leagues. Manley had been right. White baseball had looted Negro Leagues baseball of much of its talent and its fans followed those players.

More than seventy-five years after her disagreement with Robinson, Manley's career is often reduced to "the only woman in the National Baseball Hall of Fame," but there was more to her than that. She understood the power of the Negro Leagues as a place of activism and as an economic engine within her community. She also understood how integration threatened the leagues. Manley saw their value not as feeders for the majors, but as important social institutions in their own right. However flawed and underresourced the Negro Leagues were, she believed them to be worth vigorously defending, even against someone as prominent and important as Jackie Robinson. The force of her passion was an expression of all that was at stake, for her and for Black baseball. ☞

BY SHAKEIA TAYLOR

OPPOSITE Effa Manley assembled the powerful Newark Eagles teams of the 1930s and 1940s as the team's general manager. The Eagles beat the Kansas City Monarchs in the Negro World Series in 1946.

BLACK BASEBALL AS A BUSINESS

The problems with Black baseball—and with other Black businesses created by segregation—were basically economic. First, they relied on the discretionary income of a group at the bottom of the economic ladder whose position in the labor market was the most precarious. Watching baseball was not a crucial activity, but a form of entertainment. Rather than go to a baseball game, Black people could decide to go to the movies, a nightclub or tavern, a restaurant, or a concert; to buy and listen to a radio; to be actively engaged with their church most nights of the week; or to play cards with family and friends at home. If anything, an anti-sports sensibility was baked into certain segments of Black culture; many either felt that sports were sinful and decadent or saw sports as frivolous and a distraction from working to obtain their full political and civic rights in more important areas of society. Overall, it was hard to maintain a far-flung national business like a baseball league with such a customer base, and the Negro Leagues were fortunate they did so for as long as they did.

Second, the leagues were obviously undercapitalized, as so many Black businesses and institutions were. Strong Black financial institutions that were capable of underwriting that type of investment were hard, if not impossible, to find, and Black businesses had no access to white financial institutions. Organized Black baseball, in other words, was an idea that was more ambitious than its customer base could support. All of this was the result of the systemic and virulent racism that Black people faced. The dependence of the Negro Leagues on white baseball was designed, not accidental or unintentional. Moreover, Blacks had no stake in the companies that supplied baseball equipment. Outfitting a team is, of course, a significant capital cost. Another major aspect of organized baseball is recordkeeping and the preservation of statistics to provide meaning to a season. Black baseball struggled for most of its existence to keep accurate and complete records. This is, once again, for an organized baseball league, the cost of doing business. In this

Negro Leagues owners met regularly to discuss business issues
they encountered. Pictured here is a meeting that took place at
the Hotel Theresa in Harlem, New York, in June of 1946.

endeavor, the white businesses that made Black teams feasible were the landlords, and the Black teams were the tenants.

This condition of financial precariousness also made it impossible for the Negro Leagues to bargain for a fair price when their players left for white major league teams. They lacked the financial leverage to command respect and fair compensation.

Another problem, beyond economics, putting pressure on the Negro Leagues was the expectation of Black businesses that Black fans would support them out of a sense of race loyalty. In this regard, customers felt that Black business owners did not try to cater to them because they were, in effect, a captive audience. Black sportswriter Wendell Smith said: "That's the way it was with Negro Baseball. Fans who wanted to see Negro players had no choice but to attend Negro games. They did attend and the owners of those teams reaped big profits, despite the fact that they did practically nothing to improve conditions or stimulate interest." It was partly on this basis that Robinson bitterly criticized the Negro Leagues in the June 1948 issue of *Ebony* magazine as substandard operations that failed both players and fans.

Finally, supporting racially segregated businesses in effect supported the system of segregation itself and the degradation that it was meant to maintain. Continuing to support the Negro Leagues thus presented a paradoxical and difficult road to empowerment.

Once integration came and fans shifted their loyalties, the Negro Leagues had little reason to continue to exist. Nevertheless, it is a testament to the vision of the owners, no matter how flawed and selfish they were, and to the ability of the players and the support of the fans that the Negro Leagues enjoyed the considerable measure of success that they did. Their existence was, in some sense, an example of the poisoned fruits of racism, but in another way, they could be seen as a heroic and noble endeavor that pushed against the enormous odds set against Black people. The Negro Leagues were an achievement of considerable magnitude.

THE TRANSFORMATION OF INTEGRATION

On October 29, 1947, President Truman received the report of the President's Committee on Civil Rights entitled *To Secure These Rights*. The report urged the integration of the U.S. military, and Truman signed an executive order to that effect in the summer of 1948.

The report also praised National League president Ford Frick for putting down a racist rebellion in May 1947 against Jackie Robinson taking the field in St. Louis: there had been talk that some Cardinals threatened to sit out the first Brooklyn series against St. Louis in which Robinson was to play. The integration of the white major leagues, limited though it was, foreshadowed, and likely inspired, Truman's decision on the military.

Jackie Robinson was called up to play first base for the Brooklyn Dodgers in the historic year of 1947, debuting on April 15. After a highly successful season with the Montreal Royals, the Dodgers' top farm team, he was ready. His record was beyond reproach: he had won the batting crown with a .349 average, stolen 40 bases, and scored 113 runs.

As Neil Lanctot put it, "Robinson had accomplished in a single year what the NNL and the NAL had struggled to achieve in the previous decade." He made millions of Black people rabid baseball fans. No Black athlete since the heyday of boxer Joe Louis had so deeply affected so many Black folk.

Robinson quickly became the most famous Black person in America. Playing under the restraints that Branch Rickey put on him during his first three years with the Dodgers made him especially heroic. He was not permitted to retaliate in any way against the racist provocations from opposing teams or fans. Avoiding retaliation gave him the air of a martyr, but also prevented him from ever coming across as pathetic or downtrodden. Robinson's "dynamic intensity" combined with his controlled conduct during this time cloaked him with defiant dignity. "I played hard, and always to win," Robinson said.

Right after his Dodgers debut, Jackie Robinson's
popularity skyrocketed. Items such as this doll and
coin savings bank became favorites with his fans.

No Black athlete could triumph without an indomitable will to win. Robinson had that, almost too much of it, as he became one of the most argumentative players in the game once Rickey's restraints were lifted. "Ya want a guy that comes to play," said Leo Durocher, who was briefly Robinson's manager in 1947 and 1948. "This guy didn't just come to play. He come to beat ya."

Shown here is a lobby poster from the 1950 movie
The Jackie Robinson Story, featuring Minor Watson
as Branch Rickey and Jackie Robinson as himself.

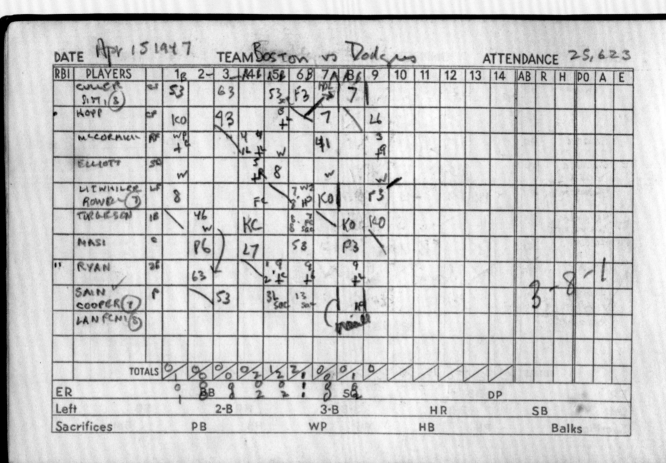

Local New York sportswriter Tom Meany documented Jackie Robinson's debut with the Dodgers on April 15, 1947, in this scorebook. Meany used "Robby" to indicate Robinson (*opposite*).

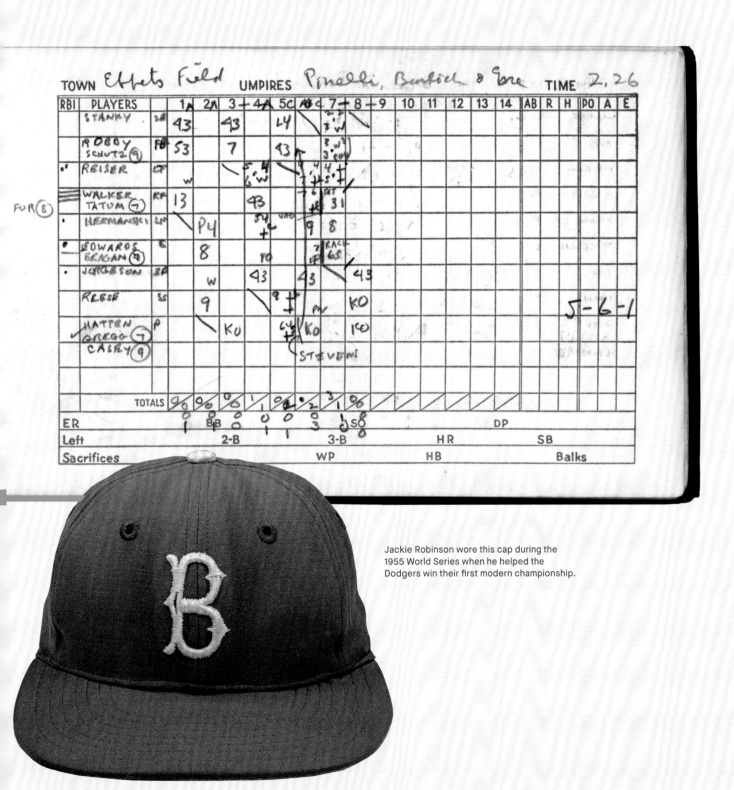

Jackie Robinson wore this cap during the
1955 World Series when he helped the
Dodgers win their first modern championship.

MR. ROBINSON'S NEIGHBORHOOD

Robinson's arrival wasn't needed to make the Dodgers contenders. The team had already won ninety-six games in 1946, finishing only two games behind the National League champions, the St. Louis Cardinals. But Robinson apparently was the Dodgers' missing piece, the spark, as the team won the National League flag in 1947. They lost the World Series, after going a full seven games, to the New York Yankees. During Robinson's tenure, Brooklyn would win the pennant five more times (1949, 1952, 1953, 1955, and 1956) and the World Series once (1955). Robinson won the Rookie of the Year Award in 1947, with a .297 batting average, 29 stolen bases, and 125 runs scored. He won the Most Valuable Player Award in 1949, the first year he was free from Rickey's directive, with a league-leading average of .342, 37 stolen bases, and 124 RBI, the last an unusually high total for a player who hit only 16 home runs that year. (In fact, Robinson never hit as many as 20 homers in a season in his entire career.)

Bill Veeck, owner of the Cleveland Indians, made the next big move. Veeck, always a maverick, had long been interested in desegregating baseball, ever since his attempt to buy the Philadelphia Phillies in 1943. Baseball commissioner Kenesaw Mountain Landis, who adamantly opposed integration of the majors, thwarted Veeck's efforts to buy the Phillies. However, former Kentucky governor Albert "Happy" Chandler, who became commissioner in 1945, was much more amenable to integrating the game. After Branch Rickey made the first move with Jackie Robinson, Veeck signed twenty-two-year-old Newark Eagles infielder Larry Doby on July 2, 1947, offering the owners, Effa and Abe Manley, $10,000, a pittance compared to what the clubs would have offered if Doby were white. (Veeck added $5,000 if Doby stuck with the Indians, which Doby did.) He also promised that Doby would not receive a salary less than $5,000 a year. When Doby debuted with the Indians on July 5, he pinch-hit, then moved to first base, not his normal position, the next day in a double header. Like Robinson, Doby felt pressure playing a strange position and, in his case, taking the place of Eddie Robinson, a popular white player.

Larry Doby became the first Black player in American League
history on July 5, 1947, when he debuted with Cleveland.

UNIFORM PLAYER'S CONTRACT

American League of Professional Baseball Clubs

Parties

Between .... CLEVELAND BASEBALL CORPORATION ....

herein called the Club, and .... **Lawrence Eugene Doby** ....

of ....**Patterson, New Jersey**..., herein called the Player.

Recital

The Club is a member of the American League of Professional Baseball Clubs, a voluntary association of eight member clubs which has subscribed to the Major League Rules with the National League of Professional Baseball Clubs and its constituent clubs and to the Major-Minor League Rules with that League and the National Association of Baseball Leagues. The purpose of those rules is to insure the public wholesome and high-class professional baseball by defining the relations between Club and Player, between club and club, between league and league, and by vesting in a designated Commissioner broad powers of control and discipline, and of decision in case of disputes.

Agreement

In consideration of the facts above recited and of the promises of each to the other, the parties agree as follows:

Employment

1. The Club hereby employs the Player to render, and the Player agrees to render, skilled services as a baseball player during the year........ 194**7**...
including the Club's training season, the Club's exhibition games, the Club's playing season, and the World Series (or any other official series in which the Club may participate and in any receipts of which the player may be entitled to share).

Payment

2. For performance of the Player's services and promises hereunder the Club will pay the Player

the sum of $ **5,000.00 (Five Thousand Dollars)** ...., as follows:

In semi-monthly installments after the commencement of the playing season covered by this contract, unless the Player is "abroad" with the Club for the purpose of playing games, in which event the amount then due shall be paid on the first week-day after the return "home" of the Club, the terms "home" and "abroad" meaning respectively at and away from the city in which the Club has its baseball field.

If a monthly rate of payment is stipulated above, it shall begin with the commencement of the Club's playing season (or such subsequent date as the Player's services may commence) and end with the termination of the Club's scheduled playing season, and shall be payable in semi-monthly installments as above provided.

If the player is in the service of the Club for part of the playing season only, he shall receive such proportion of the sum above mentioned, as the number of days of his actual employment in the Club's playing season bears to the number of days in said season.

If the rate of payment stipulated above is less than $5,000 per year, the player, nevertheless, shall be paid at the rate of $5,000 per year for each day of his service as a player on a Major League team.

Loyalty

3. (a) The Player agrees to perform his services hereunder diligently and faithfully, to keep himself in first class physical condition, to obey the Club's training rules, and pledges himself to the American public and to the Club to conform to high standards of personal conduct, fair play and good sportsmanship.

Baseball Promotion

(b) In addition to his services in connection with the actual playing of baseball, the Player agrees to cooperate with the Club and participate in any and all promotional activities of the Club and its League, which, in the opinion of the Club, will promote the welfare of the Club or professional baseball, and to observe and comply with all requirements of the Club respecting conduct and service of its teams and its players, at all times whether on or off the field.

Pictures and Public Appearances

(c) The Player agrees that his picture may be taken for still photographs, motion pictures or television at such times as the Club may designate and agrees that all rights in such pictures shall belong to the Club and may be used by the Club for publicity purposes in any manner it desires. The Player further agrees that during the playing season he will not make public appearances, participate in radio or television programs or permit his picture to be taken or write or sponsor newspaper or magazine articles or sponsor commercial products without the written consent of the Club, which shall not be withheld except in the reasonable interests of the Club or professional baseball.

Player Representations

4. (a) The Player represents and agrees that he has exceptional and unique skill and ability as a baseball player; that his services to be rendered hereunder are of a special, unusual and extraordinary character which gives them peculiar value which cannot be reasonably or adequately compensated for in damages at law, and that the Player's breach of this contract will cause the Club great and irreparable injury and damage. The Player agrees that, in addition to other remedies, the Club shall be entitled to injunctive and other equitable relief to prevent a breach of this contract by the Player, including, among others, the right to enjoin the Player from playing baseball for any other person or organization during the term of this contract.

Ability

Condition

(b) The Player represents that he has no physical or mental defects, known to him, which would prevent or impair performance of his services.

Interest in Club

(c) The Player represents that he does not, directly or indirectly, own stock or have any financial interest in the ownership or earnings of any Major League club, except as hereinafter expressly set forth, and covenants that he will not hereafter, while connected with any Major League club, acquire or hold any such stock or interest except in accordance with Major League Rule 20 (e).

Service

5. (a) The Player agrees that, while under contract, and prior to expiration of the Club's right to renew this contract, he will not play baseball otherwise than for the Club, except that the Player may participate in post-season games under the conditions prescribed in the Major League Rules. Major League Rule 18 (b) is set forth on page 4 hereof.

(3) If this contract is so claimed, the Club shall, promptly and before any assignment, notify the Player that it had requested waivers for the purpose of terminating this contract and that the contract had been claimed.

(4) Within 5 days after receipt of notice of such claim, the Player shall be entitled, by written notice to the Club, to terminate this contract on the date of his notice of termination. If the Player fails so to notify the Club, this contract shall be assigned to the claiming club.

(5) If the contract is not claimed, the Club shall promptly deliver written notice of termination to the Player at the expiration of the waiver period.

(g) Upon any termination of this contract by the Player, all obligations of both parties hereunder shall cease on the date of termination, except the obligation of the Club to pay the Player's compensation to said date.

Regulations

8. The Player accepts as part of this contract the Regulations printed on the fourth page hereof.

Rules

9. (a) The Club and the Player agree to accept, abide by and comply with all provisions of the Major and Major-Minor League Rules which concern player conduct and player-club relationships and with all decisions of the Commissioner and the President of the Club's League, pursuant thereto.

Disputes

(b) In case of dispute between the Player and the Club, the same shall be referred to the Commissioner as an arbitrator, and his decision shall be accepted by all parties as final; and the Club and the Player agree that any such dispute, or any claim or complaint by either party against the other, shall be presented to the Commissioner within one year from the date it arose.

Publication

(c) The Club, the League President and the Commissioner, or any of them, may make public the findings, decision and record of any inquiry, investigation or hearing held or conducted, including in such record all evidence or information, given, received or obtained in connection therewith.

Renewal

10. (a) On or before February 1st (or if a Sunday, then the next preceding business day) of the year next following the last playing season covered by this contract, the Club may tender to the Player a contract for the term of that year by mailing the same to the Player at his address following his signature hereto, or if none be given, then at his last address of record with the Club. If prior to the March 1 next succeeding said February 1, the Player and the Club have not agreed upon the terms of such contract, then on or before 10 days after said March 1, the Club shall have the right by written notice to the Player at said address to renew this contract for the period of one year on the same terms, except that the amount payable to the Player shall be such as the Club shall fix in said notice; provided, however, that said amount, if fixed by a Major League Club, shall be an amount payable at a rate not less than 75% of the rate stipulated for the preceding year.

(b) The Club's right to renew this contract, as provided in subparagraph (a) of this paragraph 10, and the promise of the Player not to play otherwise than with the Club have been taken into consideration in determining the amount payable under paragraph 2 hereof.

Commissioner

11. The term "Commissioner" wherever used in this contract shall be deemed to mean the Commissioner designated under the Major League Agreement, or in the case of a vacancy in the office of Commissioner, the Executive Council or such other body or person or persons as shall be designated in the Major League Agreement to exercise the powers and duties of the Commissioner during such vacancy.

Supplemental Agreements

12. The Club and the Player covenant that this contract fully sets forth all understandings and agreements between them, and agree that no other understandings or agreements, whether heretofore or hereafter made, shall be valid, recognizable, or of any effect whatsoever, unless expressly set forth in a new or supplemental contract executed by the Player and the Club (acting by its president, or such other officer as shall have been thereunto duly authorized by the president or Board of Directors, as evidenced by a certificate filed of record with the League President and Commissioner) and complying with the Major and Major-Minor League Rules.

Special Covenants

IF PLAYER DOBY IS WITH CLEVELAND CLUB 30 DAYS FROM DATE OF SIGNING HE SHALL RECEIVE AN INCREASE IN SALARY TO TOTAL INCREASE $6000. FOR BALANCE OF SEASON.

Approval

This contract or any supplement hereto shall not be valid or effective unless and until approved by the League President.

Signed in duplicate this ....5th........ day of ....July.................................., A. D. 194.7..

Larry Doby ....
(Player)

279 Hamilton Avenue ....
(Home address of Player)

Social Security No. ....

Approved ...., 194.....

CLEVELAND BASEBALL CORPORATION.......
(Club)

By ..._Bill Veeck_.................................
(President)

....
President, American League of Professional Baseball Clubs

If anything, Doby had it tougher than Jackie Robinson. He was five years younger, less mature, and less self-confident. And he was not an everyday player, so he felt he had to do something impressive whenever he did play. That expectation in fact made him perform worse. Moreover, Doby was even more isolated on his team than Robinson was on the Dodgers. However, Cleveland player-manager Lou Boudreau stuck with him. He explained that he wouldn't send Doby down to the minors because he thought Doby "would be terribly discouraged." Doby and the Cleveland Indians would come into their own in 1948.

Two other players from the Negro Leagues moved to the white major leagues in 1947. Richard Muckerman, owner of the St. Louis Browns, hastily signed Willard "Home Run" Brown, one of the greatest hitters in Negro Leagues history, and Hank "Machine Gun" Thompson, both of the Kansas City Monarchs. Neither, like Doby, was given any period of adjustment, and the white players on the Browns completely ignored them. Brown did not perform well. Thompson overcame a poor start to hit .256 with a solid .341 on-base percentage. Both players, taken on an option by the Browns, were returned to the Monarchs in a month. Neither drew more fans to the park and neither stopped the team from losing—the results that Muckerman was hoping for.

In 1948, Robinson was joined by star catcher Roy Campanella, who would win three MVP Awards and establish himself as one of the best catchers in the game. Campanella would eventually be one of the most popular players on the Dodgers' roster, surpassing even Robinson, especially as the latter became pricklier and more combative in the 1950s. The biracial Campanella—he had a Black mother and an Italian father—was more easygoing and less inclined to complain about racism. The tension between the two men grew as their careers progressed, and Robinson's relationship with the other Black Dodgers—Don Newcombe, Joe Black, and Jim Gilliam—was also sometimes uneasy. Robinson wanted his Black teammates to think and act politically as he did, and he sometimes tried to bully them. For their part, they felt that Robinson held himself out as special, being the civil rights pioneer that he was. Campanella was close to Newcombe in part because they had been in the Dodgers minor league system together and because they

PAGES 120–121 The first page and signature page of Larry Doby's contract with the Cleveland Indians, showing his $5,000 salary and the $1,000 bonus if he stayed with the team for at least thirty days.

were batterymates (pitcher-catcher partners). Campanella explained that his easy demeanor was necessary because, as the catcher, he was essentially the field general. More than any other Black player on the club, he needed to get along well with his teammates. "A catcher has to take charge," he said. In many ways, Campanella's success as the league's first Black catcher, a thinking and leadership position, was at least as important as Robinson's, if not even more remarkable. Unfortunately, a car accident in 1958 left Campanella paralyzed and ended his career.

In another major move, Veeck signed the ancient wonder and grand star of the Negro Leagues, Satchel Paige, in 1948. Paige, whose age couldn't be confirmed, was at least forty-two years old at the time, and perhaps a half dozen years more than that. Though he was past his prime, he went 6-1 with a 2.48 ERA in 1948 and was crucial in the second half of the season. Veeck respected Paige when Paige said he would not take a pay cut to pitch in the majors; Veeck paid him $25,000 for three months' work (though sources vary on the amount). But Doby and Paige did not get along at all. The generational gap was keen, and the difference in personalities was sharp as well. Unlike Doby's reception, when Paige arrived in the Cleveland clubhouse, he was warmly greeted by his white teammates. "He was funny," said Eddie Robinson, who had refused to shake Doby's hand a year earlier. Doby said of Paige, "He'd come into the clubhouse and clown around, and did some Amos 'n' Andy stuff. I didn't think it was right—at least, it wasn't right for me."

It was a slow process, but by the mid- to late 1950s, Black players were making their presence felt. Monte Irvin, Luke Easter, and Sam Jethroe, all Negro Leagues stars, joined the majors in 1949 and 1950. Between 1947 and 1956, a span of ten years, Black players won the Rookie of the Year Award seven times. Between 1949 and 1959, a span of eleven years, Black players won the MVP Award nine times. Maybe Leo Durocher was right: Black players had "come to beat ya."

The Brooklyn Dodgers won the National League Pennant in 1949, the year that Jackie Robinson (*back row, second from left*) won the league's Most Valuable Player Award. Other Black players on the Dodgers at this time were Roy Campanella (*front row, first from left*) and Don Newcombe (*back row, second from right*).

TONI STONE: IN SEARCH OF OUR MOTHERS' PLAYING FIELDS

I'm playing a man's game and I want no special considerations.
—TONI STONE, QUOTED IN ACKMANN, *CURVEBALL*, 2010

When Syd Pollock, principal owner of the Indianapolis Clowns, signed Black second baseman Toni Stone to play for his team in 1953, he suggested that she wear a short skirt, as the women of the All-American Girls Professional Baseball League (AAGPBL) did. She angrily refused. She was not on the field for sexual titillation. "I wasn't going to wear no shorts," she said. "This is professional baseball." She was as hard-bitten as the men she was used to playing with. She had played with the semipro San Francisco Sea Lions of the West Coast Negro Baseball Association and the lower professional New Orleans Black Pelicans of the Negro Southern League. Now she had her big chance: to play at the highest professional level with Black men. Her biographer noted that Stone told Pollock "she would rather quit than demean herself like that." She wound up wearing the same baggy uniform the men wore. She had applied, in fact, for a tryout with the AAGPBL, but the request was

Toni Stone chats with young fans during spring training in Florida in 1953. Stone was one of three women who played in the Negro Leagues during the 1950s.

ignored, as the women's league, which existed from 1943 to 1954, would not accept Black women. Not surprisingly, she would have been willing to play in a short skirt with other women, but not with men. They would not have taken her seriously if she had.

Pollock signed her to replace a teenage shortstop named Henry Aaron, an Alabama phenom, who was signed by the Boston Braves in the summer of 1952. For Pollock, Toni Stone was a novelty because she was a woman. The Negro American League, the last remaining all-Black league, was struggling to survive in the 1950s, as most Black fans and the Black press had transferred their loyalty to the freshly integrated National and American Leagues. Pollock needed a gate attraction, and having a woman on the field playing with men might do that.

Throughout the Negro Leagues' existence, owners placed a high premium on providing entertainment. For Black fans, going to the ballpark meant watching serious competitive baseball as well as comics like Richard "King Tut" King, Spec Bebop, a "midget," and Harlem Globetrotter Goose Tatum. Fans also loved the bands that played.

But while Stone was a novelty, she also had to be a serious ballplayer with true skills. Pollock did not expect Stone to be Aaron, but he needed her to be a credible player. And she was: Stone hit .243 in her two seasons playing for the Indianapolis Clowns.

Since childhood, Stone had thought only of playing ball. She could not find girls who could play at the intensity and with the skill she desired, so she played with boys, fighting to be accepted. She felt that only boys were taught to play sports seriously. Her family, though puzzled by her passion to play baseball, was supportive, as was the local Catholic church in the St. Paul, Minnesota, neighborhood where she grew up. She remained close to the church her entire life.

Pollock told the press that Stone's salary was $12,000 when actually she was paid much less: $400 a month. But she did increase attendance dramatically during her first year with Indianapolis. For a time, she was single-handedly saving dying Negro Leagues baseball.

From the start, Stone was a salmon swimming against the current. The Indianapolis Clowns marginalized her: she played only the first few innings of a game. When she played for the Kansas City Monarchs in 1954, manager John "Buck" O'Neil used her the same way. Without getting more playing time, she could not hope to improve her game. When she signed with Indianapolis, she was thirty-two years old and had likely passed her peak as a player. But passing herself off as ten years younger, as she did, skewed how her abilities were assessed.

The men on the team generally were jealous because, at least in her first season, Stone was a gate attraction. Also, they may have believed Pollock's press releases about her salary. In addition, some felt that she was taking a place that rightfully belonged to a man. She had to fend off sexual advances, sometimes forcefully. She could not change clothes with the men and usually asked the umpires if she could use their dressing room when they finished. Black sportswriters like Wendell Smith and A. S. "Doc" Young belittled her and said she had no business playing with men. She was often refused hotel accommodations with the men because it was thought she was a sex worker. She was directed to rooms in brothels with sex workers, who in fact became an important support for her on the road. Her experience was, if anything, worse than that of a female singer with a swing band.

Future Hall of Famer Oscar Charleston (*center*) poses with
Richard "King Tut" King (*left*) and Connie Morgan, one of three
women who played in Negro American League games in the 1950s.

A July 1953 *Ebony* article about Stone inspired infielder Connie Morgan and pitcher
Mamie "Peanut" Johnson, both teenagers, to try out for Indianapolis, becoming Pollock's
new novelties when they made the team. He thought Morgan's good looks would sell
tickets. Although both were respectable players, neither woman had the depth of Stone's
baseball experience.

After a despairing 1954 season with the Kansas City Monarchs, where she felt betrayed
by manager Buck O'Neil over a sexually obscene remark from an opposing player that
amused her teammates, Stone left Black professional baseball for good. Stone had fought
the good fight that, unfortunately, nobody else at the time believed was worth fighting. ▷

BY GERALD EARLY

In 1953, Ernie Banks became the first Black player to appear in a game for the Chicago Cubs. By the end of the 1950s, Banks would be hailed as one of the greatest power hitters in the game.

DIE HARD

Between 1954 and 1956, America experienced three events that signaled a major change in race relations. First, the 1954 *Brown v. Board of Education* Supreme Court decision declared racially segregated schools unconstitutional. Second, the grotesque lynching of Black teenager Emmett Till in Money, Mississippi, in August 1955 horrified even segments of white America. And third, on December 5, 1955, the Montgomery Bus Boycott began, launching a young minister named Martin Luther King Jr. as the voice of the Civil Rights Movement for the next decade. There was no question now that America had embarked on a social policy of dismantling racial segregation. There was no turning back, not for America and not for baseball. But racial segregation and systemic, institutionalized racism would not die easily.

By 1956, nearly seventy Black players had crossed the color barrier. Between 1951 and 1956, four Black players would shape the game with their excellence, becoming among the greatest who ever played: Willie Mays of the San Francisco Giants (1951), Ernie Banks of the Chicago Cubs (1953), Hank Aaron of the Milwaukee Braves (1954), and Frank Robinson of the Cincinnati Reds (1956). Of the four, Frank Robinson, who had not played in the Negro Leagues, would represent a new breed of Black player. Mays, Aaron, and Banks were the last great products of the Negro Leagues.

In many ways, the Negro Leagues were dead by the 1950s, having fallen to integration. But Negro Leagues games were still being played during the decade, and a few Black players were still coming from their ranks. The Negro Leagues died harder than some people were aware. There were still some Negro Leagues owners who believed in the mission of Black baseball as a cultural and economic force for the betterment of Black American life. Some Black fans continued to go to Negro Leagues games out of race loyalty, some because they preferred the style of play the Negro Leagues offered, some because they liked seeing all-Black teams, and some because they liked games tailored to please Black fans. So, in 1947, one Negro League, the NNL, died suddenly, but in the 1950s another Negro League, the NAL, would die slowly and stubbornly.

CHAPTER 4

THE
BLACK PLAYER
MEETS THE
BROWN PLAYER
1930s-1960s

IT WAS TOUGH FOR ALL THE BLACK PLAYERS,

BUT AT LEAST THE AMERICAN BLACKS SPOKE ENGLISH.

—Cuban pitcher Luis Tiant, on playing in the South in the 1960s

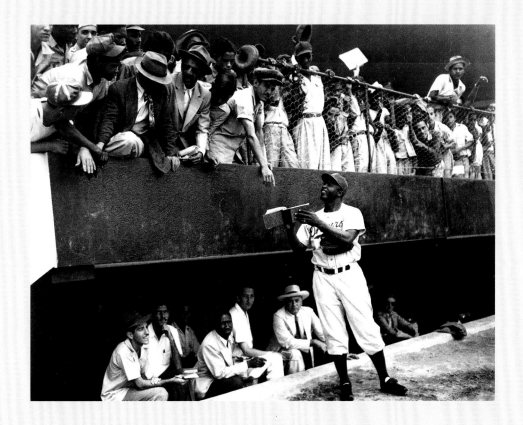

Jackie Robinson signs autographs during spring training
in the Dominican Republic in March 1948.

In 1948, a year after Jackie Robinson debuted in Brooklyn, the Dodgers held spring training in the Dominican Republic, a venue where integrated play would not trigger the animosity that Robinson had encountered in Florida in 1946. Robinson called the island "one of the most beautiful places I've been." He added: "Most of the inhabitants here are colored. They speak Spanish, but I assure you that they are conscious of their color and the things they have in common with colored people in

Page 132: Felipe Alou, Willie Mays, and Orlando Cepeda (*left to right*)

America." Twelve-year-old Felipe Rojas Alou journeyed to the capital to see the Dodgers play that spring. "On March 11, we were bused from school to see Jackie Robinson's Dodgers play the Dominican Republic All-Star team," Alou wrote years later. "I didn't even know what spring training was, but I knew this was something special. I was mesmerized seeing grown men play baseball with four real bases and wearing dazzling uniforms that shimmered in the sun."

Unable to afford a ticket to the Dodgers game against their Montreal Royals farm club, ten-year-old Manuel Mota scaled a mango tree overlooking the field two hours before the first pitch. He watched the game spellbound from his perch twenty feet above the ground. Robinson's presence stretched Alou's and Mota's horizon of what was possible. And others—Orlando Cepeda and Roberto Clemente from Puerto Rico, Orestes Miñoso and Tony Oliva from Cuba, and Juan Marichal from the Dominican Republic, to name a few—were similarly affected: the integration of the American game opened the door for these brown- and dark-skinned dreamers as well. As boys, they had learned to play in back alleys and on diamonds carved out of cane fields. As men, they were in the vanguard of players from the Caribbean making their way to the United States. And it was Jackie Robinson and the arrival of Black American players in the white major leagues that were instrumental in opening up the door for Latino players and dramatically internationalizing the game.

THE MIGRANT'S AMERICAN WELCOME

What began as a trickle of players from the Spanish-speaking Caribbean, Mexico, and South America in the 1950s became a torrent of talent, transforming baseball. Unlike the antagonistic reception Robinson and other Black players encountered in all-white franchises, Latino players were less scrutinized when they debuted in the United States. But they were not uniformly accepted, much less embraced. White fans who saw race as binary—either white or Black—were often puzzled by the Spanish-speaking, multihued players taking the field, as were some Black fans.

The transition was tough for young men like Alou, who boarded a Pan American flight in the spring of 1956 with a suitcase and rudimentary English-language skills. He headed to Lake Charles, Louisiana, to play for the San Francisco Giants' Class C minor league team in the Evangeline League. "And then the rain thundered down, a torrent of racism. . . . I started to hear words like 'monkey,' 'nigger,' and 'black son of a bitch,' all in that lilting Louisiana accent—a syrupy drawl, the sound and cadence of which have never left my ears. I knew racism existed, but nothing prepared me for this." Alou, given the legal racial segregation of the American South, had to live as an African American, and among them, when he came to the United States. This was not easy. "And then there was that division in the black neighborhoods," Alou writes, "where we were all dark-skinned, but we still weren't the same."

Black baseball in the United States had long been shaped by a Latino presence both on and off the field. One such figure was Florida-born Cuban American Alex Pompez, once owner of the New York Cuban Stars, an independent team of dark-skinned Cubans, and later the New York Cubans of the Negro National League. Also influential was Cuban Martín Dihigo, one of the greatest of all Negro Leagues players, who could play nearly every position, including pitcher, with great skill. Others included Cuban infielder and outfielder Armando Vazquez, Cuban outfielder Cristóbal Torriente, Puerto Rican outfielder Francisco "Pancho" Coimbre, and Dominican shortstop Horacio "Rabbit" Martínez.

Cuban American Alex Pompez was the owner of the
independent team the New York Cuban Stars, and later
the New York Cubans of the Negro National League.

But Alou was right: despite the cultural interactions between African Americans and players from Spanish-speaking areas south of the border, much separated them: cuisine, language, the way they experienced racism, the fact that Black Americans lived in a white-majority country. To this day, dark-skinned Latinos don't generally self-identify as Black, and intermarriage between Black Americans and Latinos is low. Whatever the differences were, however, Black Americans made it easier for Alou and other Latin players to make it in the major leagues.

A STAR IN THE MAKING

Felipe Alou grew up in Bajos de Haina along the southern coast of the Dominican Republic. His father, a carpenter, was the grandson of enslaved Africans, and his mother was of Spanish descent. Alou, using bats carved by his father and playing in a uniform fashioned from flour sacks, excelled at the sport. When the Dominican Republic beat the United States in the championship game of the 1955 Pan American Games in Mexico City, Alou starred. Intending to study medicine and represent his country in the javelin in the 1956 Summer Olympics in Melbourne, he rebuffed offers to play professionally. But after his father lost his job and the government concluded that it could not afford to send a delegation to Melbourne, Alou signed with the Leones del Escogido in the Dominican Republic to play winter ball and with the New York Giants in the States for the regular season. He was one of the first players on the island to join a white major league organization. Horacio "Rabbit" Martínez, who was Alou's baseball coach at the University of Santo Domingo and who played for Pompez's New York Cubans, was so impressed by Alou's talent that he thought the young athlete was a can't-miss prospect. Martínez, a seven-time Negro Leagues all-star shortstop regarded as one of the two greatest Dominican players prior to integration, signed Alou after he began scouting the Caribbean for the Giants during the 1950s. In addition to signing Felipe, he also signed his brothers Mateo and Jesús Alou, Manuel Mota, and Juan Marichal.

Alou did not go home after his unsettling experience at Lake Charles because of the promise he had made to Martínez and Pompez. He also didn't want to disappoint his family during hard times. At Lake Charles, Alou got nine at-bats in five games. He had two hits and one RBI and didn't play any road games. With a .222 batting average, he had an inauspicious start. The two Black Americans who were at Lake Charles with Alou never made it to the majors. Alou did.

The Giants sent Alou to Cocoa, Florida, to play in the Class D Florida State League later in 1956. Though given $12 in meal money for the two-and-a-half-day bus ride, he was unable to enter restaurants when the bus stopped. Refusing to

humiliate himself by going to the back door, he did without, other than a few bags of peanuts he had brought. He stayed at the home of "a kind [Black] woman named Blanche—his first real home in America." Blanche, with her husband, "became surrogate parents" for Alou. His manager, Buddy Kerr, told Alou he had what it took to make it to the majors, and "not to let the racial slurs and slights defeat" him. Apparently they didn't: Alou hit .380 to win the Florida State League's batting title with 21 home runs, 48 stolen bases, and 99 RBI.

In 1957, he became inseparable friends with future Hall of Famer Orlando Cepeda while playing for the Triple-A Minneapolis Millers, and fast buddies with another Puerto Rican, José Pagán, while at Class A Springfield (Massachusetts). In 1958, Alou began the year in the Pacific Coast League playing for the Phoenix Giants. He became housemates with future Hall of Famer Willie McCovey, then a promising twenty-year-old Black player from Alabama. "I loved living in the same house with McCovey," Alou recalls in his autobiography, where he reports that they shared a broken-down jalopy, which McCovey sold but made sure Alou got his share. Hitting over .300, Alou was called up in June to the major leagues, but the Giants no longer played in New York. Alou was called up to play for the freshly relocated San Francisco Giants.

OPPOSITE Felipe Alou, who joined the San Francisco Giants
organization in 1956, led the big leagues in hits in two seasons
during his seventeen-year playing career.

THE BLACK AMERICAN
PLAYER AMONG LATINOS

Black players of the Negro Leagues frequently went south of the border to play, just as Latino players went north. From the 1920s to the end of the 1940s, hundreds of Black players went to the Dominican Republic, Venezuela, Cuba, and Puerto Rico to play winter ball, and some were lured there during the regular season as well. The greatest number played in Cuba during the winter, although they experienced more than a little prejudice, and even flat-out racism, on the island. Lighter skin color was prized over darker. Of course, Black American players in Latin America faced some of the same challenges as Latino players in the United States: not knowing the dominant language, trying to navigate a different culture (including the food), and, in Mexico, adjusting to the altitude. But these were inconveniences, not daunting obstacles arising mostly from broad-based structural racism.

In 1937, star pitcher Satchel Paige, along with Josh Gibson, Cool Papa Bell, and three other members of Gus Greenlee's Pittsburgh Crawfords, traveled to the Dominican Republic to play for that country's dictator, Rafael Trujillo. This was the first time Negro Leaguers jumped to another country during the regular season. The departure of the six players gutted the Crawfords, and the team never recovered, folding in 1939, when it was sold and moved to Toledo. By June 1937, eighteen Negro Leagues players had left their teams to play in Trujillo's tournament and consequently were penalized for it on their return to the United States. Negro Leagues owners at first banned them for two years, but eventually reduced the penalty to having their salary docked one month. The Negro Leagues were hardly in a position to harshly punish some of their best players and biggest gate attractions like Satchel Paige.

Playing in the Dominican Republic had some advantages: players made more money and had an easier schedule than in the Negro Leagues, as was true of playing south of the border generally. But it was not all pleasant for them. Trujillo had little interest in baseball, but the country he ruled, the Dominican Republic, was baseball mad. He used the tournament as a gimmick to bolster his bid for reelection

The Ciudad Trujillo of the Dominican Republic fielded a
team with many players from the Negro Leagues in the
1937 tournament against the Águilas Cibaeñas.

Martín Dihigo, a star both on the mound and in the infield,
was hired as player/manager by Mexican businessman Jorge
Pasquel for his new team, the Veracruz Blues.

by creating a powerful team in the nation's capital. When he couldn't get white
American players, he did the next best thing and hired the best Black players. They
were heavily guarded, and the pressure on them to win was enormous. On July 11,
1937, Cuidad Trujillo, Trujillo's team for which many of the Black stars played, won
the tournament, eight games to six, over the Águilas Cibaeñas, with an arm-weary
Paige in relief struggling to get the last outs. Josh Gibson was the big offensive star,
hitting .453 in thirteen games. Dr. José Enrique Aybar, the Dominican dentist who
recruited the Black American players, made a dig at American racism at the end of
the tournament: "It is the general opinion here that all the imported players in this

city are the best in the world. It is my personal opinion that if our team which won the championship met any white league team, our team would win."

The most famous instance of cross-border playing, and one that most threatened the Negro Leagues, was the rise of the Mexican League. In 1940, millionaire Mexican businessman Jorge Pasquel formed the Azules de Veracruz (Veracruz Blues) and hired the great Martín Dihigo, who had been playing winter ball in his native Cuba, to be his player-manager. Dihigo, one of the players recruited to play on a rival team during Trujillo's tournament, told Pasquel to hire Negro Leagues players, whom of course Dihigo knew well, including some who were playing in Cuba that winter. The Mexican League had hired Black American players in the past, but the trend intensified in the 1940s, when the league hired Black players for its primary season, not just for winter ball. Pasquel wound up signing thirteen Negro Leagues players for the team's first season, including Gibson, Bell, "Double Duty" Radcliffe, Leon Day, and Ray Dandridge, some of the most famous Black American ballplayers of the era. Other teams hired Black American players as well: sixty-three Negro Leaguers played in Mexico in 1940, four times the number that played in 1939. Plying their trade in Mexico at some time or another during the 1940s were 120 Black American players, including such future stars as Roy Campanella and Monte Irvin.

Pasquel succeeded for two reasons: he offered the players more money than they were making in America, and they were treated better in Mexico. Infielder Willie Wells, who was known as "El Diablo" and who played and managed in Mexico, said to the Black sportswriter Wendell Smith: "Some people look at my situation simply from the standpoint of money. But there's more to it than that. In the first place, I am not faced with the racial problem in Mexico. When I travel with the Veracruz team, we live in the best hotels, we eat in the best restaurants and can go any place we care to. You know as well as all other Negroes that we don't enjoy such privileges in the United States."

As Pasquel and other Mexican League team owners continued their raid on Negro Leagues players, team owners protested, even meeting with federal officials. They would get no relief, however, until the effects of World War II were felt: when employment opportunities for Black workers increased because of Black union leader A. Philip Randolph's March on Washington Movement—which pressured President Franklin Delano Roosevelt into making political concessions—and when wages rose overall because of the high employment rates caused by the war. Negro Leagues teams began enjoying an increase in revenue as attendance rose because Black fans had greater income. This windfall allowed the Negro Leagues owners to offer competitive salaries in some cases to keep key players. They also enjoyed success in court. The Homestead Grays, for instance, sued Josh Gibson for jumping to Mexico in 1941, eventually forcing him to return.

The Mexican League's ambition was to create the future of baseball with the best American players, including white stars. Offering astronomical salaries, Pasquel signed pitcher Sal Maglie and catcher Mickey Owen. But he had limited success signing top white players because the National and American Leagues announced that jumping players would be banned for life. Nonetheless, in 1946, the Mexican League was a thorough mix of Latino, white, and Black American ballplayers. Among the forces that influenced major league baseball, the multiracial Mexican League, with its highly competent players, made it plain that keeping the white major leagues segregated would be increasingly difficult—especially during World War II, which had been fought to overthrow racist ideology.

By 1948, however, the Mexican League, too ambitious for its own good, was suffering greatly, burdened by too many big contracts and not enough revenue. And by then, the white major leagues were integrated. The game would be played together by all who qualified, as the Mexican League had shown.

OPPOSITE Negro Leagues player Ray Dandridge
spent much of his playing career—nine seasons—
in Mexico. He is seen here circa 1945.

THE LATINO PLAYER ROCKS THE GREAT AMERICAN NORTH

Felipe Alou joined a team with more Latino and Black ballplayers than any team yet in American and National League history. In 1958, the Giants, with four Black and six Latino players, was the most racially integrated team in the white major leagues, superseding the pioneering Dodgers, now in Los Angeles, who had led the way with Jackie Robinson's 1947 season.

The Giants were not signing Latino and Black players from some altruistic urge to achieve diversity. It was about money. The signing bonuses for Alou, Willie McCovey, and Orlando Cepeda were $500 each, and $4,000 for Juan Marichal. The Giants signed a white pitcher, Mike McCormick, to a bonus of $60,000. If you could find good Latino and Black players who cost a lot less than comparable white players, why wouldn't you sign them? Once integration happened, many owners discovered the economic benefit of having a pool of cheaper players.

In his first three years with the Giants, outfielder Alou improved, scoring more runs and getting more at-bats and hits each year. His batting average trended in the right direction. His breakout year would be 1961, when he had more home runs (18), more RBI (52), more hits (120), and more games played (132).

That year, however, a sort of iron triangle of race relations formed on the team, with tensions rising between the three centers of power. Horace Stoneham, the Giants owner, hired retired shortstop Alvin Dark as manager. Stoneham felt that the team required a disciplinarian, and Dark, a former marine who had just finished a successful fourteen-year playing career, including seven years with the Giants, fit the bill. Dark, who had never managed or even coached before, was a Christian teetotaler, a nonsmoker, and a Southerner from Louisiana. He was one corner of the triangle.

Star outfielder Willie Mays, arguably the best player in the game at that point, was one of the longest-tenured members of the team, having played several years for the Giants in New York. He was the second corner of the triangle. Also a Southerner, from Alabama, Mays was, whether by nature, or by conditioning,

Juan Marichal was part of a diverse Giants roster that helped
San Francisco win the 1962 National League pennant.

given that he had grown up in the South, nonconfrontational, and he usually
deflected issues about race. Dark, when appointed manager, made sure to be
supportive and complimentary of Mays. He wrote Mays a letter saying what an
honor it was to manage him. He told the press the same.

Rising Latino stars Alou and Cepeda were the third corner of the triangle.
They had no history with the team in New York and were not Americans; they
were peevish and less inclined to ignore slights. These young, competitive men
were sensitive about and less experienced with the racism they encountered in
America. What further exacerbated the situation was that Cepeda, a bona fide star
by the end of 1962, and Mays did not like each other.

DIVERSITY MEETS THE OLD SOUTH IN SAN FRANCISCO

In an effort to break up ethnic enclaves on the team—white players in a faction, Blacks in another, and Latinos in yet another—Dark rearranged lockers to mix the players. This bit of social engineering was deeply resented, and Dark soon back-tracked. In another effort to create "team" consciousness, Dark posted a sign during spring training that read: "Speak English, you're in America." Dark met with the Latino players and told them that other players on the team were complaining about them using Spanish when speaking to one another. He told them not to use Spanish while in uniform. This rule soon went by the boards. Dark could not enforce it, as the Latino players openly defied it. Dark understood "team" consciousness as a form of assimilation that the Latinos strongly opposed.

However much Dark may have been disliked, particularly by the Latino players, his presence and management style did not affect their performances on the field. Alou played even better in 1962 than in 1961. He made the National League All-Star team, hit 25 home runs, drove in 98 runs, and hit over .300. Alou appreciated that Dark talked him up to the press. Cepeda, National League Rookie of the Year in 1958, also had terrific years in 1961 and 1962, making the All-Star team each year and finishing second in the 1961 MVP voting. The Giants won the pennant in 1962 and narrowly missed beating the Yankees in the World Series. In this regard, Dark was a successful manager. Alou conceded that Dark "did excel in managing—in the strategic part of the game. I know he made me a better player."

In the midst of these conflicts, the Latino contingent of the team continued to grow and strengthen. Alou's brother Matty had joined the team in 1960, and his brother Jesús followed in 1963. Felipe described what he saw as the team pecking order: "First-class citizens were the whites, second-class citizens were the blacks, and the third-class citizens were the Latinos." Dark complained aloud to his Latino players after a bad game that they lacked hustle or baseball smarts. They were not putting out their best effort. They were dogging it, and they were dumb. He once told Cepeda to stop playing his Latin jazz records on road trips, but Cepeda

Jesús Alou, Matty Alou, and Felipe Alou (*from left to right*) became the first
"all-brother" outfield on September 15, 1963, with the San Francisco Giants.

refused to stop. On August 19, 1962, Dark, angered that Cepeda was holding up the
team bus while saying goodbye to a Puerto Rican family he knew—and kissing the
daughter, who was light enough to appear white—told the driver to leave without
him. Only the intervention of Mays, who told the driver to wait, averted a confronta-
tion between Cepeda and Dark.

WILLIE MAYS
IN THE MIDNIGHT HOUR

Mays continued his customary stellar play during Dark's four years as manager, winning the home run title in 1962 (49) and 1964 (47), earning All-Star status and Gold Gloves every year, and finishing in the top six in the MVP balloting. But Mays felt the strain of playing an expanded schedule when it went from 154 to 162 games in 1962 after the National League added two teams, the New York Mets and the Houston Colt .45s. He was also in his thirties and by 1964 had been an everyday player for ten full seasons. He felt the wear and tear, both mentally and physically. One night in 1962 he called Dark in the middle of the night, saying he had the shakes and couldn't sleep, bothered by marital problems and a slump that had the fans booing him. It was not unusual for Mays to suffer the sweats and terrors of the midnight hour, when "his self-imposed pressures" tormented him most.

In addition, the overall stress of being a Black baseball star during the civil rights era was mounting: activists were demanding a public commitment that Mays and other Black players were reluctant to give. A column by sportswriter Wendell Smith in the *Pittsburgh Courier* entitled "Isn't It About Time for Negro Athletes to Be Heard From in the Civil Rights Fight?" was published on March 14, 1964. Smith pressed his point: "The Negro baseball player particularly evades his obligation in this area. It is a rare occasion when a Negro major leaguer participates in Civil Rights demonstrations of even the mildest form. There is no recollection here that any of them, for example, participates [*sic*] in civil rights demonstrations last summer." While Mays is not mentioned in the article, the criticism seems to have been directed at him. Mays went out of his way during his career to avoid making comments about the American racial situation. He was never thrown out of a game for arguing with an umpire. He never expressed defiance or dissatisfaction. In this respect, he was the opposite of Jackie Robinson, who, once Branch Rickey's

OPPOSITE Willie Mays's career began as he helped integrate the game. By the 1960s, Mays was part of a generation of Black stars who were reshaping baseball.

three-year term of restraints was relaxed, became one of the most argumentative and fiery players in the league. He also pressed for civil rights, both during his playing career and after.

If Smith's *Pittsburgh Courier* article about Black athletes and the Civil Rights Movement did not name Mays, Robinson was willing to do so in his 1964 book, *Baseball Has Done It*. Robinson interviewed many ballplayers, Black and white, but Mays was not one of them. "Willie didn't exactly refuse to speak. He said he didn't know what to say. I hope he will think about the Negro inside Willie Mays's uniform, and tell us one day." Robinson continues: "I hope Willie hasn't forgotten his shotgun house in Birmingham's slums, wind whistling through its clapboards, as he sits in his $85,000 mansion in San Francisco's fashionable Forest Hills.... We would like to have heard how he reacted to his liberation in baseball, and to his elevation to nationwide fame."

Robinson's description of Mays's boyhood poverty is exaggerated, and his overall tone is condescending and accusatory. By virtue of his stature as a player, Mays was expected to, even pressured to, stand up against racism. Robinson sometimes chafed other Black players with his racial piety, but for him the Civil Rights Movement of the early 1960s had reached the midnight hour. Either you were committed or you weren't. In the fall of 1963, Smith wrote a sympathetic column about Mays collapsing in the dugout from extreme fatigue: "In trying to live up to the almost inhumanly high standards set for them, some Negro players exert themselves into a state of complete mental and physical exhaustion." From Mays's perspective, it might have seemed an "inhumanly high standard" that, all season, he was expected by the Giants to carry his team and by Robinson and Smith to carry his race's struggle.

OPPOSITE Alvin Dark (*right*) became the Giants manager after his playing days and—with Willie Mays in his lineup—led the Giants to the National League pennant in 1962; Dark's management style caused friction among white, Latino, and Black players on the team.

ALVIN DARK'S LOST CAUSE
AS THINGS FALL APART

Things came to a head with Dark and the Giants' Latino players in 1964, with Mays in the middle. Mays started off the year at an unbelievable pace. After one month, he was hitting .468. In May, Dark made Mays the team captain, the first time a Black player was given such an honor in the post-1947 history of the game for a formerly all-white team. Mays took his new role seriously and pridefully. Earlier that month, Robinson's *Baseball Has Done It* was released, and in it, Dark, one of the interviewees, spoke like a white southern paternalist: "The way I feel, the colored boys who are baseball players are the ones I know best, and there isn't any of them that I don't like. . . . In fact, I felt that because I was from the South—and we from the South actually take care of the colored people, I think, better than they're taken care of in the North—I felt when I was playing with them it was a responsibility for me." The timing of making Mays the captain now seemed suspicious, especially as it was unusual for a manager to do so after the season had started.

In July, things got worse for Dark when *Long Island Newsday*'s Stan Isaacs wrote an article about the Giants in which he quoted Dark: "We have trouble because we have so many Negro and Spanish-speaking players on this team. They are just not able to perform up to the white ball player when it comes to mental alertness. You can't make most Negro and Spanish players have the pride in their team that you can get from white players. And they just aren't as sharp mentally." Even though Dark denied saying these things, none of his players believed him because he had expressed sentiments of this sort in the clubhouse.

The Isaacs article nearly launched a full-scale mutiny, as the Latino players wanted to boycott Dark and sit out the games. But Mays talked them out of it. "Don't let the rednecks make a hero out of him," Mays said. Without Mays, the other players wouldn't have succeeded in a protest. Cepeda thought that Mays did not provide support or leadership for Latino players: "Mays never said anything. If I was Willie,

OPPOSITE Orlando Cepeda (*left*) and Willie Mays frequently smiled for the
camera, but they often clashed when it came to speaking out about civil rights.

The Hall of Fame collection includes the bats used by Orlando Cepeda
during a game on April 29, 1961, against the Milwaukee Braves in
Milwaukee and by Willie Mays when he hit his 512th home run—setting
a new National League record—on May 4, 1966. The homer elevated
Mays past Mel Ott, who previously held the record.

I would have spoken out more. Willie had the stature, the leverage. He was an icon, and he carried a lot of weight with management. I was very disappointed because I looked at him—we all looked at him as a leader." In the end, there was a resolution, of sorts. Stoneham fired Dark at the end of the 1964 season—not because of Dark's racist remarks, but because Dark, married and a father of four, was having an affair with a flight attendant.

Felipe Alou was not involved in any of this. In the winter of 1963, he was traded to the Milwaukee Braves. The Dominican right fielder had not endeared himself to the Giants' front office after writing *Sport* magazine's November 1963 cover story, entitled "Latin-American Ballplayers Need a Bill of Rights," in which he aired Latino players' grievances. Working with journalist Arnold Hano, Alou voiced the sentiments of most Latin players. He recounted his refusal to pay a fine of $250 for playing against Cubans in a game in the Dominican Republic that the Commissioner's Office had not sanctioned. A major league player with two or more years of service couldn't play winter ball without special consent. Alou explained

that he played winter ball because he could not refuse the military junta that governed the Dominican Republic at the time. "If I had not played," Alou proclaimed, "it would have been a slap in the face of the people of my country, who look forward to this series." He also stressed that Latino players lacked representation in the league, pointing out that the Commissioner's Office understood neither the challenges they faced, from the language to income tax disadvantages, nor the stereotyping and discrimination they withstood.

Whatever his feelings were about Dark, Alou was gone. He would play in Milwaukee for two years before the Braves moved to Atlanta, becoming the face of the majors in the former confederacy's most famous city. He would have some of his best years as a player with the Braves after leaving one legendary Black player in Mays with the Giants to share the field with another, Hank Aaron. But what happened to Aaron and Atlanta, "the City Too Busy to Hate," and other Black players in baseball in the 1960s is a different story—a story of America dramatically and sometimes violently wrenching itself out of its tarnished past to become another country.

TIME HAS COME

BLACK BALLPLAYERS AND THE CIVIL RIGHTS STRUGGLE

1960-1970

WITHOUT A DOUBT,

IT WAS AN ANGRY POINT IN AMERICAN HISTORY

FOR BLACK PEOPLE

—DR. KING'S KILLING HAD JOLTED ME; KENNEDY'S INFURIATED ME—

AND WITHOUT A DOUBT,
I PITCHED BETTER ANGRY.

—Bob Gibson, on how he turned around
his historic 1968 season

Protest in May 1963 against segregation in cafés
and restaurants in Oklahoma City.

The 1960s were the best of times and the worst of times. There was an explosion of innovation in American popular culture: Rock music would become an impressive and widely influential art form. Black music would reach its biggest audience, including both Black and white fans, and would become widely disseminated through television, the dominant medium of the era. Cinema would be transformed in both what was allowed visually on-screen and how actors were permitted to speak.

There were radical changes in fashion, architecture, painting, and literature. Molds were broken. The baby boomers, born after World War II, were rising as the major tastemakers in the world. Youth was everything, and everyone spoke of a generation gap. The problem was that change was coming faster than it could be absorbed or even understood. Americans engaged in an intense cultural battle over what they thought this powerful country was or should be. The tremors of change convulsed the country like a seizure.

And then there was baseball. In 1964, the New York Yankees, the perennial champions, lost the World Series to the St. Louis Cardinals. In 1966, the Yankees finished in last place. They would not play in the World Series again until 1976. They had more players of color by then, too.

THE CITY OF
BROTHERLY LOVE

In 1950, the Phillies—with a squad of youngsters called "the Whiz Kids" (the average age of the team was 27.6)—won the pennant but lost the World Series to the Yankees in four straight games. No Black player was on either team. Only four of the sixteen major league clubs that season had Black players: the Cleveland Indians, the Brooklyn Dodgers, the New York Giants, and the Boston Braves. The Phillies would be the last National League team to integrate when they signed Kansas City Monarchs infielder John Kennedy in 1957. Kennedy played in five games, batted twice with no hits, was optioned to the minors, and never played in the majors again. The common thought among white Philadelphians was that the Phillies had simply wanted to get the integration burden off their backs by trying out a Black player.

Whether the Phillies would have drawn more Black fans if Kennedy stayed with the team is hard to say. The Phillies had an infamous reputation among Black baseball fans because of the particularly egregious and vehement racial insults that manager Ben Chapman and his team hurled at Jackie Robinson in 1947. So vicious were Chapman's taunts that the press and Commissioner Albert "Happy" Chandler chastised him. Chapman defended himself, saying that every rookie went through this rite of passage. In the end, though, he was forced to invite Robinson to pose for a photo with him to show there were no hard feelings between them, and Robinson accepted. If Chapman became a bit more subdued, other Phillies were no less nasty to Robinson in his first year. Black Philadelphians long held this incident against the Phillies.

By 1961, the Phillies had four established Black players, three of whom were Latino—Cuban second baseman Tony Taylor, who played fifteen years for the Phillies and was one of their most popular players; Mexican shortstop Rubén Amaro, who put in six years with the club; and Cuban outfielder Tony González, who played in Philadelphia for nine years and was one of their top hitters. The lone African American was outfielder and bench player Wes Covington, who joined the

John Kennedy became the first Black player in Phillies history in 1957; Philadelphia was the last team in the National League to sign a Black player.

Wes Covington played for the Phillies from 1961 to 1965
during an era when Black players fought for acceptance
and respect in Philadelphia.

team in 1961. He stayed with the Phillies for four and a half seasons. He was a feared power hitter who was a useful utility player for the team.

But the player who was to become the Phillies' first Black superstar came up later, at the end of the 1963 season, when in ten games he hit .292. It was apparent to everyone that he was going to be an offensive force, one of the best hitters in the team's history, one of the best prospects in baseball. His name was Dick Allen, but at the time of his major league start, he was called Richie, a name he did not like. He would have a considerable impact on the city and the team during the 1960s. As time went along, however, he grew unhappy. He asked more than once to be traded. And he made sure that everyone knew about his unhappiness, just as the fans made sure to express their displeasure with him in no uncertain terms.

HOW THE MAJOR LEAGUES BECAME MODERN

Georgia-born-and-bred outfielder Dixie Walker played reluctantly and uneasily on the 1947 Brooklyn Dodgers alongside Jackie Robinson. He was a member of the uprising of white, mostly southern players who didn't want to play with Robinson. He remained on the team but still found it awkward to play with a Black man. He feared his association with a Black teammate would make him unpopular in his hometown, where he owned a hardware store. He would be branded a "nigger lover," to use racist southern parlance. Walker was traded to the Pittsburgh Pirates at the end of the season.

However, Dixie Walker's views would mellow. In Robinson's 1964 book, *Baseball Has Done It*, Walker, who had become a hitting coach for the Milwaukee Braves, was interviewed about the big leagues' acceptance of Black players. He said, "I don't know if anyone has said it yet, but I'm going to say it here—without the Negro we'd be unable to field clubs of major league quality in this expansion period." He went from seeing Black players as the death of baseball to seeing them as essential to its future. By 1960, it had become clear that all professional sports had to choose whether to grow or die. For certain sports, like baseball, Black players were key to expansion.

By the early 1960s, baseball faced a set of challenges, including the expansion and rising popularity of other professional sports such as basketball, hockey, and football. Football in particular offered the greatest competition. In addition to the enduring popularity of collegiate football, baseball faced the growth of professional football with the formation of the American Football League (AFL) in 1959, adding another dimension to the reach of professional sports. With its increase in popularity, the National Football League, which announced a merger with the AFL in 1966, would challenge baseball's place as the country's favorite sport.

The rise of television as a force in the dissemination of sports was another test for the game. Premiering in 1961 was ABC's revolutionary program *Wide World of Sports*, which not only broadcast a variety of sports but also framed sports

BROOKLYN DODGERS
WINNERS OF 1947 PENNANT IN THE NATIONAL LEAGUE

TOP ROW, L TO R

HAROLD WENDLER, DAN COMERFORD, JACKIE ROBINSON, HUGH CASEY, JOE HATTEN, DIXIE WALKER, CLYDE KING, BOBBY BRAGAN, BRUCE EDWARDS, ARKY VAUGHAN, JOHN GRIFFIN
TRAINER   PROPERTY MAN   ASST. PROP. MAN

MIDDLE ROW, L TO R

ED MIKSIS, SPIDER JORGENSEN, DAN BANKHEAD, GENE HERMANSKI, GIL HODGES, HAL GREGG, CARL FURILLO, REX BARNEY, HARRY TAYLOR, RALPH BRANCA, HAROLD PARROTT, SEC.

FRONT ROW, L TO R

PETE REISER, STAN ROJEK, AL GIONFRIDDO, ED STANKY, VIC LOMBARDI, COACH JAKE PITLER, MANAGER BURT SHOTTON, COACH CLYDE SUKEFORTH, COACH RAY BLADES,
HARRY LAVAGETTO, HANK BEHRMAN, PEEWEE REESE,
     SITTING L TO R   STAN STRULL, BATBOY, NORMAN BERMAN, BALLBOY,

EMPIRE PHOTOGRAPHERS
NEW YORK

When Jackie Robinson (*top row, third from left*) integrated the Brooklyn
Dodgers in 1947, he faced the challenge of winning over teammates who
came from segregated society, including popular outfielder Dixie Walker
(*top row, sixth from left*), who was born in Georgia.

competition as a form of personal and cultural drama. ABC would revolution-ize televised sports even further with the premiere of *Monday Night Football* in September 1970. Baseball had its *Game of the Week*, which launched in 1953, but other sports were seriously competing for viewers and fan loyalty. By 1960, televi-sion viewership had reached five hours a day; radio was down to two hours daily. From 1965 to the end of the decade, television had cut movie attendance by more than half. Baseball was not going to survive without television, but television was going to require major league baseball to expand its markets.

On October 17, 1960, the National League announced that it would add two new franchises in 1962, one in New York to replace the Giants, who had moved to San Francisco in 1958, and one in Houston that would have an ultramodern, air-conditioned, domed stadium. Almost a week later, the American League announced that it was expanding in 1961, adding a team in Los Angeles, the Angels, as a counter to the National League, which had expanded into that important mar-ket when the Brooklyn Dodgers moved there in 1958. The NL also announced the addition of a team in Washington, D.C., to replace the old Washington Senators, who moved west before the 1961 season to become the Minnesota Twins. In 1961, the American League expanded from 154 to 162 games, and by the next year, the National League followed suit. By then, each league had ten teams.

A June 1961 article in *Ebony* entitled "End of an Era for Negroes in Baseball" described integration as "old hat" and wrote that it was not the crisis it was when Robinson appeared:

> So commonplace are Negroes in baseball now, that sepia stars are added to the roster without fanfare, enter the lineup without notice and can even make an upside-down catch or swat a grand slam homer without masses of rabid race fans leaping to their feet on every great play. Indeed, most base-ball teams and stadiums have become so integrated that partisan fans find it impossible to root for their favorite teams on the basis of number of Negroes in the line-up.

The article notes that of the 450 men who played baseball in 1961—the fifteenth anniversary of Robinson's 1946 debut in Montreal with the Dodgers organization—seventy-seven were Black, or about 18 percent. (*Ebony* included Black Latinos in its count.) By 1962, each team had at least one Black player who was an important contributor, if not a major star. Standouts, not counting Latino players, included the Cubs' Billy Williams in the outfield and shortstop Ernie Banks; the Braves players Hank and Tommie Aaron, Lee Maye, and Mack Jones; Giants Willie Mays and Willie McCovey; five of the starting eight Dodgers, Jim Gilliam, Maury Wills, Tommy Davis, Willie Davis, and John Roseboro; and the Reds' Vada Pinson and Frank Robinson. Chuck Hinton patrolled the outfield for the Senators; Bob Gibson, Bill White, and Curt Flood were with the Cardinals. Even the slow-to-integrate Yankees had the stalwart Elston Howard, and the Red Sox had pitcher Earl Wilson, the first Black player to pitch a no-hitter in the American League.

In *Ebony*'s 1962 Black baseball roundup, the article bragged about the salaries of some of the leading Black players (again, Latinos included) and noted that Black men made up nearly 19 percent of MLB's rosters and earned 21 percent of the league's salary total, an indication of the recognition of their excellence. It was important that a magazine like *Ebony* touted that merit was rewarded regardless of race, once Black players had been given the opportunity to compete with white players. The article went on to note that Black players still faced racial discrimination in dealing with team accommodations at some spring training camps in Florida, but that, on the whole, the big leagues had become a poster child for how integration could work in the United States.

The big leagues made themselves modern in two distinct ways after World War II. First, adding Black players across the league made the game more inclusive and representative of the country, which helped Black fans embrace the sport, not just the Brooklyn Dodgers. And second, expanding to the West Coast made the game truly national, representing the geographically broad breadth of the country. By the end of the 1960s, expansion reached across the northern border, to Montreal, and by mid-decade the Braves would move from the North to the Deep South of the traditional Confederacy during the height of the turmoil of the Civil Rights Movement. That team would bring Hank Aaron, one of the greatest Black stars of the game, along with it. But first, there's some backstory to be told.

THE WHITE SPORTSWRITER'S SCRUTINY OF THE BLACK PLAYER

In 1961, the year the Cincinnati Reds won the National League pennant, center fielder Vada Pinson had a career year. He had a .343 batting average (second only to the Pittsburgh Pirates' Roberto Clemente), an .883 OPS, and 208 hits—the highest levels in those categories that he would ever achieve. He finished third in the Most Valuable Player voting and won a Gold Glove for his defense. Many thought that Pinson was a surefire Hall of Fame player, as much as the bona fide Black star of the Reds, take-no-prisoners outfielder Frank Robinson.

But that was 1961. On June 18, 1962, *Cincinnati Post* sportswriter Earl Lawson, convinced that, in this new season, the "laidback" Pinson was squandering his talent by swinging for the fences, wrote a highly critical article about the listless Reds, condemning the effort of many players, including the gifted center fielder. None of the Reds liked the story. Pinson was so incensed that he confronted Lawson in the locker room a few days later at Forbes Field in Pittsburgh. No player likes to be accused of dogging it, and Black players felt that they were the particular targets of that criticism,

Vada Pinson (*left*) and Frank Robinson helped form one
of the game's most formidable outfields with the Reds.

accused of not giving their best effort. Even the ultra-intense Frank Robinson was accused of this by the Reds general manager when Robinson had an off year in 1960 but still tried to get a pay raise.

The exchange between Pinson and Lawson became so heated that Pinson punched Lawson in the face. "He hit me flush on the chin," Lawson wrote. "I didn't see stars, but I did see red. Hell, I didn't kid myself. I knew I wasn't any match for him. He was 23, a well-conditioned athlete, a muscular 5-10, 185-pounder. I was 39. And if anyone were to describe me as a pudgy 5-8, 180 pounder, it would have been an act of kindness. I knew I probably would have taken a physical beating if players hadn't separated us after Pinson's first swing."

Lawson wrote about the "fight" the next day, but the matter blew over fairly quickly, somewhat surprising considering the race angle of it. Or perhaps it was thought best to let it die because of the race angle, which team officials feared. Also, Cincinnati second baseman Johnny Temple had punched out Lawson in June 1957 over a dispute about Temple being charged with an error.

Pinson and Lawson had another run-in on September 4, 1963, when Pinson pinned the journalist against a wall and tore his shirt. The cause: a Lawson article headlined "Bunts Could Make Champ of Pinson." This time Lawson had Pinson charged with assault and battery. Lawson's article suggested that Pinson could win the batting title if he bunted occasionally and used his speed more as an offensive weapon, an assertion that Pinson thought ridiculous. "My job isn't to bunt," Pinson said. "You don't drive in runs bunting." Pinson typically hit third in the Reds' order at this time. A number three hitter is not expected to bunt. But Lawson's concern was about Pinson earning a few more easy hits to beat out Pittsburgh's Dick Groat for the batting title. In this instance, Pinson and Lawson seemed to be talking past each other. Pinson was cleared of the charges on January 28, 1964.

In another incident, Frank Robinson, Pinson's best friend, star teammate, and fellow alumnus from McClymonds High School in Oakland, got into an altercation with Lawson's sportswriting colleague Si Burick of the Dayton, Ohio, *Daily News*. He accused Burick of being "just like Lawson. You're all alike." Robinson concluded, "I don't blame Vada. He should have knocked Lawson down." In response, Lawson wrote, "I was surprised to see

Robinson joining ranks with Pinson. Frank and I had very good relations since he joined the club as a rookie in 1956." Lawson had arranged with a professional bondsman to put up bail when Robinson was arrested on February 9, 1961, in Cincinnati on the charge of illegally carrying a gun. Robinson had bought an Italian Beretta .25 because he carried large sums of cash and feared being robbed. He pulled the gun during a racial altercation at a restaurant.

At Pinson's trial, Robinson was a witness for Pinson. The trial ended in a hung jury. The jurors thought Pinson was guilty of assault and battery, but also thought the encounter was too trivial to convict him. Did the fact that Pinson was a star athlete affect the jurors? If Pinson had been an ordinary Black man who struck a white reporter because of an uncomplimentary article, would he have been convicted?

Pinson's 1962 and 1963 seasons weren't as strong as 1961, but he was still a highly productive player. He had not missed a game in his first three years as a regular and never played fewer than 155 games over the next six seasons. In his first five years, he collected more hits than Willie Mays, Hank Aaron, and teammate Frank Robinson in the same time span. He finished his career with 2,757 hits, a lot for someone who is not in the Hall of Fame, and more hits than Hall of Famers Ozzie Smith, Orlando Cepeda, Ernie Banks, Ryne Sandberg, Tony Oliva, Ted Simmons, and Scott Rolen had.

During the first decade and a half of big league integration, Black players could be expected to chafe a bit under the extra scrutiny of white sportswriters and to be a bit stressed about their motives or the racist assumptions that might underlie their writing. During the Negro Leagues era, when white sportswriters had paid little attention to Black players, Black sportswriters could be cutting in their criticism, but at least Black players could feel a bit easier about their intentions. ☙

BY GERALD EARLY

RACE MAN

On January 23, 1962, Jackie Robinson, in his first year of eligibility after his retirement at the end of the 1956 season, learned that he had been elected to the Baseball Hall of Fame along with former Cleveland Indian pitching ace Bob Feller. He was the first Black major leaguer, and the first Negro Leagues player, to enter the Hall. It was an extraordinary honor that overwhelmed Robinson.

"Whether he was named to the Hall of Fame," writes *Ebony*, "for his impressive record as a ballplayer or for his pioneering feat in cracking baseball's color line is a question that will be debated for years to come." The plaque unveiled at Robinson's induction did not include a single word about his race. It did not mention that he played in the Negro Leagues. In fact, when he became eligible for election, Robinson asked that only his accomplishments on the field be considered in the voting: he clearly wanted the public to see him as a ballplayer, not a political or social symbol.

After his retirement in 1956, Robinson brought his unique experiences to a variety of endeavors. William Black, president and founder of Chock full o'Nuts, a company with shops around New York City that sold its own line of coffee and baked goods, hired Robinson to be vice president of personnel. Robinson had no expertise in this line of work, and Black, a liberal who supported Robinson's civil rights activism, admitted that he hired Robinson "because a majority of the people who work for me are colored—and I figured they would worship him." This was important as unionization loomed, although it ultimately failed. Among unions and the political left, Robinson was condemned as anti-union.

Robinson had a megaphone thanks to the syndicated columns he wrote (with ghostwriter Al Duckett) at various times for the *New York Post* and the *Amsterdam News*. This put him in the crosshairs of the Black politics of the day. After all, as a columnist dealing with current affairs, Robinson, in effect, became a political commentator. Always civil rights–minded during his baseball career, Robinson

OPPOSITE Jackie Robinson (*center*) celebrates his 1962 Hall of Fame election with Branch Rickey and his wife, Rachel Robinson.

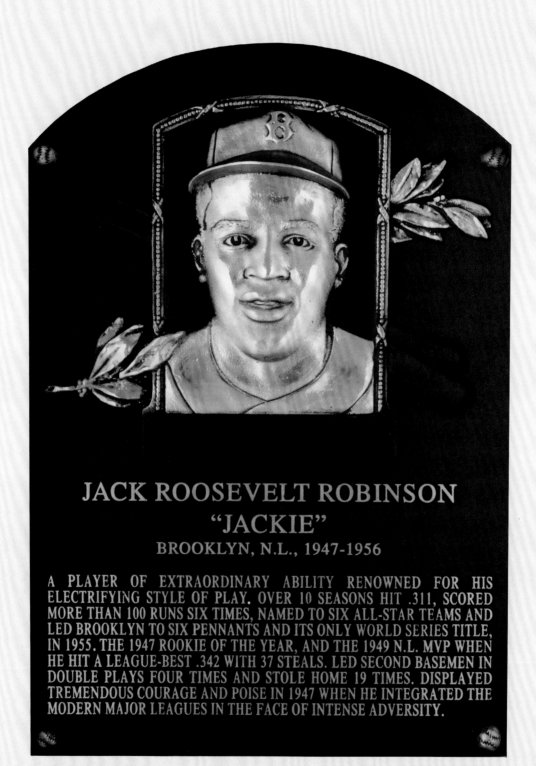

JACK ROOSEVELT ROBINSON
"JACKIE"
BROOKLYN, N.L., 1947-1956

A PLAYER OF EXTRAORDINARY ABILITY RENOWNED FOR HIS
ELECTRIFYING STYLE OF PLAY. OVER 10 SEASONS HIT .311, SCORED
MORE THAN 100 RUNS SIX TIMES, NAMED TO SIX ALL-STAR TEAMS AND
LED BROOKLYN TO SIX PENNANTS AND ITS ONLY WORLD SERIES TITLE,
IN 1955. THE 1947 ROOKIE OF THE YEAR, AND THE 1949 N.L. MVP WHEN
HE HIT A LEAGUE-BEST .342 WITH 37 STEALS. LED SECOND BASEMEN IN
DOUBLE PLAYS FOUR TIMES AND STOLE HOME 19 TIMES. DISPLAYED
TREMENDOUS COURAGE AND POISE IN 1947 WHEN HE INTEGRATED THE
MODERN MAJOR LEAGUES IN THE FACE OF INTENSE ADVERSITY.

threw himself wholeheartedly into fundraising for the NAACP in retirement, but he sometimes felt the organization was too conservative. He was attracted as well to Martin Luther King Jr. and direct-action protests. But Robinson, no fan of Malcolm X, was often rejected by younger civil rights activists and Black militants as being too conservative himself. Indeed, he began to receive hate mail from Black people who considered him an Uncle Tom. The NAACP did not heed his plea to organize direct-action protests, and Robinson became more uneasy about King when the latter came out against the Vietnam War.

Robinson was also a Republican, a party to which the Black community had become increasingly hostile given its ideological dislike of social welfare programs and its wish to distance itself from being too closely identified with Black support, as the party had been before FDR. Although Robinson was among the liberal Republicans who were still an important segment of the party in the Northeast—indeed, he worked for liberal New York governor Nelson Rockefeller for a time—many Black people saw the Republican Party, especially after World War II, as a white conservative organization that often sided with segregationist southern Democrats. In this respect, Robinson seemed out of touch, yesterday's hero.

So, too, in sports. Robinson was superseded by other Black athletes of a newer day: Jim Brown and Gale Sayers in football; Wilt Chamberlain and Bill Russell in basketball; and Bob Gibson, Bill White, Curt Flood, and a host of others in baseball. And all of them were overshadowed by a brash young boxer from Louisville who became heavyweight champion in 1964—Muhammad Ali, aka Cassius Clay. When Robinson was stricken in the 1960s with adult-onset diabetes that would ravage him, the glory days of the heroic Black ballplayer were gone. Nevertheless, in 2008, with the cooperation and agreement of Robinson's widow, Rachel, the Hall of Fame cast a new plaque for its gallery, one that reflected the pivotal role he played in the history not only of the game but of the country.

OPPOSITE Jackie Robinson's original Hall of Fame plaque made no mention, at Robinson's request, of his pioneering role in baseball. In 2008, Robinson's plaque, as seen here, was recast with the support of his widow, Rachel Robinson, to reflect the milestone he achieved when he crossed the color line.

THE QUIET MAN
AND MOVING SOUTH

When outfielder Felipe Alou, one of the first Latino players to make a mark on the game, joined the Milwaukee Braves in 1964 after being traded by the San Francisco Giants, he left the presence of one of the greatest Black players in baseball, Willie Mays, to become the teammate of another: Hank Aaron.

In 1964, Aaron was thirty years old and entering his eleventh season as a starting player for the Braves. He had won the National League's Most Valuable Player Award in 1957 when he scored 118 runs, drove in 132 runs, hit 44 home runs, and batted .322. During that same year, the upstart Braves from Bushville beat the Yankees to win the World Series. It would be the only World Series the team would win while Aaron played for them. In 1959, he had, in many respects, an even better year, hitting .355 to lead the league in batting as well as hits (223) and slugging percentage (.636). He also led the league with 400 total bases—a staggering feat.

Aaron and Mays were alike in many ways. Both were born and grew up in racially segregated Alabama, and both played with Negro Leagues teams before becoming major league players. Both won a World Series once in the 1950s, but never another. And both could hit for a high batting average, but had home run power and speed as well. The two men, however, possessed different personalities and styles of play.

This difference in temperament is clear in how each responded to being interviewed for Jackie Robinson's 1964 book, *Baseball Has Done It*. Mays, considered the more charismatic and stylish player, refused on the grounds that he didn't know what to say. Aaron, on the other hand, talked at considerable length. He said that "playing in the Sally League was quite a bad experience for me." Among the very first Black players to play in the South Atlantic League, he was called terrible names and received many threatening letters. Aaron also spoke of how some white writers tried to cast him as a "dumb Negro" who knew only how to hit a baseball. He voiced his support for Martin Luther King and mentioned reading James Baldwin, the literary voice of the Civil Rights Movement. To the white folks who counseled patience, Aaron's response was: "We're not going to wait any

Hank Aaron, playing for the Milwaukee Braves, won the National League Most Valuable Player Award in 1957. The award, seen here, is in the Hall of Fame's collection.

Hank Aaron hit his 715th career home run on April 8, 1974,
moving past Babe Ruth to the top of the all-time list.

longer!" "A quiet leader," teammate Felipe Alou called him. But even the quiet man thought Mays was too quiet. As Aaron said many years after their playing days were over, "If any part of me was not satisfied with Willie, it's that he didn't speak out enough. I couldn't understand that part of it."

In 1962, Aaron had the pleasure of having his younger brother, Tommie, join the Braves. Tommie was far more gregarious than his older brother and enjoyed hanging around the clubhouse and talking baseball after a game ended. The contrast between the two men startled Aaron's teammates. But Tommie suffered by comparison: the name carried expectations, and he was not nearly as good a ballplayer as Hank.

OPPOSITE Contemporaries in the National League, Hank Aaron
(*left*) and Willie Mays combined for 1,415 career home runs.

THE "BRAVE" NEW SOUTH

The Braves enjoyed tremendous success when the team moved to Milwaukee from Boston in 1953. They won a championship in 1957 and nearly repeated that feat in 1958, but things started to unravel in the 1960s. The Braves had been in Boston for seventy-seven seasons. They would stay in Milwaukee for only thirteen. They had broken league attendance records in the 1950s, but attendance dropped in the 1960s, owing in part to the team's underperformance in relation to its talent. The harsh spring weather in Milwaukee was also a factor. When Bill Bartholomay bought the Braves in 1962, the handwriting was on the wall: Atlanta's ambitious mayor, Ivan Allen Jr., announced that an unnamed major league team was moving to Atlanta when the city finished building a new stadium, and it was clear where the Braves were going after the 1965 season, ending a tale of anguish for both the team and Milwaukee.

Allen wanted Atlanta to become a major city, a reinvented city of the New South that would shed southern provincialism. To do this, the city needed a large, modern airport (which it had started to build in the 1950s), expressways, stadiums to attract major sports franchises, and a solution to its race situation. As Allen wrote in his autobiography, "Atlanta was still almost totally segregated when I became mayor in 1962." Segregation had to be addressed in order to convince an integrated major league baseball team to move there. Naturally, Aaron, Felipe Alou, and other Black Braves who had experienced playing in the South were not eager to move to Atlanta. "I lived in the South, and I don't want to live there again," Aaron said in 1964.

But Atlanta and the Braves *needed* Aaron to accept the move. And he needed a guarantee that he and his family would not experience any incidents of segregation or discrimination. The Black Braves were assured that the city would be completely open to them. A fuss from Aaron could have greatly embarrassed the

OPPOSITE *From left,* Felipe Alou, Joe Torre, and Hank Aaron, shown here during spring training, were part of a diverse Braves team that moved from Milwaukee to Atlanta following the 1965 season.

Much-loved superstar Roberto Clemente, a native of
Carolina, Puerto Rico, wore this Pittsburgh Pirates cap
when he hit his 3,000th career hit in 1972.

team and tarnished Atlanta's reputation as "the City Too Busy to Hate." In 1966,
his first year playing in Atlanta, Aaron led the National League with 44 home runs
and 127 RBI. He stole 21 bases and was caught only three times. Although his batting average slipped to .279, the first time he had hit under .300 since 1960, it was
another astonishingly productive year. Welcome to Atlanta, Mr. Aaron.

Alou's return to the South was equally impressive: he led the league in hits,
total bases, and runs scored and hit .327. Unbelievably, neither won the MVP that
year. Alou's hero, the Pittsburgh Pirates' Black Puerto Rican outfielder, Roberto
Clemente, was the MVP, although he did not lead the league in any offensive category. Clemente's OPS was a bit better than either Aaron's or Alou's. But it wasn't
as good as that of Dick Allen, who led the league in this category.

CRASH DIVE

Dick (Richie) Allen, the high school star from Wampum, Pennsylvania, won the National League Rookie of the Year Award in 1964, a year in which the competition was not even close. He led the league with 125 runs scored, 13 triples, and 352 total bases. He had over 200 hits and a .939 OPS. He easily beat out San Francisco Giants third baseman Jim Ray Hart and Rico Carty, the talented and temperamental Dominican Milwaukee Braves outfielder.

Allen also struck out 138 times, leading the league. Over his fifteen-year career, Allen would strike out more than 100 times in ten seasons. He joined sluggers like Mickey Mantle and an increasing number of younger power hitters like Reggie Jackson who would be prodigiously productive but strike out far more than such hitters did in the past. It was a sign of the times: hitters struck out more and pitchers had higher strikeout totals. Power was the new name of the game.

Allen's true weakness, however, was his fielding: he made a staggering 41 errors in his first full year. His teammates did not seem overly concerned about it. Phillies catcher Clay Dalrymple said, "It really didn't matter how many errors Richie made at third base because his offense more than made up for it." Allen also swung a 42-ounce bat, one of the heaviest bats in the game, and he hit monstrous home runs. The Phillies finally had their Black superstar, and so did Philadelphia.

On September 23, 1964, while Allen was still in his rookie year, the local business community, made up mostly of Jews and some Black folk, held a "Richie Allen Night." It was almost a month since the Columbia Avenue race riot on August 28, one of the worst spasms of racial violence in Philadelphia in the 1960s. The immediate cause of the riot was an unfounded rumor of police brutality, but racial tension in Philadelphia was high to begin with. The Black community was becoming more radicalized and less willing to put up with poor housing, unemployment and underemployment, crime, and inadequate health care. As the 1960s progressed, Black Philadelphians engaged in a power struggle for political control of the city with Irish, Italians, and other white ethnic groups who, though mostly New Deal Democrats, were growing increasingly more conservative. The Jewish community was caught in the middle.

The riot occurred close to Connie Mack Stadium, where the Phillies played. The neighborhood around the ballpark and across much of North Philadelphia was rapidly becoming home to Black and Latino communities. In fact, tough Black street gangs in North Philadelphia called the neighborhood "the Jungle." The riot devastated the main Black shopping drag of North Philadelphia. More than six hundred businesses, most owned by Jews, were destroyed. For weeks after the riot, many white fans were afraid to come to the ballpark; one hundred officers patrolled the neighborhood surrounding the stadium. The situation put the Phillies' front office in a quandary. As the neighborhood was changing, the Phillies hoped to attract more Black and Latino fans. But if attracting those fans came at the expense of their white fan base, was it worth it? In less than a decade, the issue would be sidestepped in a way: the new Veterans Stadium would open in 1971 on the other side of the city, deep in South Philadelphia, in an area mostly made up of white communities at the time.

But in September 1964, after the riot, it was surprising that the merchants of North Philadelphia still wanted to celebrate Richie Allen Night. And in fact, Phillies general manager John Quinn opposed it. Rookies didn't get special nights, and Quinn perhaps thought that Allen would get swellheaded or that his teammates would get jealous. But Jackie Robinson had been given a "special day" in his rookie year with the Dodgers on the exact same date, September 23, seventeen years earlier, and Black Cuban star Minnie Miñoso was also given a special day, on September 23, 1951, in his rookie year with the Chicago White Sox. Perhaps the organizers thought Allen was as important to the Phillies as Robinson had been to the Dodgers, and as impressive a rookie as Miñoso, who "is to Latin players," Orlando Cepeda said, "what Jackie Robinson is to black ballplayers." "I was presented with a television, snow tires, luggage, and a stereo . . . and those gifts were much needed," Allen said later. Robinson and Miñoso got similar gifts, but Robinson got a Cadillac as well.

OPPOSITE Dick Allen played with the Phillies for nine of his fifteen big league seasons. He was named the National League Rookie of the Year in 1964, his first full season with the team.

On Richie Allen Night, the Phillies were in the midst of a meltdown that would cost them the National League pennant. With a lead of six and a half games and twelve left to play, they proceeded to lose ten straight games. It was one of the worst collapses in baseball history. On September 23, the Phillies were in the third game of that collapse, losing that day to the Cincinnati Reds, 6–4. But in the midst of the Phillies slide, Allen hit .429 and 3 home runs as he collected 21 hits in the last twelve games of the season. It was the closest the Phillies would come to winning a pennant during Allen's first tenure with the club.

Things began to fall apart for Allen in Philadelphia in 1965 when he got into a fight with Phillies first baseman Frank Thomas, an aging but still potent slugger whom Quinn acquired from the New York Mets for the stretch run in 1964. Thomas, known for making racially insensitive remarks, bullied Phillies Black rookie out-fielder John Briggs, a close friend of Allen's. Allen resented Thomas's treatment of Briggs. Their bad feelings escalated into a fight on June 23. While Thomas was taking batting practice, Phillies outfielder Johnny Callison made a wisecrack that Thomas should try bunting. For some reason, Thomas directed his anger toward Allen, not Callison: "What are you trying to be, another Muhammad Clay, always running your mouth off?" Allen charged Thomas and knocked him down. Thomas grabbed a bat and hit Allen on the shoulder, which only further infuriated him. The players were pulled apart.

Later that day, the Phillies waived Thomas, who had been popular in Philadelphia, even having a show on WFIL radio. He also had a large family. Thomas played the victim for the press, saying he had always liked Allen and tried to help him. The white fans of Philadelphia took Thomas's side, thinking Allen was a troublemaker and that he was getting special treatment because he was Black. In addition, Allen, along with another Black player, Wes Covington, had held out in the spring of 1965 for more money. The press and a good part of the white public thought an ungrateful Black cabal was at work. Allen said, "In Philadelphia, their attitude was that I should be grateful just to be allowed on the field." Allen characterized his situation aptly: "After the Frank Thomas fight in early July, I started playing angry baseball."

Thus began Allen's long divorce from Philadelphia. Fans called him all sorts of racial epithets and threw garbage at him. Allen took to wearing a crash helmet at Connie Mack Stadium and earned the nickname "Crash." As the years went by, he

The Philadelphia Phillies pose in Connie Mack Stadium on September 24, 1964, in Philadelphia, during the National League pennant race. Dick Allen is in the second line (*second from left*), along with John Briggs and Frank Thomas (*fifth and sixth from left*). John Callison is in the front row (*third from left*).

did everything he could to force the Phillies to trade him. He sometimes did not show up for games, or showed up late. He scrawled hostile messages to the fans on the infield dirt. He dogged it on the field from time to time. He was savaged by local sportswriters and repeatedly fined and suspended by the Phillies. He sometimes showed up to play with alcohol on his breath, and in the dugout he could be found smoking, both habits possibly developed to ease his stress. Despite all of this, he remained the most productive player on the team. In 1969, his last season with the Phillies, he hit .288 with 32 home runs, 89 RBI, and a .949 OPS.

In October 1969, after five years with the Phillies, Allen got his wish. He was traded to the St. Louis Cardinals. The main player that the Cardinals sent to the Phillies in exchange, Curt Flood, never played one inning for his new team.

FLOOD PLAIN

Whatever the United States was in 1960, it was something different by the end of the decade. A president assassinated on a public street in front of thousands of witnesses was bound to unnerve the country, even shatter some of its long-held beliefs about its goodness. The Civil Rights Movement won major legislative victories with the passage of the Civil Rights Act of 1964 and the Voting Rights Act of 1965. The 1964 Philadelphia riot was a mere dress rehearsal for the 1965 Watts riot in Los Angeles, the 1967 Detroit riot, and other violent unrest that broke out across the nation in April 1968 after the assassination of Martin Luther King Jr.

Also, the rise of Black Power as a slogan and an ideology divided Black activists: some still believed in integration, but a younger and growing group felt that integration was a fraud and the United States needed to be dismantled. The cry of revolution was amplified by the New Left, whose adherents used their opposition to the Vietnam War as a fulcrum for delegitimizing the country. Even a segment of young Black athletes was radicalized, led by heavyweight champion Muhammad Ali's refusal to be inducted into the military in 1967 because he opposed the Vietnam War on religious grounds. At the 1968 Summer Olympic Games in Mexico City, sprinters John Carlos and Tommie Smith stood with clenched fists raised during the playing of the national anthem on the medalists' podium. They were greeted when they returned home as unpatriotic ingrates by some, but as liberationist heroes by others.

In the midst of all this, baseball was also trying to change, while trying to remain the same. To some members of the public, the sport seemed irrelevant, a stodgy game past its time. And yet ball games were still played, players were still developed, and fans still tuned in and turned out. In fact, from 1960 to 1970, MLB attendance went from 19.9 million to 28.7 million. However, could baseball still be regarded as the National Pastime? The AFL-NFL merger of 1966, which also created the Super Bowl, put the finishing touches on the ascendancy of professional football as "America's game." By 1970, when the merger was completed, the game on the gridiron had become a behemoth. And yet money for broadcasting baseball

Curt Flood (*left*) with Marvin Miller, head of the Major
League Baseball Players Association, on January 3, 1970,
waiting for an appearance in ABC studios in New York
during their fight with owners over the reserve clause.

continued to increase, and baseball kept expanding: four teams were added to
MLB in 1969. In the American League, the Kansas City Royals filled the hole left by
the Athletics, who had departed for Oakland in 1968, and for one season Seattle
was home to the Pilots, who would become the Milwaukee Brewers in 1970. The
National League grew to include the Padres in San Diego and the Montreal Expos,
who became the Washington Nationals in 2005. The leagues also divided into two
divisions each and introduced a playoff system. The team with the best regular-
season record was no longer guaranteed to go to the World Series.

Another development proved fateful for the game in 1966. On April 12, former
United Steelworkers economist Marvin Miller was named the head of the Major
League Baseball Players Association (MLBPA). Miller made his presence felt almost
immediately: in January 1968, the MLBPA negotiated a higher minimum salary for
players, from $7,000 to $10,000. He doubled the fee that the Topps Company paid
players for their baseball cards. He also got owners to increase their contribution
to the players' pension fund, probably the most important issue for the players.

Curt Flood was a seven-time Gold Glove Award winner, a
three-time All-Star, and a two-time World Series champion.

In keeping with the spirit of the age, they had become more militant about their
concerns and more willing to confront the owners. All of this, of course, was
mere warm-up to the big battle that awaited owners and players over the baseball
reserve clause, which bound a player to his team for life unless he was traded or
retired. St. Louis Cardinal outfielder Curt Flood would become the poster child for
that battle in its first round when he was traded to Philadelphia for Dick Allen after
the 1969 season.

If the Brooklyn Dodgers symbolized a new era of integration in the late 1940s,
with Robinson, Roy Campanella, Don Newcombe, and Joe Black, the St. Louis
Cardinals were the team of America's racial future in the 1960s. That decade, the
Cardinals captured three pennants and won two World Series, anchored by key
players of color: outfielders Curt Flood and Lou Brock; pitcher Bob Gibson; first
baseman Bill White, who was traded to the Phillies at the end of the 1965 season;
Dominican second baseman Julian Javier; and, from 1966 to 1968, first baseman
Orlando Cepeda, the Puerto Rican star, who replaced White at first base.

Flood figured large in the Cardinals' success. Born in Houston, Texas, but raised in Oakland, California, he was a graduate of McClymonds High School, which produced such players as Frank Robinson and Vada Pinson. He became a star defensive outfielder for the Cardinals, winning seven Gold Gloves, after being traded from the Cincinnati Reds. During the twelve years he was with the Cardinals, he hit over .300 six times. When the Cardinals traded him, Flood was well established in St. Louis and did not wish to leave. He objected to the trade, in part because it insulted him. "It violated the logic and integrity of my existence. I was not a consignment of goods. I was a man."

Flood was not the first ballplayer to legally challenge the reserve clause. In this instance, the MLBPA decided to support Flood's challenge to the clause once members were convinced that he was not motivated by race. The reserve clause affected all players regardless of race, and they needed a test case to reflect that. Miller told Flood that he had little chance of winning and that his baseball career would be over as a result of his challenge, but Flood persisted. Despite his protestations that he was not motivated by race, when interviewed by the ABC sportscaster Howard Cosell, who brought up his $90,000 annual salary, Flood said, "A well-paid slave is nonetheless a slave."

Despite this comment, Flood made it clear that he just did not want to play for the Phillies: "Philadelphia. The nation's northernmost southern city. Scene of Richie Allen's ordeals. . . . I did not want to succeed Richie Allen in the affections of that organization, its press and its catcalling, missile-hurling audience." But his former teammate Bill White, who had been traded to Philadelphia after the 1965 season and played there through the 1968 season, didn't have the same problems that Allen did. This aspect of Flood's complaint, by itself, would not generate much public sympathy.

More important to his case was his inability to offer his services to any team, just as any other worker could do. No baseball player was truly getting paid his market worth because the market wasn't free: a player couldn't find out what another team would pay to have him. In a telling historical twist, however, the lack of an enforceable reserve clause had contributed to the downfall of the Negro Leagues. The reserve clause was a form of salary control that worked very much against the player, but because it would have prevented players from jumping from team to team, it would have helped the Negro Leagues succeed better as a business and

as a league. The prime example was Satchel Paige, who jumped to play in Mexico or the Dominican Republic or for any team, barnstorming or league-connected, that offered more money. Others did the same. Because the Negro League teams found it hard to enforce their contracts in dealing with each other, and with leagues in other countries, they found it equally difficult to have their contracts recognized by the white major leagues. White baseball was granted the right to succeed as a monopoly. Black baseball, by virtue of its circumstances, could not—or at least not as much as it may have wanted to.

Flood lost his case before the U.S. Supreme Court purely on the basis of legal precedents that had been set in *Toolson v. New York Yankees* (1953) and *Federal Baseball Club of Baltimore v. National League of Professional Baseball Clubs* (1922). Flood made a half-hearted return to baseball in 1971, when he was traded to the Washington Senators, but his physical gifts had atrophied during his one-year absence from the game. That, plus an unhealthy consumption of alcohol and a general lack of drive, led to his departure after playing in only thirteen games that year.

But Flood's challenge was a signal to the owners that the time had come. Players were no longer passive, no longer willing to subsist on the owners' paternalism. In a sense, Black ballplayers like Flood and, to some degree, Allen forced their white peers to come to terms with reality as they made their voices heard in how the game was to be played and under what conditions they were willing to play it. One thing is sure: Allen and Flood were both angry Black players whose anger affected the history of the game. Eventually, free agency would come to the major leagues.

OPPOSITE Curt Flood (*middle*) was a three-time All-Star when he was traded from the Cardinals to the Phillies following the 1969 season. Flood refused to report to the Phillies and eventually sued MLB to contest the reserve clause, sitting out the 1970 season as a result. In 1971, Flood returned to the big leagues with the Washington Senators, who were managed by Ted Williams (*right*).

FREE AGENCY

AND

THE QUEST FOR

LEADERSHIP

1970s-1990s

I REPORTED TO THE INDIANS FOR THE
LAST THREE WEEKS OF THE [1974] SEASON . . .
AND I SAW RIGHT AWAY THAT
THIS TEAM HAD A PROBLEM.
COACH LARRY DOBY AND ALL THE BLACK PLAYERS . . .
WOULD SEAT THEMSELVES AT THE FAR END OF THE DUGOUT,
WHILE . . . THE WHITE COACHES AND PLAYERS
SAT AT THE NEAR END.
I SAT IN THE MIDDLE, OBSERVING.

—Frank Robinson, the year before he
became Cleveland's manager

Demonstration in Washington, D.C., on October 8, 1977, against the
Allan Bakke "reverse discrimination" case before the Supreme Court.

In the immediate aftermath of the civil rights era, the biggest
public policy venture to address racial inequality was affirmative action, a program meant to give America's racial minorities,
as well as women, additional consideration for employment
and promotion in the labor market. In short, qualities such as
race and gender, which had been social liabilities in the past,
would be considered in pursuit of a more equitable playing
field. Detractors referred to the policy as racial and gender
preferences, or reverse discrimination. Affirmative action has
remained controversial to the present day.

Affirmative action would have nothing to do with the number of Black MLB players on the field, as talent assessments were fairly objective, but it would come into play when calls increased for more Black managers, umpires, and front-office personnel. An old boys' network and subjective views about the intangibles of a person's administrative and interpersonal abilities were obstacles, as was the idea that white players would be uncomfortable with Black front-office personnel.

By 1970, however, Black Americans were assured of one permanent place—the major league playing field. Racial integration was no longer considered some sort of "experiment" or something that could be eliminated. No questions persisted about Black players' competitive drive and skills.

On September 1, 1971, at Three Rivers Stadium in Pittsburgh, the Pirates fielded an all-Black team of Black American and Afro-Latino players, a first for MLB. Whether Pirates manager Danny Murtaugh was conscious of the lineup's racial makeup in constructing it is difficult to say. The oddity was that Al Oliver, a solid left-handed hitter, started at first base against the Philadelphia Phillies' tough left-handed pitcher Woody Fryman. Right-hand hitting Bob Robertson, a white first baseman for the Pirates, was no mere sub or bench player. He hit 26 home runs in 1971, almost twice the offensive power of Oliver. No manager puts out a lineup to make a political statement; the lineup consists of the players the manager thinks will give the team the best chance to win. Oliver had a good game that night. Maybe Murtaugh was simply playing a hunch.

Back in 1960, Black and Latino players each made up 8.9 percent of major league players. By 1975, those percentages were 18.5 and 10.2, respectively. Black players reached their highest percentage in 1981, at 18.7 percent, but by 1990 the numbers had declined to 16.6 percent. The decline continues to the present day as Latino numbers continue to rise.

But for approximately two decades, Black Americans achieved their highest numbers as MLB players. Now the question was: Where would MLB go from here? Black players had proven that they could play the game with virtuosity. But would they be given a chance to run the game?

OPPOSITE On September 1, 1971, the Pittsburgh Pirates fielded a lineup featuring all non-white players, a first in National League and American League history.

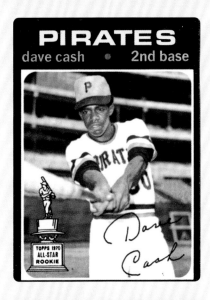

PIRATES

dave cash • 2nd base

PIRATES

roberto clemente • of

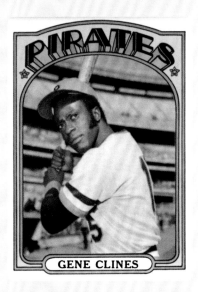

PIRATES

GENE CLINES

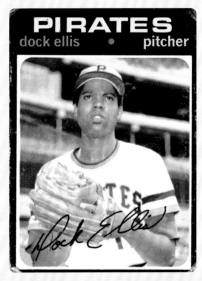

PIRATES

dock ellis • pitcher

PIRATES

JACKIE HERNANDEZ

PIRATES

al oliver • 1st base-of

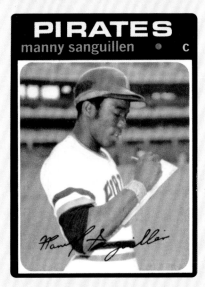

PIRATES

manny sanguillen • c

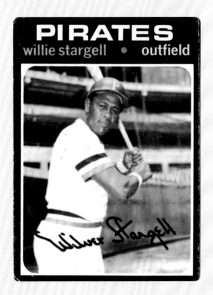

PIRATES

willie stargell • outfield

PIRATES

RENNIE STENNETT

THE SHAPE OF
BASEBALL TO COME

Baseball, perhaps more than other sports, sells tradition and its past. In this way, it seems unchanging. The statistics that Babe Ruth and Ty Cobb compiled are as universal as the stats of Ken Griffey Jr. and Mookie Betts. But the game has changed considerably over the last one hundred years.

After the 1968 "Year of the Pitcher," when Boston Red Sox outfielder Carl Yastrzemski won the American League batting title with a mere .301 average, the imbalance between hitting and pitching caused considerable concern. The pitching mound was reduced from fifteen inches high to ten, and the strike zone was narrowed the following year. But a bigger change occurred in 1973 when the American League adopted the designated hitter rule; from then on, regular hitters could bat for pitchers, who are normally poor batsmen. The designated hitter (DH) did not play in the field but only batted. After the change, the American League became the more powerful offensive league. The National League officially, and finally, adopted the rule in 2022. Filling the DH role has prolonged the careers of many aging players who could still hit well but had diminished defensive skills, and it made successful careers possible for players who never were capable in the field. In a 2013 listing of the ten greatest designated hitters in the history of the rule, five were Black (Chili Davis, Harold Baines, Frank Thomas, Hal McRae, and Don Baylor) and two were Latino (Edgar Martinez and David Ortiz).

Doubtless the biggest change to affect baseball, and indeed all sports, was the coming of free agency by 1977. Following the unsuccessful test case brought by Curt Flood in January 1970, labor arbitrator Peter Seitz ruled in 1975 that major league players would become "free agents" if they played without a contract for their team for one year. This effectively nullified the reserve clause, which wedded a player to the team holding his contract for the rest of his major league career.

The resulting free agent market drove up salaries. The year the suit was brought, Hank Aaron was the highest-paid player in MLB, making $240,000 a year. But by 1980, three years after the elimination of the reserve clause, pitcher Nolan Ryan became the first player making $1 million a year. By 1990, the Milwaukee

Hal McRae, a three-time All-Star player who later managed
the Royals and Devil Rays, was also considered one of the
top designated hitters in the game in 1983, ten years after
the rule was adopted by the American League.

Brewers' Robin Yount was making $3.2 million annually. Not only were players, particularly star players, making more money, but they were guaranteed the money over the length of multi-year contracts. If a player was injured and could not play that season, he was still paid whatever his contract demanded, and as long as he was under contract his pay could not be reduced the following year. A rising tide lifts all boats, as the saying goes, so all MLB players benefited from this change. Black players of an earlier era had felt that they were underpaid; now free agency changed that.

Escalating salaries coincided with larger television contracts and increased licensing revenue. Indeed, baseball and all of sports became an ever-growing part of television programming; then television itself radically changed with the advent of cable. The number of stations expanded dramatically from three networks and PBS in the 1960s to literally hundreds by the late 1980s. By 1994, 62 percent of American households subscribed to cable. With more stations, more programming was needed, and sports could fill the airwaves. Cable mogul Ted Turner, who started the twenty-four-hour news network CNN in 1980, used his WTCG station to broadcast Atlanta Braves games beginning in 1973, and he bought the team in 1976 so he could continue to do so. In 1979, the Entertainment and Sports Programming Network (now known as ESPN) was born, broadcasting sports twenty-four hours a day. This was the same year that Panamanian infielder Rod Carew left the Minnesota Twins for the Angels, for a salary of $800,000, the highest in baseball that year. The launching of an all-sports network may have seemed a quixotic venture at first, but as sports expanded its reach, athletes became celebrities. The high salaries of star baseball players seemed only to increase their luminescence and that of the game itself.

OPPOSITE Rod Carew became one of the game's highest
paid players when he joined the Angels in 1979.

THE YEAR
THE OLD KING DIED

Jackie Robinson's last autobiography, *I Never Had It Made*, was published on October 28, 1972, four days after he died from a massive heart attack. He was only fifty-three, but with his glassy eyes due to near-blindness, an unstable gait steadied by a cane, and snow-white hair, he gave the appearance of a man much older.

One belief was that Robinson aged as a result of bottling up anger and frustration during his ten years with the Brooklyn Dodgers. But those of this view often forget that Robinson played Branch Rickey's martyr only for three years, the first of which was for the Montreal Royals minor league team. During his final years with the Dodgers, Robinson vented his frustrations frequently. Nonetheless, the stress he had to endure as the symbol of integrating baseball—the responsibility he felt—took its toll.

His life after baseball was stressful as well. It was his dream to see business ventures flourish in the Black community, but his time as chairman of the board of the Freedom National Bank in Harlem, which officially opened its doors in 1964, proved trying for Robinson. A Black financial institution hoping to provide banking services and loans to people who found it difficult to qualify with white-owned banks, Freedom National teetered on insolvency the whole time Robinson was involved. He felt that bank regulators treated Freedom National Bank with "kid gloves" and was unhappy that the bank was not being assessed by the same standards as a white bank. To him, this paternalism was not helpful. Robinson's vigorous efforts to keep the bank afloat over the next six years, which involved ousting the president, took as much of a toll on his health as anything else. Politically, his business ambitions and his belief in capitalism as the way forward for Black people led him to the Republican Party. But Robinson grew disappointed with the Republican Party, not just with Richard Nixon and Barry Goldwater but

OPPOSITE: Jackie Robinson worked with MLB executives like Commissioner Bowie Kuhn (*right*) throughout his retirement to promote diversity in the game.

Bill Lucas became the first Black general manager in MLB in 1976,
the year he took over management of the Atlanta Braves.

with his friend Nelson Rockefeller, whom he ardently backed for the presidency. Rockefeller's suppression of the September 1971 Attica prison uprising "bitterly disappointed" Robinson.

Before Game 2 of the 1972 World Series, when Robinson appeared before the crowd at Riverfront Stadium in Cincinnati, he walked onto a baseball field for the last time in his life. He threw out the first pitch and received a "rousing and lengthy" ovation. His remarks were brief. "I am extremely proud and pleased," he said, accepting a plaque commemorating the twenty-fifth anniversary of his debut with the Brooklyn Dodgers. "But I'm going to be tremendously more pleased and more proud when I look at that third base coaching line one day and see a black face managing in baseball." Four years after Robinson's plea, in the fall of 1976, Bill Lucas in effect became the first Black general manager. Atlanta Braves owner Ted Turner put him in charge of the team, as the VP of player personnel. Lucas, who had spent his career with the Braves organization, struggled for three years in the role as Turner managed from the sidelines until Lucas died of a massive stroke in 1979. It would be some time before Robinson's wish was more fully realized.

HONORING
THE KING OF THE ROAD

When Branch Rickey signed Jackie Robinson in 1945 to play in the National League, Satchel Paige became desperate. Paige felt that he deserved to be the first one in. He felt he had earned it. What had Jackie Robinson ever done for baseball? Where was Jackie Robinson when Paige was toiling away pitching game after game as "the Emperor of Barnstormers," the king of the road? Paige was over forty years old (some believed well over forty), had been pitching since he was a teenager, and dreamed of being in the majors. He thought himself worthy of it. Paige thought he was the best pitcher to ever pick up a baseball. He might have been right. If he did not have the reams of statistics to back his claim, he had spools of anecdotal evidence. Now he saw his chance slipping away. How long could his arm hold out? If his age was against him, each passing year would simply put another nail in the coffin.

In his memoir, Paige voiced his frustration: "Signing Jackie like they did still hurt me deep down. I'd been the guy who'd started all that big talk about letting us in the big time. I'd been the one who'd opened up the major league parks to the colored teams. I'd been the one who the white boys wanted to barnstorm against. I'd been the one who everybody'd said should be in the majors. But Jackie'd been the first one signed by the white boys."

Paige was right that he was the chief attraction of the Negro Leagues. He was, without question, the most famous of all Negro Leagues players. He was among the most talented players—Black or white—of his time. But because he had always been a showman and jumped around, pitching for whoever would pay him the most, he was seen more as "being a clown, a show-off, and not a real pitcher."

When Bill Veeck signed Paige to join the Cleveland Indians in the middle of 1948, Paige helped the team win the pennant. He made an impression, but had no impact. His best days were behind him. In 1952, he won twelve games for the St. Louis Browns, made the All-Star team, and got some votes for MVP. It was his last hurrah as a professional baseball player.

Satchel Paige is congratulated by Commissioner Bowie
Kuhn at the Hall of Fame Induction Ceremony in 1971.

Satchel Paige's Hall of Fame plaque, which notes his
long years in the Negro Leagues.

In 1971, Paige was inducted into the Baseball Hall of Fame. He was not the first Black player to be so honored. Once again, Robinson beat him to it when he was inducted in 1962. But more important, Paige was the first Black player to be inducted who lacked the official stats to show how dominant he had been because he had played nearly his whole career in the Negro Leagues. His entry legitimized the Negro Leagues. Paige was the pathbreaker he finally wanted to be.

But the road to his induction was hardly smooth. In its April 1971 issue, *Ebony* offered an incensed editorial about Paige's election: "[Paige] was given a niche in the National Baseball Museum, a separate wing," the magazine pointed out. And in fact, he was not actually being inducted into the Hall of Fame, but being given a special exhibit that also featured other Black players in the Negro Leagues. The

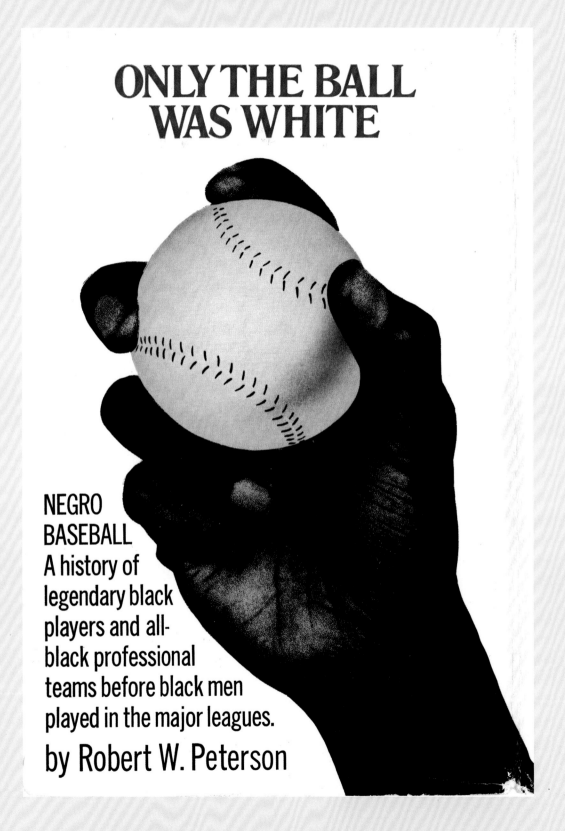

ONLY THE BALL WAS WHITE

NEGRO
BASEBALL
A history of
legendary black
players and all-
black professional
teams before black men
played in the major leagues.
by Robert W. Peterson

baseball commissioner at the time, Bowie Kuhn, explained that Negro Leagues players had come to light with the 1970 publication of Robert W. Peterson's *Only the Ball Was White*, the first history of the Negro Leagues. Kuhn held a meeting in his office in early 1970 that included National League president Ford Frick and Paul Kerr, the Hall of Fame president, both of whom adamantly opposed adding Negro Leagues players to the Hall. Among the others present, sportswriter Dick Young was the strongest advocate for the inclusion of Negro Leagues players. The meeting accomplished nothing, however, so in February 1971 Kuhn formed a committee of Negro Leagues experts to determine who were the best players, so that they could be honored in an exhibit at the Hall.

When Kuhn announced that Paige would be the first "honoree" at a press conference, the furor was deafening. There were cries of racism, Jim Crowism, and the like. Jackie Robinson, the NAACP, *Ebony*, and various activists were vehement in denouncing the arrangement. It was precisely the response that Kuhn, who favored the induction of Negro Leagues players, wanted. The outcry made Frick and Kerr give ground, and Paige was subsequently inducted as a full-fledged member. The committee that Kuhn empaneled selected Josh Gibson posthumously and Buck Leonard the following year for induction. By the end of the 1970s, Cool Papa Bell, Oscar Charleston, Martín Dihigo, Monte Irvin, Judy Johnson, and Pop Lloyd, all stars of the Negro Leagues, had been inducted. If baseball was finally and truly becoming "America's game," then the Hall of Fame was finally becoming America's shrine dedicated to remembering the whole game, not just a part of it.

OPPOSITE Robert W. Peterson's 1970 *Only the Ball Was White* detailed the history of Black baseball, and helped to urge official recognition of Negro Leagues players by the Hall of Fame.

LONG LIVE THE KING

"I suppose that first year or two in Atlanta was when I made up my mind," Hank Aaron states in his autobiography, "that if I ever got close to Babe Ruth's record for home runs, it would be mine." By the end of 1972, Hank Aaron needed 42 more home runs to break Babe Ruth's record of 714. He wanted it very much. He wanted "the recognition that I thought was long overdue me." Aaron also wanted "the financial benefits that the record would surely bring. . . . Then there was the sense of doing something for my race."

In 1973, at the age of thirty-nine, Aaron had a sensational year: 40 home runs, 96 RBI, a .301 batting average, and an OPS, amazingly, of over 1.000. He needed only two home runs in 1974 to break the record. But breaking the record had become more of an ordeal than he anticipated.

In 1973, Aaron received 930,000 pieces of mail. President Richard Nixon was the only American to receive more. The vast majority were positive, but a startling, soul-shattering number of them began "Dear Nigger." There were innumerable death threats. The Braves increased security for Aaron.

The Atlanta Braves opened the 1974 season in Cincinnati on April 4. Aaron asked the Reds for some pregame recognition of the sixth anniversary of the assassination of Martin Luther King Jr. He was ignored. The Braves had announced that Aaron would not play in any of the Cincinnati games because the team wanted him to tie and break Ruth's record when the club went home to Atlanta, right after the Cincinnati series. Commissioner Bowie Kuhn interceded, arguing that not playing Aaron, one of the team's best players, was compromising the integrity of the sport because the Braves would not field their best team.

Aaron played in two of the three contests in Cincinnati, hitting a home run in the first game. Kuhn attended that game along with Vice President Gerald Ford.

OPPOSITE Hank Aaron's remarkable consistency set the stage for him to surpass Babe Ruth's all-time home run record. Here he is on April 8, 1974, when he broke the record in Atlanta.

VIDA BLUE TELLS CHARLIE FINLEY, "THAT'S NOT MY NAME"

In the summer of 1971, Oakland A's southpaw pitcher Vida Blue was one of the most publicized Black athletes in America. Earlier in the year, on March 8, undefeated Muhammad Ali lost the heavyweight title to the undefeated Joe Frazier in New York. Ali, at that time, was the most famous athlete, Black, white, or any other color, race, creed, or gender, in the world. The fight was considered one of the most important and talked-about sporting events in history, and it caused a public frenzy. On July 25, the day before Ali fought Jimmy Ellis as he attempted to resurrect his career, Blue pitched six innings against the Detroit Tigers, giving up one unearned run and striking out six, to win his nineteenth game of the season. Could Blue emulate ace Detroit pitcher Denny McLain's 1968 feat and win thirty games or even more? Blue was all the rage. Meanwhile,

OPPOSITE Vida Blue, one of the most celebrated Black athletes in the country, won the 1971 AL's Cy Young and Most Valuable Player Awards.

Ali won a lackluster fight the next day against his former sparring partner. The public yawned. Blue became the center of a public frenzy.

Born in the small town of Mansfield, Louisiana, to the wife of a foundry worker, Blue grew up a star athlete, loving football and imagining himself a pro quarterback. "When I was a kid, my idol wasn't Sandy Koufax of the Los Angeles Dodgers, it was Johnny Unitas of the Baltimore Colts. . . . I used to dream about someday succeeding Unitas as quarterback of the Colts, of being the first big black quarterback in pro football. I still dream about it." Baseball was something he did to keep himself busy until football season came around.

His father's death in 1966, and his family's heightened poverty as a result, pushed Blue toward baseball. Four years of collegiate football was no longer feasible, as he would be playing too long without money at too big a risk of a career-ending injury. The Kansas City A's, soon to move to Oakland, drafted him in the second round, pick number twenty-seven, in 1967, and offered him a $25,000 bonus. Instead of being a left-handed quarterback, he became a left-handed pitcher.

His two short stints in the majors in 1969 and 1970 showed promise, but it was 1971 that turned out to be Blue's year—and the year of the A's. On May 9, at Memorial Stadium in Baltimore, Blue shut down the powerhouse Orioles on four hits and one run, pitching a complete game. He was then 8-1, having pitched eight complete games (one was rain-shortened) and four shutouts. He was a sensation. Reporters mobbed him after every performance. Fans pestered him endlessly for his autograph. He could hardly sleep at night for the constant ringing of the telephone.

A's owner Charlie Finley, knowing a good thing when he saw it, approached Blue after the May 9 game and asked him if he would legally change his name from Vida Rochelle Blue to Vida True Blue. "Baseball is a business," Finley said, according to Blue, "and we have to sell it. People buy colorful personalities. A colorful nickname will help you. An unusual real name will help you even more." Blue refused. "I don't like nicknames or funny names. I like my name, Vida Blue, just the way it is. It's an unusual name as it is. It was my father's name. It means 'life' in Spanish. I'm proud of it. I'd like to keep it just the way it is."

Finley saw a name change as a showbiz gimmick. People in entertainment changed their names all the time. Actors had done it, including Cary Grant, who was born Archibald Alec Leach, and Marilyn Monroe, originally Norma Jeane Mortenson. Other athletes had done it, including boxer Joe Louis (Joe Louis Barrow) and Sugar Ray Robinson (Walker Smith Jr.). Baseball players took on nicknames like Babe Ruth. Even Black players who were Blue's contemporaries had famous nicknames: Jim "Mudcat" Grant, Dennis "Oil Can" Boyd, and fellow A's teammate John "Blue Moon" Odom.

But Blue felt insulted by Finley's suggestion. Perhaps thoughts of slavery passed through his mind, the time when many slave owners gave the enslaved names like Caesar and Pompey. Maybe he thought about an actor like Lincoln Perry, who adopted the name Stepin Fetchit, which many Black people increasingly found distasteful. Among ballplayers, Richie Allen, star of the 1960s Philadelphia Phillies, made it known that he preferred Dick to Richie, which he said sounded like a little boy's name.

The most famous Black name change of the 1960s was boxer Cassius Clay becoming Muhammad Ali, a name Clay took for religious reasons, but a change that many sportswriters, as well as some of Ali's opponents, initially refused to acknowledge. In 1967, Ali fought Ernie Terrell, who, in an effort to goose the gate, taunted Ali by calling him Cassius Clay, and Ali repeatedly punched the outmatched Terrell while shouting at him, "What's my name?" In 1971, Blue's breakout year, basketball star Lew Alcindor changed his name to Kareem Abdul-Jabbar for religious reasons as well. By the time Finley made his request, the issue of name-changing by eminent Black people had become fraught. Blue clearly did not feel he should change his name for a trivial reason: it might indicate that he did not take himself seriously.

At season's end, Blue won twenty-four games, had an ERA under 2.00, completed twenty-four games, and threw eight shutouts. But having pitched more than three hundred innings that year, he was fatigued and did not pitch well in the playoffs. It was a different era, and no pitcher today would come close to achieving most of those numbers. For his accomplishments that year, Blue won both the Cy Young Award and the Most Valuable Player Award, all under the name of Vida Rochelle Blue. ⮌

BY GERALD EARLY

In the first home game, against the Los Angeles Dodgers, Aaron broke the record, hitting a home run off Black pitcher Al Downing. Kuhn did not attend that game. He sent his assistant, Monte Irvin, a former Negro Leagues and New York Giants star who, just one year earlier, had been elected to the Hall of Fame. Irvin was also the first Black man to work in the Commissioner's Office.

Kuhn was in Cleveland, speaking to the Wahoo Club, a booster group for the Indians. The commissioner said he did not want to follow Aaron around game after game until he broke the record because there was no telling when he would do it. Aaron might experience a home run drought. This excuse is plausible but not entirely persuasive. The commissioner owed Aaron at least attendance at the first few home games in Atlanta. Aaron had been miffed by the fact that Kuhn never sent him a congratulatory telegram when he hit his 700th home run in 1973. Kuhn had promised to be there for the one that broke the record. Aaron held Kuhn's absence against him for the next several years and denounced him for it publicly whenever he could.

Yet there was something fitting about Irvin being present. A fellow Black Alabamian and a fellow Negro Leagues player, Irvin broke into the majors only a few years before Aaron. Far more than Kuhn, Irvin could fully understand the magnitude of what Aaron had achieved and the odds he had to overcome to do it.

The Braves won the game, 7–4, on April 8 when Aaron hit his historic home run. The team drew nearly 54,000 fans that night. Two nights later, they drew a fraction of that—only 6,400.

THE MAN WHO MADE OCTOBER FAMOUS

Once, when Reggie Jackson was in a slump, Yankee outfielder Mickey Rivers said to him, "No wonder you're all mixed up. You got a white man's first name, a Spanish man's second name, and a Black man's third name." Jackson retorted by telling Rivers he should learn to read and write. Jackson had always highly esteemed his own intellect. He dinged Rivers once too often about being uneducated: when they were on the team bus, Jackson said that when his career was over, Rivers would wind up driving it. The two men got into a fistfight over that one. Jackson was a player that teammates loved to hate.

Reginald Martinez Jackson, power-hitting outfielder for the Oakland Athletics, the Baltimore Orioles, and the California Angels, was most famously associated with the New York Yankees. He was brash, cocky, and outspoken, often about racial issues, even though, being of mixed-race parentage, he didn't have strong attachments to the Black community. In fact, he grew up in a mostly white community in Wyncote, Pennsylvania, played on white teams while living with white roommates, dated white women, and appeared uncomfortable at times around the Black community—all of which made him unique in some ways, an exile from his race. But Reggie Jackson never lacked confidence, even if he faked it. In 1975, the last year of his debut run with the Athletics (he would play a final season in Oakland), he said, "If I played in New York, they'd name a candy bar after me." He did wind up in New York, and Standard Brands did just that. In his prime, he had more endorsement deals than any Black ballplayer had ever had, and arguably more than his white peers.

In 1977, Jackson's New York Yankees needed only to win Game 6 to win the World Series. Jackson wore a square gold medallion around his neck inscribed with Jackie Robinson's name and a button on his belt with Robinson's picture. He wore number 44 on his back, the same number as recently retired home run king Hank Aaron and San Francisco's slugger Willie McCovey. Jackson was a walking Black baseball history emblem. It is hard to know whether he wore these talismans as a tribute to greatness, as he claimed, or as a tribute to his *own* greatness.

223

The mythology of Jackson started in 1966. That year the Kansas City A's owner, Charlie Finley, drafted Jackson as the number two pick in the annual amateur baseball draft. Jackson had been a baseball star at Arizona State University. He was a key member of Finley's team, which would move to Oakland in 1968 and win three World Series in a row, in 1972, 1973, and 1974. Other key players included Bert Campaneris, Joe Rudi, Rollie Fingers, Sal Bando, and Vida Blue. Jackson was the 1973 World Series MVP with a .941 OPS and 6 RBI in seven games against the New York Mets.

Jackson and Finley had a turbulent relationship, and Jackson constantly wrangled with the owner over his salary. Black players of the past, such as Ernie Banks and Willie Mays, were quiet about contract matters, and they advised Jackson to accept his 1970 contract and not hold out. But Jackson decided to be loudly dissatisfied. He held out. After the 1975 season and the arrival of free agency, Finley, knowing that he would be unable to afford his star players, traded Jackson in April 1976 to the Baltimore Orioles. Jackson held out for $200,000 from the Orioles and eventually got it. He also made it clear that he was going to leave Baltimore in free agency at the end of the 1976 season.

Reggie Jackson would become one of the most famous free agents in the history of baseball. Yankees owner George Steinbrenner, who purchased the team in 1973, signed him for five years at $3 million, an astronomical sum at the time, although not as large as the offers from some other teams. Steinbrenner sold Jackson on playing in New York, the big stage for the big ego.

Jackson did not get along with Yankees manager Billy Martin, a brilliant but mercurial personality, nor with most of his teammates. Jackson alienated star catcher, team captain, and reigning American League MVP Thurman Munson when Jackson said in the June 1977 issue of *Sport* magazine, "I'm the straw that stirs the drink. Munson thinks he can be the straw that stirs the drink, but he can only stir it bad." When Munson referred to Jackson as "Mr. October" at the end of Game 2 of the 1977 World Series, he did not mean it as a compliment. Jackson had complained about Martin's decision to use an injured "Catfish" Hunter to start the game, and Martin said that Jackson should simply concentrate on playing right field. The men exchanged insults. It was at this point that Munson interjected, "Billy probably just doesn't realize that Reggie is Mr. October." Jackson at that point was hitting just .167 in the World Series and had hit only .136 in the 1977 postseason.

The name stuck when Jackson hit 3 home runs in Game 6, propelling the Yankees to the championship. That many home runs in a single game is noteworthy

Reggie Jackson debuted with the Oakland Athletics, but left in 1976 for the Baltimore Orioles. The next year, he joined the New York Yankees, whom he would lead to World Series titles in 1977 and 1978.

enough, but even more so considering that he hit them against three different pitchers on the first pitch thrown. In Game 5, he had hit a homer in his last at-bat on the first pitch he saw. And in Game 6, he walked in his first at-bat on four pitches, before homering on three straight pitches in his next three at-bats. Whatever the legend of Reggie Jackson had been before was magnified exponentially. For the second time in his career, he was named the World Series MVP.

THE PRICE FOR KILLING A SEAGULL

Before the bottom of the fifth inning in a 1983 night game between the visiting New York Yankees and the Toronto Blue Jays, Yankees center fielder Dave Winfield, finishing his warm-up throws with fellow outfielder Don Baylor, threw the ball to the ball boy. The ball bounced on the artificial surface and struck a seagull that had been sitting on the field, killing it instantly. As the ball boy carried the bird from the field on a white towel, as if it were a sacrifice, the crowd booed Winfield, thinking he had intentionally killed the bird, as he had thrown the ball right toward it. "Everyone is yelling, throwing stuff onto the field, and rattling the fences at me," Winfield wrote.

It got worse. Winfield was arrested after the game and charged with animal cruelty, but was released on a $500 bond. At home, Yankees fans gave him a reception similar to what he received in Toronto. All the world had become bird lovers. In the 1983 offseason, Winfield succeeded in making amends by speaking at an Easter Seals dinner and donating a painting for auction that sold for $32,000. Seagulls were expensive.

Just three years prior, Winfield had become a free agent at the end of the 1980 season. He had spent eight seasons with the Padres, collecting All-Star nods and two Gold Glove Awards, but as much as he liked San Diego, he wanted out. The Padres were going nowhere. He was twenty-eight, his years as a high-level performer were numbered, and he had to join a team that had a chance at a championship while such a team would still want him. Yankees owner George Steinbrenner saw Winfield as the big free agent prize and signed him to the biggest free agent contract of the time: $23 million for ten years and $3 million for Winfield's nonprofit foundation.

At the same time, Reggie Jackson, in the last year of his Yankees contract, was expecting Steinbrenner to re-sign him. He had encouraged Steinbrenner to sign Winfield. But Jackson, who never got along with Steinbrenner, was entering his age thirty-five season in 1981. Clearly, Steinbrenner thought he had a younger, better version of Jackson in Winfield, if more expensive. But Winfield didn't get along with Steinbrenner, either. Free agency, a strong players' union, and the example of Curt Flood had made it possible for star Black players to squabble with team owners in a way that would have been unimaginable twenty years earlier.

At six-six and 220 pounds, Winfield had been a star athlete in basketball and baseball (principally as a pitcher) at the University of Minnesota. He was the College World Series MVP in 1973. That same year, he was drafted by four different sports leagues: Major League Baseball's San Diego Padres; the National Basketball Association's Atlanta Hawks in the fifth round; the Utah Stars of the American Basketball Association in the fourth round; and, despite never having played football in high school or college, the Minnesota Vikings in the seventeenth round of the National Football League draft. Choosing baseball, he lived up to his advance billing.

Ironically, in his eight-plus years in New York, Winfield never got what he most wanted in joining the Yankees: a championship. The Los Angeles Dodgers beat the Yankees four games to two in the 1981 World Series, in what was a difficult year for MLB because of the midyear strike that canceled 38 percent of the season. The strike changed the playoff structure, adding an extra round. The Yankees changed managers with twenty-five games left in the season, replacing Gene Michael with Bob Lemon.

Winfield finally earned his World Series ring in 1992 when his Toronto Blue Jays, under the leadership of Black manager Cito Gaston, defeated the Atlanta Braves, four games to two. Forty-year-old Winfield had one of the best years of his career, hitting 26 home runs and driving in 108 runs, with an .867 OPS. It was a much better year than Reggie Jackson had when he was forty. Winfield's bat didn't do much in the World Series, but big World Series games were always more Reggie's shtick. Winfield's big year helped mightily to get the Blue Jays there. There's no doubt that 1992 was Dave Winfield's rendezvous with destiny.

THE RISE AND FALL OF THE BLACK BOY WONDERS: DWIGHT GOODEN AND DARRYL STRAWBERRY

Like many former players, Dwight Gooden and Darryl Strawberry travel to Cooperstown many summers during Baseball Hall of Fame Induction Weekend to participate in autograph shows and reminisce about their glory days—particularly the 1980s, when "Doc" and "Straw" burst onto the scene with the New York Mets and became megastars. In the first few years they trekked to the bucolic baseball village in upstate New York, they experienced mixed emotions. Reliving their pasts evoked both joy and pain. Pangs of regret haunted Gooden and Strawberry during those early visits and for years to come.

"It was tough going there at first because there was a time early in our careers when people said Darryl and me were can't-miss Hall of Famers," Gooden said. "You'd be in Cooperstown signing stuff, chatting with fans, just a block or two from the Hall, and you'd start beating yourself up, 'cause you realized you were so close and yet so far away. It entered your mind that you'd probably have a plaque [in the Hall] if it weren't for those demons that did you in."

Dwight Gooden (*left*) and Darryl Strawberry helped
power the Mets to the 1986 World Series title.

Instead of the Baseball Hall of Fame, the once-unhittable pitcher and the once-prodigious slugger wound up in the hall of justice—and in rehab centers, clinics, jails, and prisons as they battled to extricate themselves from the stranglehold of drug and alcohol addiction and numerous legal problems. They became cautionary tales, remembered as much for what wasn't as for what was.

Gooden and Strawberry would be forever linked on and off the diamond. Eventually, they would make peace with themselves and find sobriety and purpose. They would impact others in ways even more profound than they had when they were mesmerizing fans, teammates, opponents, and the media with unseeable fastballs and cloud-kissing home runs. "We've both been to the top of the highest mountain and the bottom of the lowest valley," Strawberry said. "Doc and I both have plenty of regrets, but you realize in recovery that you need to reach a point where you seek not only the forgiveness of others, but of yourself for the damage you did. Yes, we did some harmful stuff, but we also did some good, and can continue to do a lot more good."

Few young athletes ever came to the Big Apple amid greater hype and expectations than Strawberry and Gooden. And their arrival couldn't have come at a better time for the moribund Mets, whose fan base had stopped venturing out to Shea Stadium after several years of mediocre baseball. In 1980, the Mets used the first pick of the MLB draft to select Strawberry, a three-sport star out of Crenshaw High School in South Central Los Angeles. By the time the lithe, sinewy, six-foot-six Strawberry made his major league debut three years later, the forecasts for greatness were stratospheric. His "Splendid Splinter" body and majestic, sweeping swing garnered him the moniker of "the Black Ted Williams."

That season, the twenty-one-year-old slugger with the signature high-leg kick clubbed 26 homers, drove in 74 runs, and stole 19 bases to win National League Rookie of the Year honors. The following year, he smacked 26 homers again and drove in 97 runs. In 1984, he made the All-Star team for the first time, starting a streak of eight consecutive selections, including five straight as the NL's starting right fielder. He

The 1983 National League Rookie of the Year,
Darryl Strawberry, hit 335 home runs over
seventeen big league seasons.

wound up clubbing 25 or more homers during his first nine big league seasons. Given his physical stature at the plate and how hard and far he could hit a baseball, Strawberry's blasts became the stuff of legend. Former Philadelphia Phillies first baseman John Kruk admitted to fearing for his life when Strawberry stepped into the box. "If the ball was hit near you, it would go by you," Kruk said. "But if he hit it at you, it could kill you."

The year after Strawberry showed up in Queens, another phenom joined the team. Though Gooden was just nineteen and had only one full season of minor league ball after being drafted out of Tampa's Hillsborough High School, he was promoted to the Mets. Like Strawberry the year before, he justified the advance billing. Employing a 98-mph fastball and a knee-buckling curve, Gooden went 17-9 with a 2.60 ERA while establishing an MLB rookie record for strikeouts. The surgical precision he displayed fanning batters earned him the nickname "Dr. K" and prompted fans at Shea to tape large plastic *K*s to the upper-deck facade each time the six-foot-two right-hander struck someone out. Baseball writers were enamored, too, as Gooden won a landslide election as the 1984 NL Rookie of the Year.

His performance in 1985 was even better, as he delivered a pitching season for the ages, compiling a 24-4 record, a minuscule 1.53 ERA, and 286 strikeouts to win the Cy Young Award. That summer Gooden also would become the youngest player to pitch in an MLB All-Star Game, adding to his rapidly growing legend by striking out the side in his one inning of work.

"He was by far the greatest pitcher I'd ever seen," said Ron Darling, the former Mets All-Star pitcher and longtime television baseball analyst. "If you told me Dwight was going to win three hundred games and strike out four hundred people one year, I'd have believed it. That's how good he was." Gooden literally became a larger-than-life figure in New York, as evidenced by the 102-foot-high *Sports Illustrated* image of him painted on the side of a building near Times Square. "Every time I pitched at Shea, it was like a concert, and I was the performer everyone had come to see," Gooden recalled.

The meteoric starts to Gooden's and Strawberry's careers caused expectations to soar even higher. "It all happened so fast for us," Strawberry recalled. "I win Rookie of the Year, then Doc wins Rookie of the Year, and before you know it, nothing we do is good enough. People expected Doc to strike out twelve to fifteen guys and win every game. People expected me to hit a home run every day."

Strawberry believes his and Gooden's attempts to live up to impossible expectations were the main contributors to both becoming substance abusers. "I think we both were looking for some way to escape all the hype, all the pressure, all the tension," Strawberry said. "At twenty-one, my rookie year, I was already an alcoholic. I was drinking every day, and then I was introduced to cocaine. I was young, Doc was young, and we were already big-time celebrities. And the Big Apple offered all sorts of temptations—drugs, women, you name it. We were ill prepared for it, and we made bad decisions."

It didn't help that they came to MLB at a time when drug usage was rampant, and the Mets were among the hardest-partying teams. "We took big bites out of that Big Apple," Gooden said, "and it wound up taking bigger bites out of us. Not trying to make excuses. It's on us. We're responsible for our actions. Just saying there was a lot going on there, more than meets the eye."

Strawberry believes that race also played a role in the impossible expectations he and Gooden faced. "The media was mostly older white guys, and I don't think they understood my background, coming from the hard streets of South Central with an abusive father, or Doc's background, either, and the turmoil he faced growing up," he said.

"When a white player slumped or screwed up on or off the field, they'd cut him some slack, but when we slumped or screwed up, they'd come down harder on us, like we were supposed to be superhuman or something because we were Black. And the fans would pick up on what was written and said and take it as gospel. So, when I was struggling, I heard it all. The n-word and everything else."

During separate interviews in the fall of 2023, each said that he had been sober for several years. As part of their recovery, they've dedicated their lives to helping others avoid and fight addiction. An ordained Christian minister, Strawberry said that there have been years when he spoke to two hundred groups—at churches, schools, and prisons. Gooden also has shared his story of near-death and redemption with many, often focusing on young people. "You reach a point in your life when you have to stop

being a prisoner of the past in order to move forward," said Strawberry, who has helped establish rehab centers. "We don't sugarcoat our stories, but we also let people know they aren't alone in this fight. If we can bring some hope and joy to struggling people the way we once did for baseball fans, then we'll be doing greater work than anything we did in a baseball uniform."

The struggle to maintain sobriety is difficult and never-ending. The fragility of recovery is one reason the two longtime teammates check in on each other often. "Our relationship has never been stronger, never been more real," Gooden said. "There's probably no one on earth who can understand what I've been through better than Darryl. And vice versa." ⮞

BY SCOTT PITONIAK

OPPOSITE Dwight Gooden electrified baseball as a nineteen-year-old rookie in 1984, winning the NL Rookie of the Year Award and finishing second in the NL Cy Young Award race.

In 1975, Frank Robinson became the first full-time Black manager in American League and National League history when he skippered the Cleveland Indians. His jersey from that season is preserved as part of the National Baseball Hall of Fame and Museum's collection.

KODACHROME IN THE EXECUTIVE SUITE

In 1987, there were no Black MLB managers. Rachel Robinson raised this issue when she was interviewed for the news program *Nightline* in an installment that aired on April 6, 1987, to commemorate the fortieth anniversary of Jackie Robinson breaking the color barrier, which was to be officially celebrated by MLB the following week on April 15. Mrs. Robinson said in her taped interview, "It's not coincidental that baseball in the forty-year period has not been able to integrate at any other level other than the players' level. . . . We have a long way to go." Robinson had expressed the same sentiment shortly before he died.

This appeal to integrate management would have gone largely unnoticed but for the live comments of Los Angeles Dodgers general manager Al Campanis made right after Mrs. Robinson's interview aired. When asked about the lack of Black managers, Campanis said, "I truly believe they may not have some of the necessities to be, let's say, a field manager or perhaps a general manager." Unbelievably, the interview only got worse. The public furor was such that by April 8 Campanis was no longer employed by the Dodgers.

In February 1989, former first baseman and longtime Yankees broadcaster Bill White became the first Black president of the National League, thanks in good measure to the fact that MLB was still smarting from Campanis's interview. "I knew that after the spotlight the Campanis incident cast on baseball," White wrote in his autobiography, "the team owners wanted a black man for the job."

That same year saw another first: on June 27, Cito Gaston's Toronto Blue Jays played against Frank Robinson's Baltimore Orioles, marking the first time two Black MLB managers played against each other. Robinson had been the first Black field manager of an MLB team when he became the Cleveland Indians' player-manager in 1975. Rachel Robinson was a symbol and spokeswoman for the cause: she threw out the first pitch for the Cleveland Indians when Frank Robinson (no relation) took the reins on April 8. When asked if she felt that Robinson's success or failure would have any impact on the hiring of other Black managers, she responded, "Why should it? White men have failed as managers, but it has not harmed the chances of other white men."

By 1991, two years into White's term as NL president, the American League would continue to make progress: there would be three Black managers: Hal McRae, joining Gaston and Robinson, had been hired to helm the Kansas City Royals. It wasn't until 1993, the final year of White's term, that the National League caught up and had four managers of color on its docket: Dominican Felipe Alou of the Montreal Expos, Cuban Tony Pérez of the Cincinnati Reds, Dusty Baker of the San Francisco Giants, and Don Baylor of the Colorado Rockies. In all, during White's term, there were as many as six MLB managers of color, accounting for somewhat less than 20 percent of MLB teams. That was not a bad showing.

During White's presidency, Bob Watson became the second Black general manager when the Houston Astros hired him at the end of 1993. In a more unusual move, the Boston Red Sox hired Elaine Weddington Steward, a Black woman, as assistant general manager in 1990. Watson would become the general manager of the New York Yankees in 1995 and go on to become the first Black GM to win a championship. Doubtless, the Campanis flap had something to do with this progress, but White being president of the National League is also likely to have had some effect on National League clubs and maybe on MLB generally. How would it look to have a Black executive in such a high-level position and not have any Black managers at all?

However, despite progress in the management of the game, White did not enjoy his time as league president. When his term was up, his successor, Len Coleman, a Black man who had worked in MLB marketing development, asked White if he would attend a special dinner that the owners wanted to hold to acknowledge his service. He refused to go. "You can tell the owners I said the hell with them." During White's tenure, he had to deal with the blatant racism of Cincinnati Reds owner Marge Schott, who eventually was pushed out of baseball and forced to sell her interest in the team. He had to wonder how many other owners felt as Schott did, but weren't so stupid as to voice their views publicly. He had to tolerate Commissioner Fay Vincent interfering in his dealings with the umpires, whose supervision was under the league president. He had to watch as the owners fired Vincent because they thought he overstepped his authority and replaced him with an owner, Bud Selig. The vast majority of owners were, at the time of White's presidency, rich white men who believed themselves to be the smartest guys in the room.

White felt the dual nature of being a racial pioneer in this sort of job: one is hired as a Black person to be transformational but also, contrarily, to hide and even legitimize an entrenched status quo. Perhaps this is why the *New York Times Magazine* did a cover story on White during his tenure as league president called "Baseball's Angry Man."

Bill White made history when he became the
National League president in 1989.

Following his playing career, Felipe Alou embarked
on a fourteen-year career as a big league manager,
most of which was spent with the Montreal Expos.

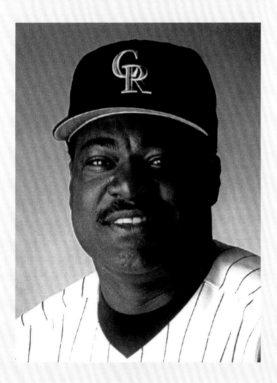

Don Baylor won the 1979 American League Most
Valuable Player Award and later managed the
Rockies and the Cubs for nine seasons.

A seven-time All-Star in his twenty-three big
league seasons, Tony Pérez later managed
the Reds and the Marlins.

CHAPTER 7

THE NIGHTCAP

BLACK PEOPLE AND BASEBALL FROM THE

1990s TO TODAY

BASEBALL WAS CONSIDERED A WHITE MAN'S GAME AND STILL IS TODAY.

—Pitcher Dennis "Oil Can" Boyd, on the dearth of Black representation in baseball

On April 15, 1997, Major League Baseball announced that Jackie Robinson's No. 42 would be retired by all teams. In attendance for the ceremony were President Bill Clinton; Jackie's widow, Rachel Robinson; and acting commissioner Bud Selig.

On April 15, 1997, for the fiftieth anniversary of Jackie Robinson's breaking the color line in professional baseball, acting commissioner and Milwaukee Brewers owner Bud Selig announced at Shea Stadium that Robinson's number, 42, would be retired across Major League Baseball. With Selig, who was also serving as acting commissioner of baseball, for the occasion was Robinson's widow and President Bill Clinton. Players who were currently wearing the number could continue to do so until they retired, but no one could adopt the number ever again. Yankees Hall of Fame reliever Mariano Rivera would be the last player to wear the number when he retired in 2013. It was the first time a gesture of this magnitude had been bestowed on a professional athlete—in this case, the only athlete to integrate his sport and influence the fate of his race through his performance.

A further step was taken on April 15, 2007, the sixtieth anniversary, when MLB players wore the number 42 in homage to Robinson. That practice has continued every Jackie Robinson Day since. Over the years, Robinson has advanced from being a sports hero to becoming an American hero. For many, he is second only to Martin Luther King Jr. in stature and more important than most other Black historical figures, artistic or political, of the twentieth century. Ken Burns's mammoth 1994 documentary, *Baseball*, did as much as anything to glorify, even mythologize, Robinson. Selig's announcement was one month before the publication of the authorized, lengthy, and deeply researched biography of Jackie Robinson by Arnold Rampersad, who was given exclusive access to Robinson's private papers. At the time, it was one of the most definitive and most highly promoted biographies ever written of a Black ballplayer, or arguably of any Black athlete.

OPPOSITE James Loney wore this number 42 jersey on Jackie Robinson Day, April 15, 2008. Loney played eleven big league seasons with the Dodgers, Red Sox, Rays, and Mets.

FATHERS AND SONS

In December 1993, the San Francisco Giants promoted one of their coaches, Dusty Baker, to be their new field manager. Baker, who had had a solid career as a ballplayer with the Atlanta Braves and Los Angeles Dodgers before closing out his playing days in the Bay Area with the Giants and Oakland Athletics, would be the seventh Black manager in the American and National Leagues. He would also be one of the longest-lasting and most successful of all Black managers, and one of the top ten managers ever (in terms of number of victories). Every team he managed over the next thirty years would make the playoffs at least once, and he won the World Series with the Houston Astros in 2022.

But Baker's ascendance was minor news that offseason for the Giants. That same month, the Giants signed former Pittsburgh Pirates outfielder, now free agent, Barry Bonds. Considered by baseball experts the best position player in the game, he was offered the biggest contract in professional baseball history at the time, for six years and $43.75 million. In his seven years with Pittsburgh, he had been voted the league's MVP twice. He would be MVP again in his first year with the Giants. He was, like his father, Bobby Bonds, a five-tool player (excelling at speed, throwing, fielding, hitting for average, and hitting for power), a once-in-a-generation phenom—except the son was living up to the hype, even helping to create it. No one thought more highly of Barry Bonds's abilities than Barry Bonds.

The signing was presented to the press as something like a homecoming. Bonds's father, Bobby, had been an outfielder for the Giants from 1968 to 1974, enjoying the best years of his career with that team. In fact, he had been labeled the next Willie Mays when he arrived in the majors. He could do what a young Mays could: hit for average and for power, run like the wind, and field his position well. The elder Bonds was an extraordinary teenage athlete, a can't-miss prospect. In his first major league game, he hit a grand slam homer, an auspicious start.

OPPOSITE Barry Bonds, son of Giants outfielder Bobby Bonds, topped the 100-RBI mark in twelve seasons and won seven National League Most Valuable Player Awards during his twenty-two-year career.

Bobby Bonds (*left*) was a three-time All-Star outfielder who
later coached his son, Barry, with the Giants. Barry Bonds holds
the MLB single-season and career records for home runs.

Incredibly, he hit 32 home runs, stole 45 bases, and scored 120 runs in 1969, his first full year. But he also struck out a great deal, 187 times, and he would continue to strike out at an alarming pace. His son struck out 100 times only once in his career, in his rookie season. While the elder Bonds enjoyed very good years with the Giants, he never quite lived up to the hype. He had an excellent career—more than 300 career home runs and more than 400 stolen bases—but did not produce the Hall of Fame numbers everyone had thought he would. His alcoholism, an addiction that started in his youth and perhaps was a way to cope with the pressure of high expectations, negatively affected him over the years, in both his personality and his playing. In addition, Bobby Bonds endured numerous injuries that diminished his productivity, especially in the later years. He was also considered a racial militant because he didn't express gratitude for the opportunity to play baseball, and he didn't think he had to.

Barry was born in 1964, when Bobby was eighteen, an age when few are prepared to be a parent. In 1968, Mays, then a thirty-seven-year-old veteran nearing the end of his career, was impressed by Bobby Bonds's talent and his inquisitive nature. "Winning is great. But look out for Number One," Mays told him. Bonds, indicating how much he admired Mays, asked the veteran star to be Barry's honorary godfather.

In spite of the connection to Mays, Barry didn't include San Francisco on his preferred list of teams during his free agent year of 1993. The older Bonds was one of Dusty Baker's coaches, and the son didn't want to be with his father every day. As a child, Bonds preferred his mother over his father, who seemed unaffectionate and detached and was often absent, because of his profession. Barry resented his father for being neither a good father nor a good husband. As his father's drunkenness became more public with a 1973 arrest for driving while intoxicated, Barry was taunted in school about it. He never performed well when his father came to see him play, even when he was a baseball wunderkind in high school and at Arizona State, but he did listen to his father's tutelage. Despite Barry's misgivings, the narrative of homecoming and playing on the team on which his father had his greatest years was touching. "Every time I step on that field," Bonds said at the press conference announcing the signing, "I know my godfather's in center field and my dad's in right field." The money was right, too.

Bonds requested that Mays's number 24 be taken out of retirement, down from its place of honor in Candlestick Park, so that he could wear it. (Bonds wore number 24 in Pittsburgh.) While the team seemed willing to do this, Giants fans were not nearly so sanguine about the matter. It struck many as disrespectful to Mays. Bonds decided to switch to number 25, the number his father wore with the Giants. But his father's number was not Barry's first choice. If the fans and the team thought Bonds was a bit of a prima donna, well, they hadn't seen nothing yet. His cockiness reminded some of Reggie Jackson. Among his peers, sportswriters, and even a segment of fans, Barry Bonds was probably the most hated player in the major leagues. Like boxer Muhammad Ali in his prime, Bonds at times seemed to court being hated. He would often blame it on his race. However valid that reasoning was, to paraphrase Nietzsche, the hatred only seemed to make him better. The more he felt he had something to prove, the more astonishing he was on the field.

On August 29, 1990, outfielder Ken Griffey Sr., forty years old and recently released from the Cincinnati Reds, signed with the Seattle Mariners. He was batting only .206 and his best years were clearly behind him. Like Bobby Bonds, he had had a fine career: more than 2,000 career hits, a .296 lifetime batting average, and two World Series rings. And like Bobby Bonds, he'd had a career that was better than most players had, but not quite good enough for the Hall of Fame. Griffey was meant to provide "some stability and experience," to serve as a veteran presence for a young but promising Mariners team. Among the young players was the twenty-year-old center fielder, who could hit for average and power, run, throw, and field. He was "the Kid." Griffey would bat second in the lineup and the Kid would bat third.

The Kid, the new boy wonder of baseball, was Griffey's son, Ken Griffey Jr., and like Barry Bonds, Griffey Jr. would exceed what his father accomplished as a player. They got back-to-back singles in their first at-bats together. The father-son duo increased attendance for the Mariners so dramatically that Cincinnati Reds owner Marge Schott, the team from which Griffey Sr. retired (his second time with the Reds) before the offer to play for the Mariners materialized, wanted half the gate receipts when the two played together. She was ignored. The father and son played together in fifty-one games until the father retired in 1991, undone by a herniated disc in his neck.

When Griffey Sr. was traded from the Reds to the New York Yankees in 1981, Griffey Jr., who had become difficult for his family to handle, was sent to live in New York with his father. Griffey Sr. was nineteen when Junior was born and trying to make it as a professional athlete, much as Bobby Bonds was when Barry was born. Neither man was in a good position to be a fully attentive dad to his son. Griffey Sr. worked out with Junior during the time they spent together in New York, putting his son through strenuous hitting drills every day. He realized that Junior

Ken Griffey Sr. (*left*) and Ken Griffey Jr. became
the first father-son combination to play simultaneously
for the same team in 1990.

had special talent and could become a successful pro player. But all was not easy during Junior's teenage years. At seventeen, he became so depressed and stressed by both his family and baseball that he attempted suicide. But he was happy to be playing with his father in 1990. Baseball, it is said, is a game of fathers and sons, but for Black fathers and sons the stakes are high because Black manhood is so fraught with tension and expectations.

While in Seattle, Ken Griffey Jr. won ten Gold Gloves and the MVP in 1997, and he was named to the All-Century team in 1999. He hit 398 home runs in eleven seasons with Seattle and won the home run title in the American League four times in those years. Despite the success with the Mariners, he wanted to return home to Cincinnati to live closer to his family, and so, in February 2000, he accepted a trade to the team that had shaped the most important years in his father's career, a return reminiscent of Bonds going to the Giants several years earlier. When he arrived in Cincinnati, he initially adopted his father's number 30. He had worn number 24 while in Seattle. The years in Cincinnati were not as bountiful as the Seattle seasons, mostly because Junior was stricken by a number of injuries. But he was still putting up good enough numbers to be a cinch for the Hall of Fame.

Griffey Jr. might be remembered for donning number 42 in 1997, the fiftieth anniversary of Robinson's breaking the color line, when Robinson's number was officially retired across the majors. Griffey's tribute, coming from arguably the most idolized and admired Black player in the game at that time, inspired MLB to adopt the practice of all players wearing the number on Jackie Robinson Day after 2007. The idea for Griffey Jr. to wear number 42 originated with the Robinson family. Griffey said, "Actually, the Robinson organization asked me to wear it all year. My dad said on the 15th, I should wear it, that it's a number that is something special. This is his day. [Robinson] worked hard for each and every one of us in this locker room."

But Griffey Jr. might be remembered just as well for something he didn't do. In his MVP year of 1997, Griffey hit 56 home runs and drove in 147 runs. For a player to hit over 50 home runs is a notable feat, but Griffey did not lead the majors in home runs in 1997. St. Louis Cardinals first baseman Mark McGwire did, with 58. Both men were considered the favorites going into the 1998 season to break the single-season home run record of 61 set by Roger Maris of the New York Yankees in 1961. In 1998, Griffey, hampered by injuries, dropped out of the home run chase that electrified baseball and the entire nation that year. He wound up duplicating his 1997 total with 56. The chase was between McGwire and Chicago Cubs outfielder Sammy Sosa, who hit 66. McGwire hit 70, a number most thought to be unobtainable.

Barry Bonds had few friends among his baseball peers, but among those few was Ken Griffey Jr. Bonds, five years older, acted a bit like an older brother when the two first met in 1987. They had much in common: their prodigious athletic talent, the burden of famous baseball fathers, privileged upbringings. Whenever either was in the other's hometown, they would go out for dinner.

Bonds had dinner at Griffey's Florida home, according to Jeff Pearlman's 2007 book about Bonds, *Love Me, Hate Me*, during the winter of 1998, the winter of Bonds's discontent. Sammy Sosa had won the National League's MVP Award. Bonds finished eighth in the voting. He was livid because he thought that Sosa cheated, using steroids to balloon his power numbers. Bonds hit only 37 home runs that season—what had once been a more than respectable total—and had otherwise had an excellent year. He drove in 127 runs and scored 120 runs. He also walked 130 times. Those numbers, in normal times, would probably get a player higher than an eighth-place finish in the MVP voting. But it was not a normal time. PED use had become rampant in baseball. The increase in home runs brought fans to the games, and MLB needed all the goodwill it could get after the 1994 labor stoppage that deeply tarnished the sport with the public. The spectacle of the home run purchased a great deal of goodwill. And home runs got players bigger contracts. According to Pearlman, at the dinner at Griffey's home, Bonds said that he felt compelled to use steroids almost as a way to level the playing field, as a kind of justice. What was fair if players could do steroids and get rewarded for it? Griffey, who finished fourth in the American League MVP voting, was not nearly as upset as Bonds. He felt that Bonds's points were valid, but he didn't think taking steroids was a good idea. He feared that doing so would ruin his reputation. Bonds was thirty-five, though, and felt he needed an edge in his waning years.

At the start of the 1999 season, Bonds was a completely different-looking person—everything about him was bigger, his legs, his chest, his neck. Everyone noticed that he was transformed. For four years, from 2001 through 2004, Bonds won the National League MVP. During this time, he broke the single-season home run record with 73. He broke the career home run record set by Hank Aaron in 1974. But these were seasons when Bonds went from age thirty-six to thirty-nine. He was accomplishing incredible offensive feats that no player at those ages had ever achieved. Griffey hit 48 home runs in 1999 and 40 in 2000. He never hit 40 home runs again for the remaining eleven years he played.

Griffey was voted into the Hall of Fame in 2016. Bonds, despite putting up better career numbers than Griffey, has not come close to getting into the Hall. In his last year on the Baseball Writers of America Association ballot in 2022, Bonds got 66 percent of the vote, better than the 61.8 percent he got in 2021, but not close to the 75 percent required for induction. But Bonds might wonder, in fairness, how the baseball writers could vote to make him the MVP for four straight years, when most were convinced he was taking steroids, but not vote to put him in the Hall of Fame for that reason.

In 2003, in the midst of Bonds's improbable late-career bloom, his father died, having suffered a host of illnesses, including lung cancer, a brain tumor, heart problems, and kidney cancer. Bobby Bonds had been a heavy smoker and struggled with alcoholism. Barry's relationship with Bobby had improved once his father underwent treatment for his alcoholism. "I've never played baseball without my dad," Bonds said while his father was dying. "Now I play alone."

THE QUEST FOR
THE BLACK GAME MASTERS

In 1997, the year Selig and MLB retired Robinson's number, the major leagues faced a racial quandary that Selig at least partly acknowledged and partly exacerbated. Of the thirty-one major league managers of 1997 who helmed twenty-eight teams, three were Black and one Latino: Felipe Alou of the Montreal Expos, Don Baylor of the Colorado Rockies, Dusty Baker of the San Francisco Giants, and Cito Gaston of the Toronto Blue Jays. Collectively, by season's end, they made up a bit more than 10 percent of the total. African Americans were 15 percent of MLB players and Latinos nearly 24 percent, a fact that underscored the underrepresentation of both groups in management.

Selig conceded in a *Washington Post* article the existence of an "old boy" network in which white executives hired people they knew and trusted, who were usually other white men. That network had to be disrupted. "We need to do better and we know we need to do better," he said. But after the dismissal of Commissioner Fay Vincent in 1992, when Selig took over as acting commissioner, the owners moved to centralize the structure of the sport—including eliminating the league presidencies, adopting interleague play, and unifying umpires under the aegis of the commissioner. Selig also created the position of major league president with three vice presidents under him. No Black candidates, however, were even interviewed for these posts, let alone offered any of the jobs. Leading Black players criticized Selig for this, disappointed that when Len Coleman's National League presidency ended in 1999, he was never considered for baseball commissioner or one of the new jobs. Coleman was the highest-ranking Black baseball executive at the time. Selig had served as acting commissioner for more than five years before being given the job officially in July 1998. In this regard, he and the rest of the "old boy" network did not "do better" or even try.

The one Black general manager in 1997 was Bob Watson of the New York Yankees. Yankees owner George Steinbrenner hired Watson away from the Houston Astros, where Watson had success in the two years—1994 and 1995—that he ran the club. Watson took the Yankees job despite the fact that Steinbrenner had gone through

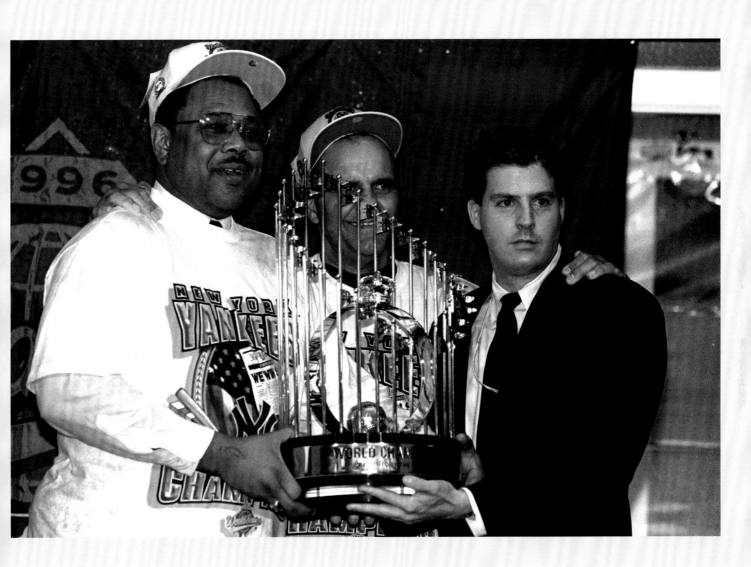

Bob Watson became the first Black general manager to lead his team to a World Series win with the Yankees in 1996. Watson is shown here (*left*) with Yankees manager Joe Torre (*center*) and Hal Steinbrenner, representing Yankees ownership.

fifteen GMs in twenty-three years. It was the Yankees, after all! Watson became the first Black GM to win a World Series when the Yankees were crowned champions in 1996, beating the Atlanta Braves in six games. Watson was voted the 1996 Executive of the Year. But on February 3, 1998, Watson signaled that his tenure was over when he introduced Brian Cashman as the new Yankees GM. Watson had quit when Steinbrenner ordered him to trade outfielder Bernie Williams and pitcher Andy Pettitte for Minnesota Twins second baseman Chuck Knoblauch. Watson had felt that the trade would hurt the team, about which he was surely right. Steinbrenner was also annoyed with Watson for failing to get pitcher Pedro Martínez when the Montreal Expos made him available. Watson, Steinbrenner likely thought, could not pull the trigger on deals quickly enough. And in fact Cashman was able to consummate a deal for Knoblauch without trading either Williams or Pettitte and without orders from Steinbrenner about whom to trade. Watson's bowing out so soon from the Yankees, where he had had considerable success, only intensified cries for more integration of front offices and also cries of institutional racism against MLB.

Two decades later, in 2017, the seventieth anniversary of Robinson's breakthrough, Robinson's stature was never higher. Hollywood had produced a Robinson biopic in 2013, called *42*, which had been endorsed by Rachel Robinson, who was involved in its making, and became a commercial and critical success. Just one year before, filmmaker Ken Burns's four-hour, two-part documentary, *Jackie Robinson*, was aired on PBS to great acclaim. On the ground with MLB, however, matters were a little different. There were two Black managers, Dusty Baker of the Washington Nationals and Dave Roberts of the Los Angeles Dodgers. Kenny Williams of the Chicago White Sox was the highest-ranking front-office Black administrator, serving as his team's executive vice president after twelve years as general manager; Williams was also the first Black GM to work with a Black manager, Jerry Manuel. Williams had a few successful years with the White Sox—winning the World Series against the Houston Astros in 2005—mixed with more years of mediocrity. Owner Jerry Reinsdorf finally pulled the plug on Williams in August 2023 as the White Sox were en route to losing more than one hundred games. On the whole, if anything, the numbers were slightly worse in 2017 than twenty years earlier.

OPPOSITE Dusty Baker managed for twenty-six seasons after his nineteen-year playing career, winning three Manager of the Year Awards and the 2022 World Series title. His first managing stint began in the 1993 season for the San Francisco Giants. He is pictured here in 1997 at Candlestick Park in San Francisco.

"THE PAST IS NEVER DEAD. IT'S NOT EVEN PAST."

Comedian Chris Rock, in condemning the whiteness of baseball in his famous 2015 seriocomic takedown of the sport, complained that the game is stuck too much in the past, that Black fans aren't interested in baseball's white past. But that is not quite true: while baseball has a segregated past, it is not only white. The preoccupation with unearthing the history of the Negro Leagues is proof that the story of American baseball is vastly incomplete without Black baseball. More and more people are coming to accept that today.

In discussing his 1994 *Baseball* documentary with his consultants, Ken Burns made a point to say that he was treating the Negro Leagues as the equal of the major leagues and giving both equal coverage in his segment devoted to baseball in the 1930s. Burns, with his scriptwriter Geoffrey C. Ward, published as a companion to the documentary *Shadow Ball: The History of the Negro Leagues*. It joined Dick Clark and Larry Lester's *The Negro Leagues Book* and James A. Riley's *The Biographical Encyclopedia of the Negro Leagues*, both published in 1994. Later explorations of Black baseball included, among others, Neil Lanctot's 2004 *Negro League Baseball* and Leslie Heaphy's 2003 *The Negro Leagues, 1869–1960*. Children's books, like Patricia and Fredrick McKissack's *Black Diamond: The Story of the Negro Baseball Leagues* (1994) and Kadir Nelson's *We Are the Ship: The Story of Negro League Baseball* (2008), also began to tell the story.

Black baseball continues to be memorialized and honored in ways that directly reach the public. In 1990, the Negro Leagues Baseball Museum, the only museum dedicated to telling the story of the leagues, opened in Kansas City, Missouri. More recently, in 2015, the Negro Southern League Museum opened in Birmingham to shine a light on a lesser-known enterprise that fed players to the Negro American and Negro National Leagues. Negro Leagues apparel is also popular, and for more than thirty years MLB has adopted the uniforms of Negro Leaguers for a few games every year. In addition, MLB officially recognized the Negro Leagues as major leagues as of December 2020, and record books are now being rewritten to reflect

Actor and comedian Chris Rock, a fan of big
league baseball, has been known to criticize the
whiteness emphasized in the history of the game.

the statistics of Negro Leagues players. In May 2024, MLB announced a new all-time
batting leader, Negro Leaguer Josh Gibson, who displaced Ty Cobb in career batting
average. All of this points to baseball's Black past becoming just as important as its
white past, as well as its growing importance to Black history and to the history
of the nation as a whole. Surely, Rock would approve of *this* preoccupation with
baseball's past. But does the current preoccupation with the Negro Leagues attract
more Black Americans to play baseball or attend ball games?

HERE COMES
MR. JORDAN

On October 6, 1993, Michael Jordan announced that he was retiring from basketball. Leaving the game was a decision that shocked even people who had no interest in sports. Jordan was not just the most famous Black athlete in the world, he was the most famous person in the world.

He was thirty years old and still had plenty left in the tank as a high-performance hoops player. In nine seasons, he was named to nine NBA All-Star Games, collected three MVP Awards, and won seven scoring titles. The Chicago Bulls won three straight championships (1991–1993) with him as the team's engine, driven by his indomitable will to win. He was brilliant *and* durable, the two necessary qualities of the star athlete. Why this abrupt departure right before the start of the NBA season? As he said, "I went through all the different stages of getting myself prepared for the next year, and the desire was not there."

OPPOSITE While taking a year off from the NBA, Michael Jordan played
for the White Sox Double-A team in Birmingham, Alabama, in 1994.

Basketball Hall of Famer Michael Jordan used this bat in 1994
when he played for the Birmingham Barons, a minor league
affiliate of the Chicago White Sox.

One theory was that Jordan was grieving. His father, James R. Jordan Sr., had
been murdered on a North Carolina highway as he slept in his Lexus that previous July.
Two young men were convicted of the murder, motivated by robbery (though one has
maintained his innocence). Jordan was close to his father, and he would surely have been
devastated by his tragic and untimely death. Another theory was that he was tired of the
attention, the glare of his celebrity. He said that he wanted to spend "more time with my
family, my wife, my kids, and just get back to a normal life, as close to it as I could."

If his departure from basketball was unsettling, his decision to sign a contract in
the spring of 1994 to play for the Birmingham Barons, the Double-A team of the Chicago
White Sox, was positively quixotic. Jordan, who had last played baseball in high school,
was now thirty-one years old—not an age to consider trying one's hand at another sport.
But Jordan would get his shot at baseball—and get high-level instruction in it—because
Jerry Reinsdorf owned the White Sox as well as the Bulls.

Jordan knew nothing about playing the game at this level. He needed to learn the
difference between a two-seam and four-seam fastball, how to position his feet to play
the outfield, how to charge a ball, and how to throw to the cutoff man (and what a cutoff
man was). All the other men he was playing with had had to learn to play at this level,
too, but they had learned these basics at a much younger age and had been training for
years to master the craft. Essentially, Jordan was just being introduced to it. Reps are
everything in learning a sport, particularly in baseball. What Jordan needed, according to
the old heads, was not 10,000 reps, but 300,000 reps. The article in the March 14, 1994,
issue of Sports Illustrated, with Jordan on the cover flailing away at an outside pitch, was
entitled "Bag It, Michael!" clearly not hiding the contempt with which the magazine held
his effort. Jordan never forgave them for it.

If nothing else, he was a gate attraction. The press packed each game as if they were covering the World Series. Birmingham drew sellout crowds at home and on the road. People not only asked for his autograph—he accommodated them as much as he could—but also wanted to see him play. He was cheered whenever he got a hit, stole a base, or made a play in the field. It was hard to know whether people wanted him to succeed or found him a sort of celebrity curio. One thing is almost a certainty: probably a lot of Black kids who bought Air Jordans, who lived and breathed basketball, now suddenly were aware of baseball, especially minor league baseball. They surely wanted to know why Michael Jordan thought it was worth playing. And if he thought it was worth playing, it was worth their while to at least pay some attention to it. If Jordan had made the big leagues, his presence would have done more to attract young Black fans than all the feats of the Black stars playing the game at that time.

Was Jordan serious? His manager, Terry Francona, who went on to considerable success as a major league skipper, said that not only was Jordan serious but "he respected the game"—the highest praise a baseball lifer could have offered. Jordan worked very hard, enjoyed his teammates, and never threw his fame around. He was not playing as a stunt. As sportswriter Jim Patton noted, "there are easier ways for a proud man to get publicity than by struggling with a difficult sport in full public view."

"I do think with another 1,000 at-bats he would have made it," Francona said, speaking of Jordan's chances of making the majors. Maybe. Jordan hit .202 in 127 games with Birmingham. He had 3 home runs, an on-base percentage under .300, and a slugging percentage under .300, all terrible numbers. On the other hand, he drove in 51 runs, stole 30 bases, and walked 51 times, all promising numbers. He was thrown out 18 times, a 37 percent rate of failure, which is high, but he would have improved his technique with practice. His lean, lanky body, similar to Dave Winfield's, probably would have generated more power as he became more experienced and actually learned how to swing a bat with proper technique, which, in fact, even experienced, high-level ballplayers find difficult to do on a consistent basis.

Jordan played right field at Birmingham, which meant that Francona and the other coaches thought he had more promise as a fielder; otherwise, he might have been hidden in left field, where the weakest fielding outfielder usually plays. He hit .252 in the Arizona Fall League, so in many respects he was doing well for a man with so little experience playing serious competitive baseball. Of course, he was relying on his athleticism rather than his training, but he was teachable.

Sportswriter Tom Verducci, in reassessing Jordan's baseball career, thought he was good enough to make the White Sox as, at least, the twenty-fifth man. Verducci also thought that Jordan greatly benefited baseball with his presence: in choosing to play minor league baseball, he showed that he wanted to learn and earn his way. What Jordan did was "an incredible affirmation for the sport." That Jordan was Black gave this affirmation even more resonance: that he *could* give it and that he *wanted to*.

In 1995, Jordan was ready to report to Triple-A Nashville. However, the lingering MLB strike, which had started on August 12, 1994, put Jordan in the position of crossing a picket line, as minor leaguers were being asked to be replacement players in spring training and regular-season games. Jordan, realizing that being a strikebreaker would destroy his reputation, said no thank you, returned to basketball, and led the Bulls to three more championships. ☞

BY GERALD EARLY

OPPOSITE Michael Jordan retired from the NBA following the 1993 season and played minor league baseball with the White Sox organization in 1994.

Tony Reagins, whom Commissioner Manfred hired in 2015 to help
address the waning involvement of Black players and fans in baseball,
served as the Angels general manager for five years.

REVIVING THE BLACK RELATIONSHIP TO BASEBALL

In an effort to grow the game at the grassroots level and reverse the current trend of Black estrangement from baseball, MLB commissioner Rob Manfred hired Tony Reagins in March 2015. Many believed that Reagins, who eight years earlier had become only the fourth Black general manager in MLB history, was the ideal person to help baseball play catch-up after decades of neglecting the African American community.

Before taking the job as baseball's senior vice president for youth programs, Reagins spent nearly two decades with the Los Angeles Angels, slowly climbing the franchise's front-office ladder to the GM position. During his four years running the show, he guided the Angels to a 363-285 record—a robust .560 winning percentage—and two American League West titles. Reagins resigned following the 2011 season after the Angels missed the postseason two years running, and he stepped back from the sport for three years.

Manfred's intriguing offer convinced him to return. Reagins, the son of a single mother, thought back to his childhood experiences, remembering how greatly influenced he was by the male mentors he interacted with at the Boys & Girls Club in Coachella Valley, California. Now he believed he could have a similar impact, only on a much wider scale. "To have someone who has lived this life and has had the struggle and has had to work really hard to get recognized and move up," said Darrell Miller, a Black executive who works with Reagins as MLB's vice president of youth and facility development, "it gives a lot of peace—because he knows [what it takes]."

Although Reagins and his staff made steady progress in growing participation overall, particularly among girls, their efforts to strike a chord with Black America have proven more difficult than first imagined. "As we drilled down and started talking about our expectations and what we were trying to accomplish, the more excited I got," he recalled. "But I was naive. I thought we would be able to make dramatic changes in just a few years. I quickly discovered there were some deep-rooted issues and that it would take time to make the impact we were hoping to make."

Just how much work remains to be done was underscored by Black participation figures from Opening Day 2023. The share of African American players in major league baseball had dropped to 6.1 percent—about one-third of their peak share in 1981 of 18.7 percent—and it marked a continuation of a three-decade-long decline. A 2023 survey by *USA Today* revealed that five teams didn't have a single African American on their Opening Day roster, while nine other clubs had just one. "It is frustrating," said former All-Star pitcher C. C. Sabathia, vice president of the Players Alliance, a nonprofit organization of current and former players working to increase Black involvement in the game at all levels. "I'm not seeing the light at the end of the tunnel, but I am starting to see it dig, and there's some headway. It's right there under the surface."

The 2022 draft brought encouraging news with the selection of nine African American players in the first round, the most since 1992, including four of the top five picks. That trend continued into the 2023 draft, with ten Black players among the first fifty picks. "We're trying to create pathways, not just get drafted, but actually make it to the big leagues," Sabathia said. "The efforts are being made. We're starting to see some of the stuff pay off."

Much of the credit for that belongs to Reagins, who was promoted to MLB's chief baseball development officer in 2020, making him the highest-ranking Black executive in baseball. He's responsible for nurturing existing programs as well as planting seeds for new initiatives that are now bearing fruit. At his urging, MLB has pledged $150 million in a ten-year partnership with the Players Alliance. About three hundred current and former MLB players have assisted in the staging of elite Black prospect camps and tournaments. "There are a number of promising players in the pipeline rubbing shoulders with guys who have made it in college ball or minor league ball or the major leagues," Reagins said. "So that gives the guys coming through this program an 'I can do this, too, if I put in the work' attitude. We believe this giving back by people who look like them and went through what they are going through is going to pay dividends long-term."

Many players in the pipeline got their start in the Reviving Baseball in Inner Cities (RBI) program, which has a presence in more than one hundred cities nationwide and has been bolstered by a sponsorship deal with Nike that MLB brokered in 2023. "To have credibility in the Black community, you have to keep coming back, you have to be consistent, you have to be authentic, and we've tried to be that," Reagins said. "This is not a onetime thing; it's a continuous thing. We've

Through the Reviving Baseball in Inner Cities (RBI) program, MLB has promoted efforts to diversify the youth game. Young participants in the RBI program in New York City celebrate the 2013 All-Star Weekend by taking a ceremonial ride on the number 7 subway, which stops at the Mets stadium at Citi Field.

been involved with the Black churches, which is crucial. We've taken a hands-on approach, whether it's providing financial resources or equipment or instruction."

MLB's two-pronged approach works from the bottom up and the top down. If more Black superstars like Aaron Judge and Mookie Betts are developed, more young African American athletes are likely to want to play and follow the game, as was the case in the 1950s through the 1990s, when the likes of Hank Aaron, Willie Mays, Bob Gibson, Frank Robinson, Reggie Jackson, Vida Blue, Darryl Strawberry, Doc Gooden, Dave Winfield, Rickey Henderson, Ken Griffey Jr., Barry Bonds, and Derek Jeter dominated. To get more Black players into the big leagues as quickly as possible, Reagins and his colleagues created numerous elite camps and programs that focus on developing baseball and life skills and on showcasing players to scouts and college recruiters. Between 2015 and 2022, more than 250 Black players from the Hank Aaron Invitational, the DREAM Series, and the Breakthrough Series were drafted. "Nine years ago, these elite programs didn't exist," Reagins said. "The last five years, there's been an uptick and improvement. Today there's definitely more of these high-profile, high-end Black players involved in the game. They just needed an opportunity."

In 2022, MLB started the Identification Tour in underserved communities across the country for players in the eighth and ninth grades. Baseball set up shop in eighteen cities, including Oakland; Detroit; Chicago; St. Louis; Atlanta; Sacramento; Gary, Indiana; and Flint, Michigan, in search of athletes with raw skills that would translate to the baseball diamond. Additionally, MLB has been providing financial assistance to address the economic disparities of travel youth baseball, which has priced many Black players and families out of the game and made it difficult for them to compete with white kids on a level playing field and receive a similar amount of exposure to scouts and college coaches. "We didn't have travel ball, summer ball, legion ball, daddy ball, and all of that," said LaTroy Hawkins, a former three-sport scholastic star who pitched in 1,042 games during his major league career. "That started to make baseball expensive—a sport minorities couldn't afford to play in the United States."

The dearth of Black men playing college baseball is another enormous hurdle. Compared to football and basketball, college baseball lags far behind in the number of scholarships it offers, and that gap isn't likely to change because there are far fewer college baseball programs. Unlike with football and basketball, only a handful of them are revenue producers. As of 2023, Black players made up roughly 4 percent of college baseball players, a significantly low percentage, considering that nearly 70 percent of all MLB draftees came from the college ranks in recent years. MLB has tried to combat this problem by staging more showcase tournaments for Black players, such as the Aaron Invitational and the Andre Dawson Classic, and by providing additional resources to baseball programs at historically Black colleges and universities (HBCUs).

To address the lack of Black representation in managerial and front-office positions, MLB University was formed. This ten-month career development program provides educational training in a variety of areas, including the ever-expanding field of analytics. Reagins credited Manfred for further diversifying the commissioner's office, an effort that he believes has trickled down to the front offices of several clubs, though the number of Black managers, whether in front offices or dugouts, remains distressingly low.

Some have theorized that young Black athletes gravitated away from baseball to basketball and football because those sports are more exciting. Reagins acknowledged that was a problem, but said that baseball's appeal has been growing and will probably continue to grow thanks to rule changes MLB implemented during the 2023 season that sped up the pace of the game and placed a greater emphasis on athleticism, particularly on the bases and in the field. Sabathia agreed. "I think the rule changes will have an impact for sure," he said. "Teams may have to draft more athletes, more people who are what they call 'raw.' The field is more wide open now."

Despite the declining number of Black players in MLB, baseball continues to become a more diverse and international game. The percentage of white players declined from 70.3 percent in 1989 to 63.7 in 2016, according to SABR research, owing to the share of Latino big leaguers more than doubling (from 13.2 to 27.4 percent) and the number of Asian players climbing to 2 percent. The dramatic jump in foreign-born players is attributable to the stature the sport holds in countries like the Dominican Republic, Venezuela, and Japan, where baseball academies are more prevalent and sporting alternatives less diverse than in the United States.

These trends are expected to continue, but Reagins sees no reason for the diversification percentages to not also include a noticeable jump in the number of Black players and fans at all levels. It took Reagins himself eighteen years to become a big league general manager and another several years to become baseball's top Black executive, so when he becomes frustrated that things aren't progressing quickly enough, he reflects on his own journey and remembers how he persisted.

This section was written by Scott Pitoniak.

WRECKING STADIUMS AND REPPING CITIES: HIP-HOP REMIXES THE SONIC LANDSCAPE OF BASEBALL

At the end of the 2008 Philadelphia Phillies World Series DVD, Jimmy Rollins and Ryan Howard offer a remix to the classic baseball song "Take Me Out to the Ball Game." Rollins provides the production, making a beat with his hands on the table, while Howard serves as MC and DJ, rapping the lyrics to the tune and mixing on imaginary turntables. The soundtrack of baseball is frequently associated with an organ music tradition, updated to include country, rock, or the everlasting jock jam; the Rollins/Howard remix defies the sonic expectations of the sport. While baseball fans gravitate toward the nostalgia of John Fogerty's 1985 classic "Centerfield," or see themselves in *Field of Dreams* (1989), some of us are more *Hardball* (2001), both the film *and* the song featuring Lil Wayne, Lil Zane, Lil Bow Wow, and Sammie. Hip-hop's integration into the National Pastime has infused new Black cultural forms in distinct, crucial ways that continue to shape the contours of the sport.

Howard and Rollins, as they playfully bring the beat into "Take Me Out to the Ball Game," are reminiscent of rapper Drake on "Thank Me Now": "Damn, I swear sports and music are so synonymous / 'Cause we want to be them, and they want to be us." Rollins would eventually start his own music label and claim the rap alter ego J-Roll; other players, including Lastings Milledge, José Reyes, and Deion Sanders, have all tried their hands at the rap game.

At the intersection of music and sport, DJ Severe mixes the sound of the Los Angeles Dodgers each season, curating two to three hip-hop mixes in collaboration with players that he denotes as "batters-only music." In an interview on the podcast *Sounding Off*, he shared how the genre is sometimes heard by those off the field: "Some people complain about hearing hip-hop. Sometimes at the stadium when I first started, they would say, 'Do you think the players want to hear that?' And I always say, 'You realize the players are like 21, 22, 23. You think they wanna hear what *you* grew up on?' Like, that's not gonna get them pumped up. You have to kind of put yourself in their shoes."

Hip-hop loves to step into the players' cleats. While Jack Norworth, the Tin Pan Alley cowriter of "Take Me Out to the Ball Game," had never seen baseball when he helped pen its unofficial anthem, rappers have long pined after the sport. On the Ultramagnetic MCs 1993 album, *The Four Horsemen*, an entire song, "Saga of Dandy, the Devil & Day," is dedicated to Negro Leagues legends and notes both the successes and the struggles of players under segregation.

The perennial swagger of baseball players is an ideal match for the sound and feel of hip-hop. Whether rappers are lyrically comparing themselves to players or visually representing the game in music videos, the fashion and form of baseball do important narrative work. Take, for example, Nelly (himself a former baseball player) and the St. Lunatics with jerseys and bats on "Batter Up" or Da Band (first introduced via MTV's *Making the Band*) with their baseball-themed video for "Bad Boy This, Bad Boy That." Baseball can match the bravado of the brag; Pharoahe Monch can show better than he can tell when he raps that he's got "more range than Rey Ordoñez." Phife Dawg of A Tribe Called Quest offers endless baseball references, coming for Bo Jackson on "Scenario" and making it known that he has "more hits than the Braves and the Yankees" on "Award Tour." The sport has been taken up in hip-hop to exaggerate everything from one's sexual prowess to record sales. There are many, many comparisons to Barry Bonds. The game also functions as a metaphor for darker themes, such as police brutality in Main Source's "Just a Friendly Game of Baseball," or when Eazy-E apologizes to his Louisville Slugger for using it to inflict violence in "Sorry Louie."

Like baseball, hip-hop is grounded in rooting for the home team. In the "Welcome to Atlanta (Coast 2 Coast Remix)" video, each city   Atlanta, New York, St. Louis, Long Beach—features baseball merch, with the St. Lunatics shooting their segment inside of the old Busch Stadium flanked by Fernando Viña. On UGK's "The Game Belongs to Me," Bun B raps, "Like Dontrelle Willis, we the trillest / On the mound, I'm holdin' that whole South down." Bun's relationship to the Houston Astros also includes "Crush City," an entire ode to the team that booms inside the stadium on game day with an accompanying video, cementing the relationship between the 'Stros and the city's storied rap history. Furthermore, while you will hear Frank Sinatra's rendition of "New York, New York" at Yankee Stadium, you won't make it to the ninth inning without hearing Jay-Z and Alicia Keys dote on the city via "Empire State of Mind."

In many ways, the relationship between hip-hop and baseball has emerged primarily from below, fed by the fans, athletes, and artists who love the game *and* the culture. We see this in the wholesale embrace of the iconic black Chicago White Sox fitted cap, worn by Ice Cube in the "Steady Mobbin' " video, a move in 1991 that mobilized hip-hop fans around the country to deck themselves out in ChiSox gear. As Shakeia Taylor notes, the rise in White Sox merch sold that year placed the team behind only the Yankees and A's in sales. Now documented in a New Era–produced segment titled "Fitted in Black," teams such as the Chicago White Sox can claim their own relationship to hip-hop and give due credit to the visionaries and artists who remixed an otherwise static cultural relevancy. In tandem with this, Major League Baseball's partnership with Mass Appeal and Hip Hop 50 Live at Yankee Stadium served as a direct connection to the genre's birth in the Bronx. With this, Chuck D of Public Enemy was named a music ambassador for MLB's Hip Hop 50 celebrations and released his *We Wreck Stadiums* album, which offers a lyrical interrogation of the game over a rugged wall of sound that feels higher than the original Great Wall of Flushing.

While hip-hop has always paid homage to the game's best, MLB is just now showing love. It's a new era for a sport and a genre, a remix rooted in capitalist gain and popular culture relevance, but a crucial collabo nonetheless. ☞

BY COURTNEY M. COX

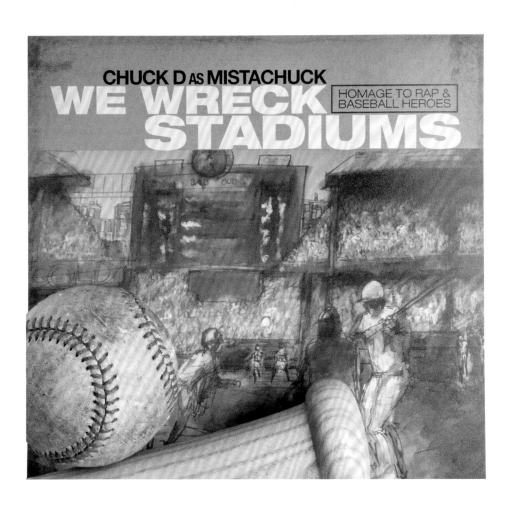

Chuck D's *We Wreck Stadiums* album cover.

THE LONG HELLO

In 1987, at the tail end of his Hall of Fame career, Reggie Jackson offered this hypothetical among his reflections about the impact of the Al Campanis debacle in a cover story in *Sports Illustrated*: "If a black hitting instructor is let go because, say, he spends a lot of time at the racetrack, you can be almost certain that no one in the organization sat down with him and asked him to change. With a white hitting instructor who spends time at the track, they'd talk to him."

What Jackson suggested is that even after forty years of integrated baseball, Black players, despite their importance, were still outsiders, a part of the professional baseball community, but apart from it. Outfielder Preston Wilson's denunciation of baseball thirty-three years later, in the July 17, 2020, issue of *Sports Illustrated*, made a similar point. Wilson, nephew and stepson of the popular New York Mets outfielder Mookie Wilson, complained about MLB's statement condemning racism and injustice in the light of the police killing of George Floyd, whose death had rocked the nation. It "could have been stronger," Wilson said. He was annoyed that the statement did not contain the words "police brutality," an omission he considered an evasion. MLB was the last major professional sports organization to issue a statement on the matter, which indicated a reluctance to issue a statement at all. For Wilson, the statement seemed to hold Black concerns at arm's length. Wilson was the only African American on the 2006 St. Louis Cardinals championship team and he felt terribly isolated. After more than seventy years since Jackie Robinson, many Black people do not feel quite welcomed by organized baseball. Wilson felt like an exile *in* the kingdom.

Despite the nation's polarizing racial issues and the underrepresentation of Black American players, there are still Black stars in the game. Los Angeles Dodgers outfielder/infielder Mookie Betts is probably one of the most popular and gifted players on the scene. The 2018 winner of the MVP in the American League, he came in second for the award in 2016, 2020, and 2023. Yankees outfielder Aaron Judge,

Mookie Betts wore this shirt in support of diversity in baseball during the 2019 All-Star workout day. He won the 2018 American League Most Valuable Player Award with the Red Sox before being traded to the Dodgers following the 2019 season.

another popular player, broke the American League home run record set by Roger Maris by hitting 62 in 2022. He won the Most Valuable Player Award that year for his efforts. Judge was also the 2017 Rookie of the Year. Both men have signed huge multi-year contracts. And there are younger Black players who have the makings of stardom, such as Atlanta Braves outfielder Michael Harris II and Cincinnati Reds pitcher Hunter Greene.

Yet it is still disturbing to see so few Black American players today when baseball was once a Black cultural and economic institution of enormous importance. Black baseball teams and leagues showed Black people's determination to build something for themselves despite adverse circumstances, despite living in a country whose majority population thought they were not only inferior but possibly not even human. Playing baseball was also Black people's ticket into the society in which they lived, for it was their strenuous claim that they, too, were Americans. Black people playing baseball has made America a better country.

Before playing harder, before the commitment, the dedication, the sacrifice, to become a major league player, there is the dream of being a baseball player. Black people, too, believed, and believe, in an American dream. In 2025, though, we are not living in the America of Jackie Robinson but of his great-great-grandchildren, a line of descent that has more and wants more. What we have learned from the history of Black baseball, Black players, and organized baseball is this: the future of the game and the fate of Black Americans are inextricably bound forever. Black Americans are not saying a long goodbye to Major League Baseball; they are simply at another stage, beyond Jackie Robinson, of saying a proud, but challenging, hello.

OPPOSITE Aaron Judge became one of the faces of baseball when he hit 52 home runs during his rookie season with the Yankees, in 2017. Five years later, Judge set an American League record with 62 home runs in one season.

Hunter Greene debuted with the Reds in 2022
as one of the hardest-throwing pitchers in baseball.

OPPOSITE Michael Harris II debuted with the
Braves in 2022 and went on to win the National
League Rookie of the Year Award.

NOTES

INTRODUCTION

xiv "knights of the diamond—the ballplayers": Art Rust Jr. with Edna Rust, *Recollections of a Baseball Junkie* (New York: William Morrow, 1985), 69.

1 allegiance from cricket to baseball: Rust, *Recollections of a Baseball Junkie*, 11–12.

3 "That's no life for you," he said: John Holway, *Voices from the Great Black Baseball Leagues*, rev. ed. (New York: Da Capo Press, 1992), 191.

3 before she began to cry: Roy Campanella, *It's Good to be Alive* (Boston: Little Brown, 1959), 62–63.

3 "dressing room, dining room, and hotel": Campanella, *It's Good to be Alive*, 66.

3 "but *working* the position": Campanella, *It's Good to be Alive*, 65, italics Campanella's.

3 "probably the sorriest idols I had": Rust, *Recollections of a Baseball Junkie*, 37.

3 he had new heroes: Rust, *Recollections of a Baseball Junkie*, 20.

3 about to enter college, "nearly cried": Rust, *Recollections of a Baseball Junkie*, 31.

4 today's effort by Major League Baseball (MLB): Major League Baseball didn't form as we know it today until 1969, hence the use of the term as a proper noun only during or after that year.

6 "lot of little boy in you too": Campanella, *It's Good to be Alive*, 182.

6 "the game of ball is glorious": *Brooklyn Eagle*, July 23, 1846; reported in *Medium* by John Thorn, June 15, 2012; https://ourgame.mlblogs.com/whitman-melville-and -baseball-662f5ef3583d.

CHAPTER 1

10 Black national anthem: James Weldon Johnson, *Along This Way: The Autobiography of James Weldon Johnson* (New York: Penguin Books, 1990, originally published in 1933), 36.

13 pogroms of the Reconstruction period: Stephen V. Ash, *A Massacre in Memphis: The Race Riot That Shook the Nation One Year After the Civil War* (New York: Hill and Wang, 2013).

13 take over the local courthouse: Philip Dray, *Capitol Men: The Epic Story of Reconstruction Through the Lives of the First Black Congressmen* (Boston: Houghton Mifflin, 2008), 135– 50.

13 in the country's financial institutions: Carl R. Osthaus, *Freedmen, Philanthropy, and Fraud: A History of the Freedman's Savings Bank* (Chicago: University of Chicago Press, 1976), 183–85, 191.

13 jumped to 55.5 percent by 1890: Rayford W. Logan, *The Betrayal of the Negro: From Rutherford B. Hayes to Woodrow Wilson* (New York: Collier Books, 1972), 325.

14 social engineering at its most brutal: Douglas O. Linder, "Lynchings, by Year and Race" (data from Tuskegee Institute Archives), UMKC School of Law, Famous Trials, http://law2.umkc.edu/faculty/projects/ftrials/shipp /lynchingyear.html.

15 "to the feelings of our masters": Frederick Douglass, *Narrative of the Life of Frederick Douglass, an American Slave. Written by Himself* (Boston: Anti-Slavery Office, 1845), chap. 10, para. 15 and 16, https://www.gutenberg .org/cache/epub/23/pg23-images.html.

15 a form of rounders or town ball: Michael E. Lomax, *Black Baseball Entrepreneurs, 1860–1901: Operating by Any Means Necessary* (Syracuse, NY: Syracuse University Press, 2003), 11.

17 "Fred Douglass Sees a Colored Game": There is some confusion about the date when this story appeared. John Muller, in his book *Frederick Douglass in Washington, D.C.: The Lion of Anacostia* (Charleston, SC: Arcadia, 2012) (https://thelionofanacostia.wordpress.com/2012/05/28 /fred-douglass-sees-a-colored-game-ny-clipper-july -13-1867/), offers the date of July 13, 1867, in the *New York Clipper*. In Ryan A. Swanson, *When Baseball Went White: Reconstruction, Reconciliation, and Dreams of a National Pastime* (Lincoln: University of Nebraska Press, 2014), the date cited (217) is October 10, 1868.

17 Racial lines had already been drawn: Swanson, *When Baseball Went White*, 108.

17 an honorary Mutual in September 1870: Muller, *Frederick Douglass in Washington, D.C.*

17 played catch with his grandchildren: Muller, *Frederick Douglass in Washington, D.C.*

18 "an estimable young teacher, Octavius V. Catto": W. E. B. Du Bois, *The Philadelphia Negro: A Social Study* (New York: Schocken Books, 1967), 39.

18 join his Black National Guard unit: Lawrence D. Hogan, *Shades of Glory: The Negro Leagues and the Story of African American Baseball* (Washington, DC: National Geographic, 2006), 18; Daniel R. Biddle and Murray Dubin, *Tasting Freedom: Octavius Catto and the Battle for Equality in Civil War America* (Philadelphia: Temple University Press, 2010), 427–29.

18 permit employees to attend the funeral: Swanson, *When Baseball Went White*, 147.

19   necessary to lead the race: Hogan, *Shades of Glory*, 13–14.

19   ancient Greece and the Olympic Games: Biddle and Dubin, *Tasting Freedom*, 361.

19   the money to play baseball: Biddle and Dubin, *Tasting Freedom*, 361.

19   lower-class Black citizens: Julie Winch, *Philadelphia's Black Elite: Activism, Accommodation, and the Struggle for Autonomy, 1787–1848* (Philadelphia: Temple University Press, 1988), chap. 1.

19   William Wells Brown, and Frederick Douglass: Biddle and Dubin, *Tasting Freedom*, 364.

20   running the Institute for Colored Youth: Biddle and Dubin, *Tasting Freedom*, 364.

20   *Sunday Mercury* and the *Philadelphia Inquirer*: Swanson, *When Baseball Went White*, 69.

20   had no chance of success: Swanson, *When Baseball Went White*, 79.

22   heroes rather than traitors: Edward H. Bonekemper III, *The Myth of the Lost Cause: Why the South Fought the Civil War and Why the North Won* (Washington, D.C.: Regnery History, 2015).

22   any club with a Black member: Swanson, *When Baseball Went White*, 101.

22   he was a white Southerner: Swanson, *When Baseball Went White*, 18.

22   because of the way he died: Swanson, *When Baseball Went White*, 148.

23   "white, professional rosters": Leslie A. Heaphy, *The Negro Leagues, 1869–1960* (Jefferson, NC: McFarland, 2003), 12.

25   "no more with the nigger in": David L. Fleitz, *Cap Anson: The Grand Old Man of Baseball* (Jefferson, NC: McFarland, 2005), 111–12.

25   no one of this Black Bohemia: Lomax, *Black Baseball Entrepreneurs, 1860–1901*, 76.

25   "minor leagues in an 18-year period": Hogan, *Shades of Glory*, 50.

25   Crawfordsville, Indiana; and Topeka, Kansas: Heaphy, *The Negro Leagues, 1869–1960*, 12.

25   "and in cities in the East," writes one scholar: Lomax, *Black Baseball Entrepreneurs, 1860–1901*, 64.

26   with whom he played until 1891: Heaphy, *The Negro Leagues, 1869–1960*, 12. Fowler played in other places after he was released from the Bingos. Lomax writes, "After leaving the Gorhams in 1887, Bud Fowler continued his itinerant ways, playing on white minor league clubs that offered the opportunity. He played in the minor leagues throughout the West and Northwest in cities such as Santa Fe, New Mexico; Terre Haute, Indiana; Burlington, Iowa; and Lincoln, Nebraska. By 1894, Fowler played on an independent club based in Findlay, Ohio." Lomax, *Black Baseball Entrepreneurs, 1860–1901*, 135.

26   no "colored league" at the time: Jeffrey Michael Laing, *Bud Fowler: Baseball's First Black Professional* (Jefferson, NC: McFarland, 2013), chap. 7, loc. 2956, Kindle.

26   college-educated, respectable men: Lomax, *Black Baseball Entrepreneurs, 1860–1901*, 137.

28   in the nineteenth century: It has been uncovered that William Edward White, who played one game for the Providence Greys of the National League in 1879, was Black. This is irrelevant, as White passed as white for the one game he played as a substitute for an injured player and never played in the major leagues again. The race question is contingent on a person's race not being concealed but publicly known and acknowledged, and for that person's interaction with the particular institution or organization to have been sustained for longer than a day. Race must be a salient aspect of the situation and the person must be trying to endure in the situation despite the disadvantages of his or her race.

28   all of his white teammates: Hogan, *Shades of Glory*, 54.

28   fifty-four games in 1884 and hit .251: There is some difference in accounts here. The numbers cited here are from Heaphy, *The Negro Leagues, 1869–1960*, 14. Hogan writes that Walker "played in 42 of Toledo's 110 games. . . . He hit .263 without much power." Hogan, *Shades of Glory*, 54–55.

28   best catcher he ever threw to: Hogan, *Shades of Glory*, 55.

29   give the customers what they wanted: Sol White, *Sol White's History of Colored Base Ball, with Other Documents on the Early Black Game, 1886–1936* (Lincoln: University of Nebraska Press, 1995), 76–77.

36   So ended our knight: David W. Zang, *Fleet Walker's Divided Heart: The Life of Baseball's First Black Major Leaguer* (Lincoln: University of Nebraska Press, 1995), 122–24.

CHAPTER 2

40   "the American dollar": Booker T. Washington, *The Negro in Business* [1907] (New York: AMS Press, 1971), 14.

41   "Black Star Line owned by black men": Colin Grant, *Negro with a Hat: The Rise and Fall of Marcus Garvey* (New York: Oxford University Press, 2008), 191.

42   thought it should have: "Later when he began to collect money for his steamship line I characterized him as a sincere and hard-working idealist but called his methods bombastic, wasteful, illogical and almost illegal. . . ."; W. E. B. Du Bois, *The Autobiography of W. E. B. Du Bois* [1907] (New York: International Publishers, 1975), 273.

43   unbearable for Black families: Ethan Michaeli, *The Defender: How the Legendary Black Newspaper Changed America* (New York: Houghton Mifflin Harcourt, 2016), 63–64.

43   Foster saw a great opportunity: Michaeli, *The Defender*, 67, 70.

44   cornerstone of Foster's league: Information about Foster in the preceding paragraphs is from Robert Charles Cottrell, *The Best Pitcher in Baseball: The Life of Rube Foster, Negro League Giant* (New York: New York University Press, 2001), 7, 9, 62, 63.

44   fans would be attracted to the games: Cottrell, *The Best Pitcher in Baseball*, 145–46.

46   Black umpires fared no better: The information on umpires is from Leslie A. Heaphy, *The Negro Leagues, 1869–1960* (Jefferson, NC: McFarland, 2003), 52–54. See also Cottrell, *The Best Pitcher in Baseball*, 162.

47   carbon monoxide poisoning?: Cottrell, *The Best Pitcher in Baseball*, 168–69.

55   "That's who we played": quoted in Brent Kelley, *"I Will Never Forget": Interviews with 39 Former Negro League Players* (Jefferson, NC: McFarland Publishing, 2003).

56   "big store by book learning": Leroy Satchel Paige, as told to David Lipman, *Maybe I'll Pitch Forever: A Great Baseball Player Tells the Hilarious Story Behind the Legend* [1962] (South Orange, NJ: Summer Game Books, 2018), 17.

56   looked like "a walking satchel tree": Paige, *Maybe I'll Pitch Forever*, 18.

59   "instead of just some more trash": Paige, *Maybe I'll Pitch Forever*, 19.

59   "a big bum, a crook," as Paige put it: Paige, *Maybe I'll Pitch Forever*, 24.

59   "woman first baseman, and a Negro pitcher": Booker T. Washington, "Letter to F. C. Lane, January 21, 1913," in *The Booker T. Washington Papers*, vol. 12, edited by Louis R. Harlan and Raymond W. Smock (Urbana: University of Illinois Press, 1982), 108.

59   rehabilitating wayward Black boys: Donald Spivey, *"If You Were Only White": The Life of Leroy Satchel Paige* (Columbia: University of Missouri Press, 2012), 29–30.

64   "institution of its kind in the United States": Courtney Michelle Smith, *Ed Bolden and Black Baseball in Philadelphia* (Jefferson, NC: McFarland, 2017), chap. 1, loc. 399, Kindle.

65   be involved in Black enterprises: "To many Blacks, Jews were a separate category of white, different, though not always in a positive way, from gentiles. They were not themselves a separate race, but neither were Jews just a religious group. There was something else bound up in their long history and distinct culture that set them apart in some palpable way."—Nadine Cohodas, *Spinning Blues into Gold: The Chess Brothers and the Legendary Chess Records* (New York: St. Martin's Press, 2000), 110. " 'Thus the story of the black entertainer angry at his Jewish agent who he is sure is exploiting him. He tells his friends how angry he is, but then admits, "If the Jews didn't get us bookings or parts, we wouldn't work—they make a gold mine out of us." ' "—Black scholar C. Eric Lincoln, quoted in Cohodas, *Spinning Blues into Gold*, 110.

66   winning 137 games and the pennant: Smith, *Ed Bolden and Black Baseball in Philadelphia*, 35.

67   a knuckleball and two curves: Lonnie Wheeler, *The Bona Fide Legend of Cool Papa Bell: Speed, Grace, and the Negro Leagues* (New York: Abrams Press, 2020), 30.

67   "you'd really fool the batter": John Holway, *Voices from the Great Black Baseball Leagues*, rev. ed. (New York: Da Capo Press, 1992), 132.

67   the opposition flat-footed: Wheeler, *The Bona Fide Legend of Cool Papa Bell*, 34–36.

68   stopped pitching and played center field: Wheeler, *The Bona Fide Legend of Cool Papa Bell*, 44–45.

68   with eleven hits in that series: Wheeler, *The Bona Fide Legend of Cool Papa Bell*, 74.

71   ridicule them as Uncle Toms: About Stepin Fetchit (Lincoln Perry), one of the biggest Black stars of the late 1920s and '30s: "The inequity with regard to most appraisals of his career is that he is often singled out as the inventor or lone perpetrator of what, in retrospect, was generally regarded as a deplorable stereotype. In reality, Perry was not imitating white purveyors of racist stereotypes, as many critics have asserted. He was working within the parameters of an established and accepted comic representation that, at the time, dominated the era's theatrical world. He stands out from the hundreds of black comedians who were working variations of the same character only because, ultimately, he was far superior to most of them."—Mel Watkins, *Stepin Fetchit: The Life and Times of Lincoln Perry* (New York: Pantheon Books, 2005), 61–62.

71 Homestead Grays were also a powerhouse: James
Bankes, *The Pittsburgh Crawfords* (Jefferson, NC: McFarland,
2001), 16.

74 "Pittsburgh, the End of Philadelphia, and the Death and
Resurrection of Satchel Paige": This section was written
in large part by Rob Ruck.

74 "Grays dominated baseball at that time": Irvin quoted in
Kings on the Hill: Baseball's Forgotten Men (video), first aired
on WQED-TV, PBS (Pittsburgh: San Pedro Productions,
1993).

77 potential economic and political clout: Laurence Glasco,
"Double Burden: The Black Experience in Pittsburgh," in
City at the Point: Essays on the Social History of Pittsburgh,
edited by Samuel P. Hays (Pittsburgh: University of
Pittsburgh Press, 1989), 69–70; John Bodnar, Roger Simon,
and Michael Weber, *Lives of Their Own: Blacks, Italians,
and Poles in Pittsburgh, 1900–1960* (Champaign-Urbana:
University of Illinois Press, 1983), 185–86.

79 "from the very first day": Rob Ruck, *Raceball: How the Major
Leagues Colonized the Black and Latin Game* (Boston: Beacon
Press, 2012), 38.

79 "that's when we beat the Grays": Tinker quoted in Irvin
quoted in *Kings on the Hill: Baseball's Forgotten Men* (PBS,
1993).

80 he contributed to the team's demise: Donald Spivey,
"If You Were Only White": The Life of Leroy Satchel Paige
(Columbia: University of Missouri Press, 2012), 144–49.

81 just given Paige an arm massage: Spivey, *"If You Were Only
White,"* 169.

81 "nothing and killing off attendance": Paige, *Maybe I'll Pitch
Forever*, chap. 16, loc. 1473.

84 "nobody guarding him": Edward Kennedy Ellington, *Music
Is My Mistress* (Garden City, NY: Doubleday, 1973), 18.

85 "meant a lot to me": Ellington, *Music Is My Mistress*, 17–18.

86 the Senators' owner, Clark Griffith: Blair A. Ruble,
Washington's U Street: A Biography (Washington, DC, and
Baltimore: Woodrow Wilson Center Press and Johns
Hopkins University Press, 2010, 2012), 158.

86 "and working-class African Americans": Ruble,
Washington's U Street, 158.

86 any other team in the Negro Leagues: Ruble, *Washington's U
Street*, 162.

86 but nothing came of it: Ruble, *Washington's U Street*,
159–60.

86 "hardworking white people here": Ruble, *Washington's
U Street*, 161.

CHAPTER 3

90 "you right out of the park": Roger Kahn, *The Era, 1947–1957:
When the Yankees, the Giants, and the Dodgers Ruled the World*
(New York: Ticknor & Fields, 1993), 36.

93 permanently blinded him: Richard Gergel, *Unexampled
Courage: The Blinding of Sgt. Isaac Woodard and the Awakening
of President Harry S. Truman and Judge J. Waties Waring* (New
York: Sarah Crichton Books, 2019), 14–23.

93 filed federal charges against Shull: Michael R. Gardner,
*Harry Truman and Civil Rights: Moral Courage and Political
Risks* (Carbondale: Southern Illinois University Press,
2002), 17–18.

93 President's Committee on Civil Rights: Gardner, *Harry
Truman and Civil Rights*, 14–15.

94 told to sit in the back of a military bus: For a full account
of Robinson's military career and court-martial, see
Michael Lee Lanning, *The Court-Martial of Jackie Robinson:
The Baseball Legend's Battle for Civil Rights During World War
II* (Guilford, CT: Stackpole Books, 2020). In a nutshell: on
July 6, 1944, Lieutenant Robinson boarded a military-base
bus at Camp Hood, Texas. He sat next to Virginia Jones,
the light-skinned wife of a lieutenant Robinson knew. The
bus driver grew angry, possibly thinking Jones was white,
and ordered Robinson to the back of the bus. Robinson
refused on the grounds that, under new army regulations,
there could be no racial discrimination on military buses,
so he could sit wherever he wanted. The driver reported
Robinson to MPs, and Robinson, in the dustup that
followed, was charged with insubordination to a superior
officer and subjected to a general court-martial. He was
ultimately acquitted.

94 rebuked him for failing to finish: Arnold Rampersad, *Jackie
Robinson: A Biography* (New York: Alfred A. Knopf, 1997), 81.

94 college degree meant that much: David Falkner, *Great
Time Coming: The Life of Jackie Robinson from Baseball to
Birmingham* (New York: Simon & Schuster, 1995), 64.

94 "He was so close to finishing": Quoted in Lanning, *The
Court-Martial of Jackie Robinson*, 28.

96 one season as a shortstop was dismal: Falkner, *Great Time
Coming*, 56–57.

96 impressed Booker T. Washington: Booker T. Washington,
"Letter to F. C. Lane, January 21, 1913," in *The Booker T.
Washington Papers*, vol. 12, edited by Louis R. Harlan and
Raymond W. Smock (Urbana: University of Illinois Press,
1982), 108.

96   where he went 0-for-5: Larry Lester, *Black Baseball's National Showcase: The East-West All-Star Game, 1933-1953* (Lincoln: University of Nebraska Press, 2002), 229.

96   thirty-four league games: Rampersad, *Jackie Robinson*, 118.

97   Branch Rickey about Robinson: Falkner, *Great Time Coming*, 101–3.

99   Rachel Robinson said: Rampersad, *Jackie Robinson*, 139.

100   Black baseball endured, even thrived: For a record of the Kansas City Monarchs' profits during the war years, see Neil Lanctot, *Negro League Baseball: The Rise and Ruin of a Black Institution* (Philadelphia: University of Pennsylvania Press, 2004), 293.

102   for which he then played: Lanctot, *Negro League Baseball*, 243.

102   $156,000 in 1946 to $83,000 in 1948: Lanctot, *Negro League Baseball*, 340.

102   reduction that alienated players: Lanctot, *Negro League Baseball*, 328.

102   had New York all to themselves: Lanctot, *Negro League Baseball*, 327–28.

103   to continue operation: Lanctot, *Negro League Baseball*, 329.

103   "Negro league game any time": Quoted in Lanctot, *Negro League Baseball*, 330.

103   good at promoting their game: Lanctot, *Negro League Baseball*, 331.

112   a captive audience: "Both inside and outside of the entertainment industry, the lack of consistently good service was often cited as the primary cause for the failure of black business ventures," Roberta J. Newman and Joel Nathan Rosen, *Black Baseball, Black Business: Race Enterprise and the Fate of the Segregated Dollar* (Jackson: University Press of Mississippi, 2014), 57.

112   "improve conditions or stimulate interest": Leslie A. Heaphy, *Negro League Baseball, 1869–1960* (Jefferson, NC: McFarland, 2003), 182.

113   entitled *To Secure These Rights*: President's Committee on Civil Rights, *To Secure These Rights: The Report of the President's Committee on Civil Rights* (Washington, DC: U.S. Government Printing Office, 1947).

113   in the summer of 1948: Steven F. Lawson, ed., *To Secure These Rights: The Report of President Harry S. Truman's Committee on Civil Rights* (Boston: Bedford/St. Martin, 2004), 176–77.

113   which Robinson was to play: Lawson, *To Secure These Rights*, 60.

113   "achieve in the previous decade": Lanctot, *Negro League Baseball*, 316.

113   cloaked him with defiant dignity: Jules Tygiel, *Baseball's Great Experiment: Jackie Robinson and His Legacy* (New York: Oxford University Press, 1993), 190.

113   "always to win," Robinson said: Jackie Robinson, *Baseball Has Done It* [1964] (Brooklyn, NY: Ig, 2005), 42.

114   "He come to beat ya": Roger Kahn, *The Boys of Summer* (New York: Harper & Row, 1972), 393.

118   salary less than $5,000 a year: Effa Manley and Leon Herbert Hardwick, *Negro Baseball . . . Before Integration* (Chicago: Adams Press, 1976), 74–77.

122   "would be terribly discouraged": Lou Boudreau with Russell Schneider, *Covering All the Bases* (New York: Sports Publishing, 2017), 133.

122   civil rights pioneer that he was: Neil Lanctot, *Campy: The Two Lives of Roy Campanella* (New York: Simon & Schuster, 2011), 310–11; William C. Kashatus, *Jackie & Campy: The Untold Story of Their Rocky Relationship and the Breaking of Baseball's Color Line* (Lincoln: University of Nebraska Press, 2014), 130, 132–33, 136–60.

123   "A catcher has to take charge," he said: Robinson, *Baseball Has Done It*, 92.

123   sources vary on the amount: The figure of $25,000 is mentioned in Donald Spivey, *"If You Were Only White": The Life of Leroy "Satchel" Paige* (Columbia: University of Missouri Press, 2012), 225. In *Veeck as in Wreck: The Autobiography of Bill Veeck* (Chicago: University of Chicago Press, 2001), Bill Veeck never mentions how much he paid Paige. Nor is a figure mentioned in Paul Dickson, *Bill Veeck: Baseball's Greatest Maverick* (New York: Walker and Company, 2012).

123   "at least, it wasn't right for me": Luke Epplin, *Our Team: The Epic Story of Four Men and the World Series That Changed Baseball* (New York: Flatiron Books, 2021), 233–34.

126   quoted in Ackmann, *Curveball*, 2010: Ackmann, *Curveball*, 137.

126   "This is professional baseball": Martha Ackmann, *Curveball: The Remarkable Story of Toni Stone, the First Woman to Play Professional Baseball in the Negro League* (Chicago: Lawrence Hill Books, 2010), 123.

126   "than demean herself like that": Ackmann, *Curveball*, 123.

127   not accept Black women: Ackmann, *Curveball*, 108–9.

127 Harlem Globetrotter Goose Tatum: "King Tut," *Baseball History Daily*, January 30, 2022, https://baseballhistorydaily.com/tag/spec-bebop/; "Spec DeBop," Trading Card Database, https://www.tcdb.com/GalleryP.cfm/pid/175863/Spec-BeBop.

128 much less: $400 a month: Neil Lanctot, *Negro League Baseball*, 381; Ackmann, *Curveball*, 164, 142.

128 skewed how her abilities were assessed: Ackmann, *Curveball*, 98, 126.

128 sexual advances, sometimes forcefully: Ackmann, *Curveball*, 155.

128 no business playing with men: Ackmann, *Curveball*, 136, 189.

128 support for her on the road: Ackmann, *Curveball*, 156.

129 Stone's baseball experience: Ackmann, *Curveball*, 160.

129 professional baseball for good: Ackmann, *Curveball*, 189.

CHAPTER 4

134 "Blacks spoke English": Luis Tiant with Saul Wisnia, *Son of Havana: A Baseball Journey from Cuba to the Big Leagues and Back* (New York: Diversion Books, 2019), 41.

135 "colored people in America": Jackie Robinson, "Jackie Robinson Says," *Pittsburgh Courier*, March 13, 1948, 15.

136 "uniforms that shimmered in the sun": Felipe Alou with Peter Kerasotis, *Alou: My Baseball Journey* (Lincoln: University of Nebraska Press, 2018), 22.

136 making their way to the United States: Rob Ruck, *Raceball: How the Major Leagues Colonized the Black and Latin Game* (Boston: Beacon Press, 2012), 144.

138 Black Americans and Latinos is low: Denise-Marie Ordway, "Intermarriage and U.S. Hispanics: New Research," *Journalist's Resource*, August 3, 2017, https://journalistsresource.org/politics-and-government/interracial-intermarriage-hispanic-population-research/; "Interracial Marriage and Latino/a Racial Identity," *Fordham Law News*, May 19, 2017, https://news.law.fordham.edu/blog/2017/05/19/interracial-marriage-and-latinoa-racial-identity/.

139 white major league organization: Ruck, *Raceball*, 149.

139 disappoint his family during hard times: Alou, *Alou: My Baseball Journey*, 38.

139 never made it to the majors. Alou did: Alou, *Alou: My Baseball Journey*, 34, 36.

141 "became surrogate parents" for Alou: *Alou: My Baseball Journey*, 38–39.

141 "slurs and slights defeat" him: Alou, *Alou: My Baseball Journey*, 44.

141 shared a broken-down jalopy: Alou, *Alou: My Baseball Journey*, 55.

142 flat-out racism, on the island: Alou, *Alou: My Baseball Journey*, 173.

142 during the regular season: John Virtue, *South of the Color Barrier: How Jorge Pasquel and the Mexican League Pushed Baseball Toward Racial Integration* (Jefferson, NC: McFarland, 2008), 58.

145 "our team would win": Quoted in Averell "Ace" Smith, *The Pitcher and the Dictator: Satchel Paige's Unlikely Season in the Dominican Republic* (Lincoln: University of Nebraska Press, 2018), 112–13. Smith also provides an account of the championship game (107–11) and tournament statistics (166–17).

145 Roy Campanella and Monte Irvin: Smith, *The Pitcher and the Dictator*, 173.

145 "such privileges in the United States": Jim Reisler, *Black Writers/Black Baseball: An Anthology of Articles from Black Sportswriters Who Covered the Negro Leagues* (Jefferson, NC: McFarland, 1994), 45, 46.

146 eventually forcing him to return: Reisler, *Black Writers/Black Baseball*, 102–3.

148 to a bonus of $60,000: James S. Hirsch, *Willie Mays: The Life, the Legend* (New York: Scribner, 2010), 283.

149 told the press the same: Hirsch, *Willie Mays*, 333.

149 did not like each other: Orlando Cepeda with Herb Fagen, *Baby Bull: From Hardball to Hard Time and Back* (Dallas: Taylor, 1998), 65.

150 Latinos strongly opposed: Hirsch, *Willie Mays*, 351.

150 talked him up to the press: Alou, *Alou: My Baseball Journey*, 103.

150 "made me a better player": Alou, *Alou: My Baseball Journey*, 92.

150 "third-class citizens were the Latinos": Alou, *Alou: My Baseball Journey*, 89.

151 between Cepeda and Dark: Hirsch, *Willie Mays*, 351.

153 had the fans booing him: Hirsch, *Willie Mays*, 349.

153 when "his self-imposed pressures": Hirsch, *Willie Mays*, 333.

155 "his elevation to nationwide fame": Jackie Robinson, *Baseball Has Done It* [1964] (Brooklyn, NY: Ig, 2005), 208–9.

155 "mental and physical exhaustion": Wendell Smith, "Negro Players in the Majors Have a Huge Responsibility to Meet," *Pittsburgh Courier*, September 21, 1963, 23.

156 after the season had started: Hirsch, *Willie Mays*, 414.

156 "aren't as sharp mentally": Hirsch, *Willie Mays*, 418.

156 "make a hero out of him," Mays said: Willie Mays and John Shea, *24: Life Stories and Lessons from the Say Hey Kid* (New York: St. Martin's Press, 2020), 220.

158 "looked at him as a leader": Cepeda and Fagen, *Baby Bull*, 76.

159 discrimination they withstood: Felipe Alou with Arnold Hano, "Latin-American Ballplayers Need a Bill of Rights," *Sport*, November 1964. The article is reprinted in Alou, *Alou: My Baseball Journey*, 128–40.

CHAPTER 5

162 "I pitched better angry": Bob Gibson with Lonnie Wheeler, *Stranger to the Game: The Autobiography of Bob Gibson* (New York: Viking Press, 1994), 188.

165 trying out a Black player: Christopher Threston, *The Integration of Baseball in Philadelphia* (Jefferson, NC: McFarland, 2003), 89.

165 and Robinson accepted: Arnold Rampersad, *Jackie Robinson: A Biography* (New York: Alfred A. Knopf, 1997), 172–76; Jules Tygiel, *Baseball's Great Experiment: Jackie Robinson and His Legacy* (New York: Oxford University Press, 1993), 182–85.

168 "in this expansion period": Jackie Robinson, *Baseball Has Done It* [1964] (Brooklyn, NY: Ig, 2005), 57.

170 attendance by more than half: "The Year of Transition: 1959," *Britannica*, https://www.britannica.com/art/television-in-the-United-States/The-year-of-transition-1959.

170 "number of Negroes in the line-up": "End of an Era for Negroes in Baseball," *Ebony*, June 1961, 36.

171 recognition of their excellence: "1962: Year of the Big Money," *Ebony*, June 1962, 81.

174 still tried to get a pay raise: Frank Robinson and Berry Stainback, *Extra Innings* (New York: McGraw-Hill, 1988), 49.

174 "after Pinson's first swing": Earl Lawson, *Cincinnati Seasons: My 34 Years with the Reds* (South Bend, IN: Diamond Communications, 1987), 122.

174 "You don't drive in runs bunting": UPI, "Pinson Arrested after Tiff with Sports Writer," *Desert Sun*, September 5, 1963.

174 "should have knocked Lawson down": UPI, "Pinson Arrested after Tiff with Sports Writer."

175 "the club as a rookie in 1956": Lawson, *Cincinnati Seasons*, 125.

175 Robinson was a witness for Pinson: Lawson, *Cincinnati Seasons*, 128.

177 "will be debated for years to come": "From First to Fame," *Ebony*, October 1962, 85.

177 "they would worship him": Rampersad, *Jackie Robinson*, 322.

179 being too conservative himself: Rampersad, *Jackie Robinson*, 372.

179 against the Vietnam War: David Falkner, *Great Time Coming: The Life of Jackie Robinson from Baseball to Birmingham* (New York: Simon & Schuster, 1995), 323.

180 received many threatening letters: Robinson, *Baseball Has Done It*, 132.

180 knew only how to hit a baseball: Robinson, *Baseball Has Done It*, 134.

180 voice of the Civil Rights Movement: Robinson, *Baseball Has Done It*, 138, 139.

180 "not going to wait any longer!": Robinson, *Baseball Has Done It*, 139.

183 "couldn't understand that part of it": Quoted in James S. Hirsch, *Willie Mays: The Life, The Legend* (New York: Scribner, 2010), 473.

183 as good a ballplayer as Hank: Howard Bryant, *The Last Hero: A Life of Henry Aaron* (New York: Pantheon Books, 2010), 292.

184 "when I became mayor in 1962": Ivan Allen Jr. with Paul Hemphill, *Mayor: Notes on the Sixties* (New York: Simon & Schuster, 1971), 82.

184 "don't want to live there again": Quoted in Bryant, *The Last Hero*, 306.

187 Dominican Milwaukee Braves outfielder: Hank Aaron with Lonnie Wheeler, *I Had a Hammer: The Hank Aaron Story* (New York: HarperCollins, 1991), 261–62.

187 "more than made up for it": William C. Kashatus, *Dick Allen: The Life and Times of a Baseball Immortal* (Atglen, PA: Schiffer, 2017), 67–68.

187 monstrous home runs: Matt Breen, "The Legend of Allen's 42-Ounce Bat," *Philadelphia Inquirer*, December 10, 2020, https://www.inquirer.com/newsletters/phillies/phillies-dick-allen-42-ounce-bat-louisville-slugger-bobby-wine-20201210.html.

188 the neighborhood "the Jungle": "Philly Gang Members Tell Their Own Story," from *The Jungle* (documentary), 1967, https://www.youtube.com/watch?v=CpODLe15q4c&t=3s.

188 neighborhood surrounding the stadium: Kashatus, *Dick Allen*, 74.

188 with the Chicago White Sox: Minnie Miñoso with Fernando Fernandez and Robert Kleinfelder, *Extra Innings: My Life in Baseball* (Chicago: Regnery Gateway, 1983), 67–68.

188 "Robinson is to black ballplayers": Orlando Cepeda with Herb Fagen, *Baby Bull: From Hardball to Hard Time and Back* (Dallas: Taylor Publishing, 1998), 13.

188 "were much needed," Allen said later: Dick Allen and Tim Whitaker, *Crash: The Life and Times of Dick Allen* (New York: Ticknor & Fields, 1989), 56.

190 twelve games of the season: Kashatus, *Dick Allen*, 82.

190 escalated into a fight on June 23: Kashatus, *Dick Allen*, 89.

190 players were pulled apart: Kashatus, *Dick Allen*, 89.

190 "to be allowed on the field." Allen and Whitaker, *Crash*, 64.

190 "playing angry baseball": Allen and Whitaker, *Crash*, 58.

195 "I was a man." Curt Flood with Richard Carter, *The Way It Is* (New York: Trident Press, 1971), 15.

195 "is nonetheless a slave": Interview with Howard Cosell, *ABC's Wide World of Sports*, January 3, 1970.

195 "missile-hurling audience": Flood, *The Way It Is*, 188.

CHAPTER 6

200 "I sat in the middle, observing": Frank Robinson and Barry Stainback, *Extra Innings* (New York: McGraw-Hill, 1988), 108.

202 a first for MLB: Nathalie Alonso, "The Pirates Lineup That Changed Baseball," *MLB News*, September 1, 2022, https://www.mlb.com/news/featured/the-day-the-pirates-fielded-the-first-all-black-and-latino-lineup; "Philadelphia Phillies vs. Pittsburgh Pirates—September 1, 1971," Baseball Almanac, https://www.baseball-almanac.com/box-scores/boxscore.php?boxid=197109010PIT.

202 Latino numbers continue to rise: Mark Armour and Daniel R. Levitt, "Baseball Demographics, 1947–2016," Society for American Baseball Research, https://sabr.org/bioproj/topic/baseball-demographics-1947-2016/.

204 (Edgar Martínez and David Ortiz): Joel Reuter, "Ranking MLB's 10 Greatest Designated Hitters of All Time," *Bleacher Report*, July 11, 2013, https://bleacherreport.com/articles/1700743-ranking-mlbs-10-greatest-designated-hitters-of-all-time.

209 paternalism was not helpful: Mehrsa Baradaran, *The Color of Money: Black Banks and the Racial Wealth Gap* (Cambridge, MA: Harvard University Press, 2019), 198.

209 toll on his health as anything else: Arnold Rampersad, *Jackie Robinson: A Biography* (New York: Alfred A. Knopf, 1997), 396.

210 "bitterly disappointed" Robinson: David Falkner, *Great Time Coming: The Life of Jackie Robinson from Baseball to Birmingham* (New York: Simon & Schuster, 1995), 339.

210 "see a black face managing in baseball": Rampersad, *Jackie Robinson*, 459.

211 "signed by the white boys": Leroy Satchel Paige, as told to David Lipman, *Maybe I'll Pitch Forever: A Great Baseball Player Tells the Hilarious Story behind the Legend* [1962] (South Orange, NJ: Summer Game Books, 2018), 173.

211 "and not a real pitcher": Paige, *Maybe I'll Pitch Forever*, 150.

213 "a separate wing," the magazine pointed out: "A Hollow Ring to Fame," *Ebony*, April 1971, 124.

215 first history of the Negro Leagues: Robert Peterson, *Only the Ball Was White: A History of Legendary Black Players and All-Black Professional Teams* (Oxford, UK: Oxford University Press, 1992).

215 Negro Leagues players, wanted: Bowie Kuhn, *Hardball: The Education of a Baseball Commissioner* (New York: Times Books, 1987), 110.

216 "home runs, it would be mine": Hank Aaron with Lonnie Wheeler, *I Had a Hammer: The Hank Aaron Story* (New York: HarperCollins, 1991), 260.

216 "doing something for my race": Aaron, *I Had a Hammer*, 308.

216 only American to receive more: Michael MacCambridge, *The Big Time: How the 1970s Transformed Sports in America* (New York: Grand Central, 2023), 162.

220 "I still dream about it": Bill Libby and Vida Blue, *Vida: His Own Story* (Englewood Cliffs, NJ: Prentice-Hall, 1972), 24.

220 "real name will help you even more": Libby and Blue, *Vida: His Own Story*, 74.

220 "keep it just the way it is": Libby and Blue, *Vida: His Own Story*, 75.

221 insulted by Finley's suggestion: Libby and Blue, *Vida: His Own Story*, 75.

221 like a little boy's name: William C. Kashatus, *Dick Allen: The Life and Times of a Baseball Immortal* (Atglen, PA: Schiffer, 2017), 9.

222 a home run drought: Kuhn, *Hardball*, 123.

222 700th home run in 1973: MacCambridge, *The Big Time*, 167.

222 the one that broke the record: MacCambridge, *The Big Time*, 167.

222 publicly whenever he could: Kuhn, *Hardball*, 124–25.

223 teammates loved to hate: Willie Randolph, *The Yankee Way: Playing, Coaching, and My Life in Baseball* (New York: It Books, 2014), 99–100.

223 dated white women: Jackson always said that the reason the New York Mets did not draft him in 1966 when they had the first pick was because he had a white girlfriend (she was actually Mexican). "Reggie Jackson Wasn't the #1 Pick Because of Mets 'Racism,'" *New York Post*, October 6, 2013, https://nypost.com/2013/10/06/reggie-details-yankees-rivalries-mets-racism-in-tell-all/. Jackson dating white women is discussed in Dayn Perry, *Reggie Jackson: The Life and Thunderous Career of Baseball's Mr. October* (New York: HarperCollins, 2010), 327–28.

223 "name a candy bar after me": MacCambridge, *The Big Time*, 269.

223 more than his white peers: Perry, *Reggie Jackson*, 271–72.

223 with Robinson's picture: Perry, *Reggie Jackson*, 2.

224 He held out: Perry, *Reggie Jackson*, 91.

224 big stage for the big ego: Willie Randolph, *The Yankee Way: Playing, Coaching, and My Life in Baseball* (New York: It Books, 2014), 66.

224 "but he can only stir it bad": Quoted in MacCambridge, *The Big Time*, 270.

224 "Reggie is Mr. October": Quoted in Perry, *Reggie Jackson*, 303, 304.

225 on the first pitch he saw: Perry, *Reggie Jackson*, 306.

226 "Everyone is yelling, throwing": Dave Winfield with Tom Parker, *Winfield: A Player's Life* (New York: W. W. Norton, 1988), 201.

228 "The Rise and Fall of the Black Boy Wonders": Sources consulted in the writing of this section essay: Michael Bamberger, "Darryl Strawberry Is Not Trying to Save You," *New York Times*, August 18, 2023; Baseball Almanac, https://www.baseball-almanac.com; Baseball Reference, Baseball-reference.com; "Doc & Darryl" (documentary), *ESPN 30 for 30*, 2016; Dwight Gooden, and Ellis Henican, *Doc: A Memoir* (Boston: Houghton Mifflin Harcourt/New Harvest, 2013); Lee Kluck, "Dwight Gooden" (biography), Society of American Baseball Research, sabr.org/bioproj/person/dwight-gooden/; Shawn Morris, "Darryl Strawberry" (biography), Society of American Baseball

Research. sabr.org/bioproj/person/darryl-strawberry/; Jeff Pearlman, *The Bad Guys Won! A Season of Brawling, Boozing, Bimbo Chasing, and Championship Baseball with Straw, Doc, Mookie, Nails, the Kid, and the Rest of the 1986 Mets, the Rowdiest Team Ever to Put on a New York Uniform—and Maybe the Best* (New York: HarperCollins, 2004); Shawn Powell with David Blair Miller et al., *Don't Give Up On Me: Shedding Light on Addiction with Darryl Strawberry* (Milwaukee: HenschelHAUS, 2017); Erik Sherman, *Kings of Queens: Life Beyond Baseball with the '86 Mets* (New York: Berkley, 2016); Darryl Strawberry with John Strausbaugh, *Straw: Finding My Way* (New York: Ecco Press, 2010); Tom Verducci, "The High Price of Hard Living," *Sports Illustrated*, February 27, 1995.

228 "those demons that did you in": Quotes from Dwight Gooden in this essay are from a phone interview on October 24, 2023.

230 "continue to do a lot more good": Quotes from Darryl Strawberry in this essay are from a phone interview on November 17, 2023.

237 "We have a long way to go": William Weinbaum, "The Legacy of Al Campanis," ESPN, March 29, 2012, https://www.espn.com/espn/otl/story/_/id/7751398/how-al-campanis-controversial-racial-remarks-cost-career-highlighted-mlb-hiring-practices.

237 "wanted a black man for the job": Bill White with Gordon Dillow, *Uppity: My Untold Story About the Games People Play* (New York: Grand Central, 2011), 189.

237 "the chances of other white men": Russell J. Schneider, *Frank Robinson: The Making of a Manager* (New York: Coward, McCann & Geoghegan, 1976), 64–65.

238 assistant general manager in 1990: Gordon Edes, "Elaine Steward: 30 Years Later, First Female Assistant GM Reflects on Making History with Red Sox," MLB, https://www.mlb.com/redsox/fans/elaine-steward.

238 "said the hell with them": White, *Uppity*, 7.

238 called "Baseball's Angry Man": White, *Uppity*, 7.

CHAPTER 7

242 "game and still is today": Dennis "Oil Can" Boyd with Mike Shalin, *They Call Me Oil Can: Baseball, Drugs, and Life on the Edge* (Chicago: Triumph Books, 2012), 34.

249 his personality and his playing: Jeff Pearlman, *Love Me, Hate Me: Barry Bonds and the Making of an Antihero* (New York: It Books, 2007), 19, 31.

249 he didn't think he had to: Pearlman, *Love Me, Hate Me*, 40.

249 "look out for Number One," Mays told him: Pearlman, *Love Me, Hate Me*, 26.

249 Barry's honorary godfather: Pearlman, *Love Me, Hate Me*, 26.

249 his free agent year of 1993: Pearlman, *Love Me, Hate Me*, 137.

249 neither a good father nor a good husband: Pearlman, *Love Me, Hate Me*, 32.

249 taunted in school about it: K. P. Wee, *The Case for Barry Bonds in the Hall of Fame: The Untold and Forgotten Stories of Baseball's Home Run King* (Riverdale, NY: Riverdale Avenue Books, 2021), 14.

249 listen to his father's tutelage: Pearlman, *Love Me, Hate Me*, 137.

249 "my dad's in right field": Pearlman, *Love Me, Hate Me*, 142.

250 number his father wore with the Giants: Pearlman, *Love Me, Hate Me*, 143.

250 young but promising Mariners team: Ken Griffey with Phil Pepe, *Big Red: Baseball, Fatherhood, and My Life in the Big Red Machine* (Chicago: Triumph Books, 2014), 11.

250 She was ignored: Griffey, *Big Red*, 184.

250 when Barry was born: Griffey, *Big Red*, 163.

251 that he attempted suicide: Associated Press, "Griffey Jr. Recalls Attempted Suicide," *New York Times*, March 16, 1992, https://timesmachine.nytimes.com/timesmachine /1992/03/16/704092.html?pageNumber=30.

252 "in this locker room": Richard Cuicchi, "April 15, 1997: Ken Griffey Jr. Wears Number 42 to Honor Jackie Robinson on 50th Anniversary," Society for American Baseball Research, https://sabr.org/gamesproj/game/april-15 -1997-ken-griffey-jr-wears-number-42-to-honor-jackie -robinson-on-50th-anniversary/.

253 an edge in his waning years: Pearlman, *Love Me, Hate Me*, 198–99, offers a complete account of the dinner at Griffey's Florida home.

253 "Now I play alone": Pearlman, *Love Me, Hate Me*, 285.

254 both groups in management: Mark Armour and Daniel R. Levitt, "Baseball Demographics, 1947–2016," Society for American Baseball Research, https://sabr.org/bioproj /topic/baseball-demographics-1947-2016/.

254 "know we need to do better," he said: Mark Maske, "Off the Field, the Barriers Still Stand," *Washington Post*, March 27, 1997, https://www.washingtonpost.com/archive /sports/1997/03/28/off-the-field-the-barriers-still-stand /a68a9472-9805-4173-9a86-5cefd96e9473/.

254 or one of the new jobs: Jon Pessah, *The Game: Inside the Secret World of Major League Baseball's Power Brokers* (New York: Little, Brown, 2015), 250.

256 fifteen GMs in twenty-three years: Pessah, *The Game*, 161.

256 1996 Executive of the Year: Pessah, *The Game*, 221.

256 as the new Yankees GM: Pessah, *The Game*, 224.

256 Montreal Expos made him available: Pessah, *The Game*, 221.

256 pull the trigger on deals quickly enough: Pessah, *The Game*, 221.

256 against the Houston Astros: Houston was still in the National League at that time.

258 aren't interested in baseball's white past: "Chris Rock's Take on Blacks in Baseball: Real Sports (HBO)," YouTube, April 22, 2015, https://www.youtube.com /watch?v=oFFQkQ6Va3A.

260 "and the desire was not there": "Michael Jordan's Statement from His 1993 Press Conference to Announce His Retirement from the NBA," *Chicago Tribune*, October 6, 1993, https://www.chicagotribune.com/sports/bulls/ct -michael-jordan-statement-1993-retirement-20200509 -3jewwci7pnbztlmpjdlhftcxqe-story.html.

262 "as close to it as I could": "Michael Jordan's Statement from His 1993 Press Conference," October 6, 1993.

263 praise a baseball lifer could have offered: Anthony Castrovince, "The Real Story of MJ's Baseball Career," MLB, February 7, 2024, www.mlb.com/news/featured /michael-jordan-the-real-story-of-his-baseball-career.

263 "difficult sport in full public view": Jim Patton, *The Rookie: When Michael Jordan Came to the Minor Leagues* (Reading, MA: Addison-Wesley, 1995), 2.

263 chances of making the majors: Ryan Fagan, "Was Michael Jordan Good at Baseball? A Look Back at His Brief Career with the White Sox," *Sporting News*, October 6, 2021, https://www.sportingnews.com/us /mlb/news/michael-jordan-baseball-career-white -sox/1lir1a7ewr0e91okm55a0njkr6.

264 "affirmation for the sport": Tom Verducci, "Michael Jordan Chose Baseball. Baseball Never Chose Him Back," *Sports Illustrated*, May 11, 2020, https://www.si.com/mlb/2020 /05/11/michael-jordan-baseball-career-white-sox.

267 Reviving the Black Relationship to Baseball: This section was written by Scott Pitoniak.

267 from the sport for three years: Bill Ladson, "Reagins Recounts His Path to Trailblazer GM," MLB, December 18, 2020, https://www.mlb.com/news/tony-reagins-intern -to-mlb-chief-baseball-development-officer.

267 "because he knows [what it takes]": Jack Harris, "A Familiar Face Leads MLB Efforts to Grow Baseball in Underprivileged Communities," *Los Angeles Times*, April 15, 2021, https://www.latimes.com/sports/angels /story/2021-04-15/familiar-face-tony-reagins-leads -mlb-grow-baseball-underprivileged-communities.

267 "the impact we were hoping to make": Tony Reagins, MLB Chief Development Officer, interview with Scott Pitoniak, February 1, 2024.

268 "It's right there under the surface": Bob Nightengale, "MLB's Percentage of Black Players Is Lowest Since 1955. What's Baseball Doing to Fix That?" *USA Today*, April 14, 2023, https://www.usatoday.com/story/sports /mlb/columnist/bob-nightengale/2023/04/14/mlb -percentage-black-players-baseball-jackie-robinson -day/11657961002/.

268 "see some of the stuff pay off": Nightengale, "MLB's Percentage of Black Players Is Lowest Since 1955."

268 "going to pay dividends long-term": Reagins, interview with Pitoniak.

270 "financial resources or equipment or instruction": Reagins, interview with Pitoniak.

270 "They just needed an opportunity": Reagins, interview with Pitoniak.

270 "couldn't afford to play in the United States": Nightengale, "MLB's Percentage of Black Players Is Lowest Since 1955."

271 on the bases and in the field: Reagins, interview with Pitoniak.

271 "The field is more wide open now": Nightengale, "MLB's Percentage of Black Players Is Lowest Since 1955."

271 less diverse than in the United States: Brandon Jones, "73 Years after Robinson Broke Barrier, Baseball Still Struggles," *Cronkite News*, January 6, 2021, https:// cronkitenews.azpbs.org/2021/01/06/seventy-three-years -after-robinson-broke-color-barrier-baseball-still-struggles -to-lure-african-americans/#:~:text=baseball%20still%20 struggles-,73%20years%20after%20Robinson%20broke %20barrier%2C%20baseball%20still%20struggles,the%20 lowest%20percentage%20since%201957.

273 "and they want to be us": Drake, "Thank Me Now," by Drake, Timbaland, T. Mosley, Noah "40" Shebib, Anthony Palman, Ghazi Hourani, Jas Prince, and Chris Godbey, track 14 on *Thank Me Later,* Universal Motown B0014325-02, Cash Money Records B0014325-02. Drake, "Thank Me Now," *Thank Me Later* (Aspire Music Group, 2010).

273 "put yourself in their shoes": Perry B. Johnson and Courtney M. Cox, *Sounding Off* (podcast), "Sounding Off: DJ Severe," 2021, season 2, episode 3, https://open.spotify .com/episode/5Lf33k2aHHSVjY2Vspk1em?si=d7caa2ca3 c2a42a5. In case you were wondering, his walk-up song would be "Made You Look" by Nas.

274 "holdin' that whole South down": UGK, "The Game Belongs to Me," Jive 88697-05287-2, Zomba 88697-05287-2, compact disc. Originally released in 2006. *Underground Kingz* (Jive Records, 2007).

274 only the Yankees and A's in sales: Shakeia Taylor, "The White Sox and Hip-Hop Culture," FanGraphs, April 13, 2018, https://blogs.fangraphs.com/the-white-sox-cap -and-hip-hop-culture/.

276 "they'd talk to him": Reggie Jackson, "We Have a Serious Problem That Isn't Going Away," *Sports Illustrated*, May 11, 1987.

276 omission he considered an evasion: Stephanie Apstein, "Why Baseball Is Losing Black America," *Sports Illustrated*, July 17, 2020.

AUTHORS AND CONTRIBUTORS

Gerald Early is the Merle Kling Professor of Modern Letters in the African and African American Studies Department at Washington University in St. Louis. An award-winning essayist and culture critic, Early has published extensively, winning a National Book Critics Circle Award for *The Culture of Bruising: Essays on Prizefighting, Literature, and Modern American Culture*. He has been a consultant on the Ken Burns documentaries *Baseball*, *Jazz*, *The Tenth Inning*, *The Roosevelts*, and *Jackie Robinson*. In 2013, President Obama appointed Early to a five-year term at the National Council on the Humanities. Early recently served as curatorial consultant for *The Souls of the Game: Voices of Black Baseball* exhibit at the National Baseball Hall of Fame and Museum.

Courtney M. Cox is an assistant professor in the Department of Indigenous, Race, and Ethnic Studies (IRES) at the University of Oregon, whose research examines issues related to identity, technology, and labor through sport and wine. She is also co-director (with Dr. Perry B. Johnson) of The Sound of Victory, a multi-platform project at the intersection of music, sound, and sport. She previously worked for ESPN, Longhorn Network, NPR-affiliate KPCC, and the WNBA's Los Angeles Sparks.

Leslie Heaphy is an associate professor of history at Kent State University at Stark and publishes in the area of the Negro Leagues and women's baseball. In 2008, she became the founding editor of the journal *Black Ball*, published by McFarland. She was the 2014 winner of the Bob Davids Award, SABR's highest honor, and received the Henry Chadwick Research Award in 2024. Heaphy recently served as curatorial consultant for *The Souls of the Game: Voices of Black Baseball* exhibit at the National Baseball Hall of Fame and Museum.

David Winfield, a native of St. Paul, Minnesota, was a five-tool player who starred in both baseball and basketball at the University of Minnesota. Winfield never spent a day in the minor leagues, making his major league debut in 1973 after being drafted by the San Diego Padres in the first round of that year's amateur draft. He utilized his superb athleticism to amass 3,110 hits, 465 home runs, 7 Gold Glove Awards, and 12 All-Star selections in a twenty-two-year career, earning election to the Baseball Hall of Fame in 2001.

Larry Lester is co-founder of the Negro Leagues Baseball Museum in Kansas City, Missouri, and served as its research director and treasurer for five years (1991–1995). Up until 2021, he was chairman of the Society for American Baseball Research's (SABR) Negro Leagues Committee for more than thirty years. In 2023, he served as historical consultant for the documentary *The League*, produced and directed by three-time Emmy winner Sam Pollard. Lester most recently served as curatorial consultant for *The Souls of the Game: Voices of Black Baseball* exhibit at the National Baseball Hall of Fame and Museum.

Rowan Ricardo Phillips, professor of English at Stony Brook University, is the author of three books of poetry and two books of nonfiction—*The Ground, Heaven, Living Weapon, The Circuit,* and *When Blackness Rhymes with Blackness*—all published by Farrar, Straus and Giroux. A prodigious sportswriter, Phillips has written on sports for *The New York Times Magazine, The New Yorker, The New Republic,* and *The Paris Review.* He recently served as curatorial consultant for *The Souls of the Game: Voices of Black Baseball* exhibit at the National Baseball Hall of Fame and Museum.

Scott Pitoniak is a nationally honored sports journalist and author of nearly forty books. The Rome, New York, native is a frequent contributor to the Hall of Fame's *Memories & Dreams* magazine. Scott's books include *Remembrances of Swings Past: A Lifetime of Baseball Stories* and *Memories of Yankee Stadium.* He was inducted into the Rochester Red Wings Hall of Fame in 2013.

Rob Ruck is a historian at the University of Pittsburgh, where he teaches and writes about sports. He focuses on how people use sport to tell a collective story about who they are—to themselves and to the world. His books and documentaries include *Sandlot Seasons, Rooney: A Sporting Life, Raceball: How the Major Leagues Colonized the Black and Latin Game,* and *Tropic of Football: The Long and Perilous Journey of Samoans to the NFL.* Ruck recently served as curatorial consultant for *The Souls of the Game: Voices of Black Baseball* exhibit at the National Baseball Hall of Fame and Museum.

Shakeia Taylor is a writer and storyteller whose work focuses on the intersection of culture and sport. She is an avid baseball historian; her primary areas of research are the Negro Leagues and women in baseball. She is currently a deputy senior content editor for the *Chicago Tribune,* where she covers sports, history, and culture.

ACKNOWLEDGMENTS

FROM GERALD EARLY

My involvement with *Play Harder: The Triumph of Black Baseball in America* would not have been possible without Tom Shieber, head curator at the National Baseball Hall of Fame and Museum, who recruited me in 2022 to be one of the consultants for the Hall's project of reimagining its Black baseball exhibit. I am not sure what made him think I could be helpful to him and the other curators in this endeavor, but I am eternally gratefully that he thought I had something to offer. At the time he reached out to me, I had not been thinking about Blacks and baseball very much at all in recent years. I was following Major League Baseball—it is almost a crime not to in St. Louis—but had not been engaging it in quite the way I had back in the 1990s when Ken Burns recruited me for his documentary, *Baseball*, and so fired a latent passion in me that I became a Cardinals season ticket holder for many years and once attended fifty games in one season. In any case, Tom, as Ken Burns did before him, placed a lot of faith in me, and I did not want to disappoint him.

Among other things, in my efforts to be a good consultant, I read a lot of Black baseball books while working for the Hall: and probably invented my own graduate course. These books included works by my fellow consultants—we collectively became known as the Fab Five: Rob Ruck, whom I had encountered several years earlier at an American Studies Association conference; Larry Lester, the emperor of the study of Black baseball; Leslie Heaphy, who astonished me with her work on Black baseball; and Rowan Ricardo Phillips, whom I had known only as a poet, not as the fine sportswriter that he also is. This book would not have been possible without their contributions to it as writers and without my being party to our many discussions in planning the new exhibit, where I learned more about Black baseball than I ever thought possible. Talk about a graduate seminar, those sessions with Tom, the curators, and my fellow consultants were exactly that!

I am also grateful to the other key curators: Nicole Retzler (the nicest, most dedicated team player I have ever met), Mary Quinn (one of the ablest and most down-to-earth persons I have ever met), Gabrielle Augustine (the knitter with astute observations), and R. J. Lara (one hardworking fellow). Interacting with these people also made writing the book possible for me. I learned a lot from them, especially about how to blend discrete elements into a narrative whole.

Josh Rawitch, president of the Hall of Fame, always enlivened our group sessions whenever he sat in, and I much appreciate his kindness to my wife when she called the Hall to make arrangements for our visit for the opening of the exhibit in May 2024.

I want to thank Scot Mondore and Sean Gahagan for all their counsel and help with the book, and their belief that I could write it. I am deeply indebted to Valerie Tomaselli for being the taskmaster and getting the book out of me and the contributions from our guest contributors in a timely manner. She is a fine editor and an even finer person. I wish to thank Aaron Wehner and Kim Keller at Ten Speed Press for rolling the dice with me to write the book and particularly for going along with me about the title. Thanks as well to contributors Courtney Cox, Scott Pitoniak, and Shakeia Taylor. Without their work, this book would be deeply impoverished.

My wife, Ida, does not like baseball but has always supported my love of the game. In the year I went to fifty

St. Louis Cardinals game, she came with me to every one of them. For this project, she helped me schlep suitcases of baseball books between St. Louis and Las Vegas (my writing retreat) while I was working on the book. She even read parts of the manuscript and let me talk to her about Black baseball incessantly.

Finally, I would like to thank Dave Winfield for his wonderful foreword. It was an honor to have him do it. And, of course, I thank all the Black people who gave their time, their talent, their being, to the game of baseball. I became deeply reacquainted with many of my boyhood and young adult heroes, now gone, including Hank Aaron, Ernie Banks, Willie Mays, Jim Gilliam, Earl Battey, Dick Allen, Curt Flood, Bob Gibson, Vada Pinson, Frank Robinson, and Vida Blue. It was nice to have a chance to think about them again and what they meant to me as a Black kid growing up in Philadelphia. Now the book is finished and my heroes dim in the mist of memory. As Woody Guthrie once sang, "So long, it's been good to know you."

FROM THE HALL

A project of this scope and importance involves a big team, and the Hall of Fame would like to sincerely thank them all here. In particular, the entire group behind our new groundbreaking exhibit, *The Souls of the Game*, lent their expertise to this book. The exhibit is part of our institution-wide Black Baseball Initiative, which has been guided by our Board of Directors and Chairman Jane Forbes Clark and spearheaded by our president Josh Rawitch. It has focused on honoring and celebrating the history of Black baseball from a new perspective.

Among the most important collaborators are the project's curatorial consultants, including the Fab Five—Gerald Early, Leslie Heaphy, Larry Lester, Rowan Ricardo Phillips, and Rob Ruck—scholars and lovers of baseball whose new insights from the growing body of knowledge about Black baseball were harnessed for the exhibit, and were applied to the book here. Their contributions all grace the manuscript.

Chief among these five scholars is, of course, our main author, Gerald Early, whose ability to envision and set to paper the best way to tell this important history always amazed us. His uncanny talent in uncovering the core of each movement and facet of the history of Black baseball and telling it with the full humanity the narrative deserves makes *Play Harder* what it is.

Hall of Famer Dave Winfield, a man of many talents both on and off the field, answered the Hall of Fame's call by contributing the foreword, one that offers a perfect framing of the book.

The team also includes curator Gabrielle Augustine, whose thoughtful input helped guide the development of the manuscript. Our library director, Cassidy Lent, and her staff, including reference librarian Rachel Wells, painstakingly fact-checked every word, phrase, and sentence, and saved us from mistakes that might have slipped in.

Sean Gahagan, VP of retail merchandising and licensing, and Scot Mondore, director of licensing, were at the helm from the start and guided the project with good humor and careful stewardship throughout the process. Scot was particularly important to the success of the project as he adeptly coordinated the Hall's resources with the author and publishing team.

The visuals in a book like this are as critical as the text, and for this we have to thank John Horne, from our photo department, who scoured our archives and other sources to help enliven the narrative; our communications director, Craig Muder, who wrote the photo captions; and Kimberly Adler, who assisted with rights clearances. Talented graphic artist Oboh Moses provided the beautiful illustrations that adorn the chapter openings. Our staff photographer, Milo Stewart, photographed the artifacts included in the book. And the design team at Ten Speed, led by Isabelle Gioffredi, took this complex narrative and imagined a beautiful visual framework for it.

This book would not have been possible without the steady guidance and many contributions made by our literary agent, Valerie Tomaselli. She not only found the perfect publishing partner but worked tirelessly in helping to manage the project from concept to finished product. We are forever grateful for all she's done in support of the Hall of Fame.

This leads us to our final thanks—to Kim Keller and Kelly Barrales-Saylor, our editors at Ten Speed, who worked with us with patience and equanimity as they helped us to bring this important history to the page; and to Aaron Wehner, publisher at Ten Speed, who saw the importance of this book from the first inklings in its earliest form. They have our deep gratitude for helping to bring this story to life.

PHOTO CREDITS

INDEX

299

Photograph credits appear on page 298.

Library of Congress Cataloging-in-Publication Data
Names: National Baseball Hall of Fame and Museum, author. |
Early, Gerald Lyn, author.
Title: Play harder: the triumph of black baseball in America /
National Baseball Hall of Fame and Gerald L. Early. Identifiers:
LCCN 2024027011 (print) | LCCN 2024027012 (ebook) | ISBN
9781984863225 (hardcover) | ISBN 9781984863232 (ebook)
Subjects: LCSH: African American baseball players—History. |
Baseball—United States—History. | Racism in sports—United
States—History. | Discrimination in sports—United States—
history. | United States—Race relations—history. | National
Baseball Hall of Fame and Museum.
Classification: LCC GV863.A1 N38 2025 (print) | LCC GV863.A1
(ebook) | DDC 796.357092/396073—dc23/eng/20240727
LC record available at https://lccn.loc.gov/2024027011
LC ebook record available at https://lccn.loc.gov/2024027012

Hardcover ISBN: 978-1-9848-6322-5
EBook ISBN: 978-1-9848-6323-2

Printed in China

Acquiring editor: Kim Keller
Project editor: Kim Keller
Production editor: Patricia Shaw
Designer: Isabelle Gioffredi
Production designers: Mari Gill, Claudia Sanchez, and Faith Hague
Production manager: Dan Myers
Copy editor: Cindy Buck | Proofreaders: Rob Sternitzky,
Sigi Nacson, and Ishan Taylor
Indexer: Cathy Dorsey
Publicist: Lauren Chung | Marketer: Chloe Aryeh
Illustrations: Oboh Moses

National Baseball Hall of Fame and Museum team
Project supervisors: Sean Gahagan and Scot Mondore
Developmental and project editor: Valerie Tomaselli
Curator and content reviewer: Gabrielle Augustine
Fact checkers: Cassidy Lent and Rachel Wells
Photo coordinator: John Horne
Visit www.BaseballHall.org to learn more about the National
Baseball Hall of Fame and Museum.

10 9 8 7 6 5 4 3 2 1

First Edition

THERE WAS NO COLOR LINE IN MONTREAL, BUT AS SOON AS I CROSSED THE BORDER AND PLAYED IN SYRACUSE, I FOUND A LOT OF PREJUDICE, HOOTING AND HOLLERING, NAME-CALLING. I'D PLAYED IN BALTIMORE WITH THE ELITE GIANTS, BUT NOT IN THE ORIOLES' BALLPARK, AND NEVER HEARD A WORD ABOUT MY COLOR. BUT WHEN I CAME THERE WITH THE [MONTREAL] ROYALS, THE FANS GOT ON ME. HEARING THOSE NAMES, I JUST BORE DOWN HARDER.

—Jim Gilliam, All-Star second baseman, 1946–1948 and 1953–1966

DO I NEED TO PLAY HARDER? DO I NEED TO PRAY HARDER?

—Toni Stone, Negro Leagues second baseman, 1953–1954,
first woman to play in the Negro American League

I SOLVED MY PROBLEM BY PLAYING MY GUTS OUT. I RAN MYSELF DOWN TO LESS THAN 135 POUNDS IN THE BLISTERING HEAT. I COMPLETELY WIPED OUT THAT PECKERWOOD LEAGUE. I LED IT IN EVERYTHING BUT HOME RUNS—ALTHOUGH I HIT 29. I PLAYED IN ALL 154 GAMES. I BATTED .340, DRIVING IN 128 RUNS WITH 190 HITS. THE BETTER I DID, THE TOUGHER I GOT.

—Curt Flood, All-Star center fielder, 1956–1969 and 1971 and baseball broadcaster